THE FRUGAL GOURMET WHOLE FAMILY COOKBOOK

Recipes and Reflections for Contemporary Living

JEFF SMITH

TV STAR AND BESTSELLING AUTHOR
FRUGAL GOURMET JEFF SMITH
"IS COOKING ON ALL BURNERS . . .
FIFTEEN MILLION WEEKLY TV VIEWERS
OBVIOUSLY THINK SO,
AND SO DO THE COOKBOOK BUYERS
WHO HAVE PUT HIS BOOK AT THE TOP
OF THE *NEW YORK TIMES* BESTSELLER
LIST."

People Magazine

"THE FRUGAL GOURMET IS KNOWN
AS THE LEO BUSCAGLIA OF COOKING . . .
BUT HE'S INVARIABLY TRUE TO HIS TITLE—
AND FRUGAL DOESN'T MEAN CHEAP;
IT MEANS NOT WASTING ANYTHING."

Newsweek

D0381408

THE FRUGAL GOURMET WHOLE FAMILY COOKBOOK

Recipes and Reflections for Contemporary Living

JEFF SMITH

Craig Wollam, Culinary Consultant
Chris Cart, Illustrator
D.C. Smith, Research Assistant

AVON BOOKS NEW YORK

Grateful acknowledgment is made to the following for use of material in this book: ''Milk Bones'' recipe from Frances Sheridan Goulart, *Bone Appétit* (Seattle: Pacific Search Press, 1976). ''Potato Gnocchi'' recipe from Lidia Bastianich, *La Cucina di Lidia* (New York: Doubleday, 1990).

AVON BOOKS
A division of
The Hearst Corporation
1350 Avenue of the Americas
New York, New York 10019

Copyright © 1992 by The Frugal Gourmet, Inc.
Illustrations copyright © 1992 by Chris Cart
Cover photograph by Anthony Loew
Published by arrangement with William Morrow and Company, Inc.
Library of Congress Catalog Card Number: 92-8582
ISBN: 0-380-72062-0

The William Morrow and Company edition contains the following Library of Congress Cataloging in Publication Data:
Smith, Jeff.
    The Frugal gourmet whole family cookbook : recipes and reflections for contemporary living / Jeff Smith : Craig Wollam, culinary consultant : D. C. Smith, research assistant.
        p.   cm.   Includes bibliographical references and index.
1. Cookery for one.   2. Cookery for two.   3. Quick and easy cookery.
4. Frugal gourmet (Television program).   I. Wollam, Craig.   II. Title.
TX652.S555   1992   92-8582
641.5'61—dc20   CIP

First Avon Books Printing: March 1994

AVON TRADEMARK REG. U.S. PAT. OFF. AND IN OTHER COUNTRIES, MARCA REGISTRADA. HECHO EN U.S.A.

Printed in the U.S.A.

OPM   10   9   8   7   6   5   4   3   2   1

Acknowledgments

Every time we do a new book and a new television series, the list of persons who have contributed to same seems to grow longer and longer. What does that say about my job? It says that I am simply learning to become more dependent upon more wonderful people.

I am often asked which comes first. Is it the book or the television show? The answer is simply, yes! One feeds the other and thus the two grow together.

With this book and this family cooking series we mark a major change in our production and location. I cannot believe this but I did my first *Frugal Gourmet* show twenty years ago, in Tacoma, Washington. In 1983 WTTW, Channel 11, Chicago, invited us to do the shows in that wonderful city. This last year, after a fine relationship of eight years and five full television series, we have moved the production of the shows from Chicago back to the Pacific Northwest. We now tape in Seattle, near the Pike Place Public Market. So our first bit of thanks is due to Dr. William McCarter, president of WTTW, Chicago, who actually helped us pack up our gear and sent us off with his blessings. Please understand that this is a most gracious and unusual act, given the television business. Thanks, Bill.

We thank WTTW a second time for allowing my director

of many years, Tim Ward, to come out to Seattle and direct our new series. Tim is the best!

Nat Katzman, of A La Carte Productions, San Francisco, helped put this whole concept together, along with Lonnie, Barb, Bonnie, and John. Such skilled and patient people.

KQED, Channel 9, San Francisco, jumped into this new relationship with us. And, without the support of National Public Broadcasting, these shows would have been impossible. My affection for PBS remains firm and steadfast.

We again thank the In-Sink-Erator Corporation for their generous contributions to what we do. They are our national corporate underwriters and we have great fun together. Good people, that bunch!

Thanks to Elkay sinks, General Electric, Wolf gas ranges, and KitchenAid for their contributions to a new kitchen set in Seattle. Designed by Diane and Jim Elofson, the set feels very much like my beloved Seattle.

When the set is up, it is at Pinnacle Post Studios, under the able and charming supervision of Vance, J. P., and Angela. A most patient audio and camera crew was provided by Northwest Mobile Television. Those guys can go anywhere and catch anything!

Many thanks to the young co-stars who appeared with us during the series. Such neat kids, and so kind to be with us on camera.

The young stars were: Nick Benfield, Christopher Campbell, Nicolas Campbell, Marlin Chan, Phyllis Chan, Emily Ching, Sara Cohen, Nykeesha Davis, Nick Doner, Keith Dunn, Mitch Freeman, Rebecca Galavan, Shanti Giese, Brian Gilmore, David Gilmore, Paul Goodman, Nick Kwan, Kelsey Laderriere, Travis Lambert, Kiel Lunsford, Brook Otto, Ryan Rautio, Brian Ruttkay, Brianna Ruttkay, Ryon Sellers, Angela Snyder, Briana Treusch, Amanda Treusch, Zana Tsutakawa, and Anthony White.

Special recognition is due the many people who helped through their appearance on the series and their kind contributions in terms of ideas.

Charlie and Itsey Brenner, Brenner Bros. Bakery
Lidia Bastianich, chef/owner of Felidia, New York

Sue and Mike Verdi, Verdi Farms

Bill Street, Jr., Ostrom's Mushroom Farm

Rabbi Marc Gellman, from New York, author of *Does God Have a Big Toe?*

Randy Cade, Pacific Fish Company

Solly and Pure Food Fish, Pike Place Farmer's Market

Robin and Emil Giese, Riverview Herb Farms

Nancy and Kaspar Donier, Kaspar's by the Bay, Seattle

Sarah Lea, of the Lennox House, Chicago

Barrie Wilcox and family, of Wilcox Farms

Sara Little, designer, scholar, and dear friend

Sosio's Fruit and Produce, Pike Place Farmer's Market

Frank's Produce, Pike Place Farmer's Market

Emely Smith, the author's wise and frugal mother

Tony Scoccolo, Italian cook and wise householder

Dale Chihuly, founder of the Pilchuck Glass School

Lino Tagliapietra, glassblower and artisan from Venice, Italy

Kevin Clash, the brilliant man behind the beloved Elmo puppet of *Sesame Street*. Sheer genius!

Alice and Phil Chan, owners of the wonderful Sea Garden Seafood Restaurant, Seattle

Mark Hogan, top student from Edmonds Community College Culinary Arts Program, assisted Craig and me with the preparation of each show. Steve Miller, assistant chef at Kaspar's by the Bay, was diligent and creative in his daily support. Certainly Marion Schiewe, the woman to whom this book is dedicated, is to be thanked again and again.

While I am no expert on health, I certainly know one when I meet one. We must thank Dr. Evette Hackman for her creative and patient additions to the section on healthy eating.

Jason Lynch helped with the preparation of the series and continuously cleaned up after Craig and me. What kind of a medal should be offered to this lad?

Thanks to Karen Wollam, Craig's mother and closest friend of the famous dog Gus.

Our office could not function without Jim Paddleford, our business manager, and Dawn Sparks, our administrative assistant. And thanks to D. C. Smith, who can research the most obscure subjects.

We thank Bill Alder, our book agent in New York, for his constant support. And to our publisher, William Morrow and Company, and Al Marchioni, president and chief executive officer. Maria Guarnaschelli, our editor, causes our friendship to grow with each and every book. She is a genius and she is wonderfully creative.

Patty, my wife, deserves a great deal of credit for keeping me out of trouble. I mean with this book! She carefully read and criticized the articles so that they were consistent and could be understood. She knows how I babble on, and she is willing to tell me to cool it and calm down. I am most thankful that I have her.

Finally, I personally am tickled to thank Craig Wollam, my chef and right hand (all right, left hand, too) for his patient presence, insight, and skill in working with someone such as I, someone who becomes so frustrated when there is so much to do. I cannot rattle this fine young man and I thank him for his support.

Now, does that answer the question that is most often asked of me? "Who eats all of that food?" Count the above names, add twenty more for fine crew members, and then figure it out. We do *The Frugal Gourmet* . . . so nothing is wasted. Nothing! They eat everything.

Thanks to all . . . and blessings.

Contents

To Marion Schiewe—
who came to us as an orphan in
a night of sorrow—and who
is now our set mother

To Maid Marion

Jeff and Craig

INTRODUCTION

The Changing American Family

This book, these articles, these recipes attempt to help those of us who find ourselves in a new family form to be more creative with our food and our life-styles. The family is so very different from what it was four decades ago that we must admit to changes in eating habits, life-styles, and thus kitchen preparation. But I am optimistic about what is going on. I am anxious to bring us all together around one stove, especially the kids. If we don't all cook for one another, we are going to be in a very hungry state!

The Traditional Family
in America

The changes that have come upon the American family during the last four decades have caused more guilt and confusion than even the social psychologists seem willing to admit. Consider what has happened. Prior to the Second World War the family was defined as a mother, father, and two to three children. The whole family was supposed to behave like the books I read in first grade. Mother was always home, always. Father went to work each day. Dick and Jane played after school and always got along with each another. And then, of course, there was Spot, the dog, Puff, the cat, and Baby Sally, who was always sitting on the floor in a freshly pressed little dress. Dinner was celebrated at the table and never was an argument heard. This crowd made Ozzie and Harriet look like gangsters!

With the coming of World War II many moms went off to work in places like the Boeing Airplane Company, and they have not been home since. The family unit changed drastically during that war and during the decade that followed, but all of us still seem to harbor dreams of being part of that "normal" family, Dick and Jane style. Yet it is obvious that such a thing will become more and more rare in our future. Further, the guilt that all of us still feel when we see one of Norman Rockwell's Thanksgiving dinner paintings, with every family member smiling and happy and the bird just so . . . well, we all wonder about whether or not our family is strange, what with the arguing and the unemployed brother and all. No, we are not strange, not in the least.

During the sixties it became more and more necessary for the woman of the house to join in the work force and help with the family finances. Thus she was stuck with two jobs, one in the workplace and one in the home. The American male ego seems to have been terribly wounded during this time and I hope we are seeing signs of recovery.

During that time we should have redesigned our kitchens so that we could all cook together, Dick, Jane, Puff, the whole crowd. But we continued to design kitchens as if only Jane would work in that special room, and thus we continued the course of guilt caused by change unaccepted.

We did this despite the fact that during the fifties we began to seek new methods of feeding the family since often both parents were working. The first frozen chicken pot pie was developed by Swanson in 1952, and it changed the eating habits of America. It was followed by the inevitable TV dinner in 1957, and America was off on a whole new image of the table and of the family, and certainly a new image of eating.

While a college chaplain during the late sixties I began

to understand the reason why so many students were will-ing to live together but were reluctant to consider marriage. The usual critics of the young claimed that the students were not up to the commitments that their parents made, and that the antimarriage feeling was simply another mark of the decay of lasting values in our culture. However, I saw these same students move into communes and form sound relationships with other persons, many of these re-lationships lasting for decades, but still marriage and a "normal" family life seemed out of the question. Then it hit me. As the students and I talked together on the campus, more and more of them expressed a desire to celebrate feasts, and, of course, the Chaplain was a good cook. So I began cooking and feasting with these young college stu-dents and I learned a profound lesson. They were not will-ing to involve themselves in a traditional marriage because they felt the marriage of their parents lacked depth and insight. Why? Because they always ate from TV dinner trays and seldom communicated. Dinner was served on those shaky aluminum trays in front of the television . . . and *Gunsmoke,* or perhaps the evening news, was always on at dinnertime. Each person chose his/her private dinner and then went into the TV room and ate from a private tray. No one spoke if "Doc" was speaking for fear of an instant gunshot wound. And, come to think of it, the TV room where all of this took place was called the "family room." You remember, I am sure.

These kids were so hungry for communication that they wound up in communes, where there would be someone to talk to day and night, and where every meal was celebrated in the midst of close friends, even though the food, as I remember it, was little more than brown rice and fried cel-ery. The point of a feast does not always center around the food but around the reason for the gathering.

Years later these very same students became parents and they built homes with kitchens and dining rooms . . . but few have "family rooms," a leftover from a time they would just as soon forget. I see hope for this age group, great hope indeed.

For the rest of the culture strange changes are coming rapidly. Everyone still seems to feel that the basic family unit is a great thing, but this style and structure are becoming less and less common in our time and more difficult to achieve. Increasingly, living units consist of parents without partners, of two or more single people living in a common dwelling, both fathers and mothers who have children and intend to raise them on their own. Finally, we have single people who live by themselves, the current number being twice the figure reported in the 1970 census. Many of these are elderly and living on a fixed income that is becoming less valuable day by day.

Given all of this, we must recognize that the family in our time is very different from that of thirty years ago, but family structures still exist and are to be celebrated. People who live alone are adopting family members, people who have nothing to do with blood ties. The fact that we continue to be a very mobile culture means that such adoptions are going to increase as we live farther and farther away from our original homes and parents. While some bemoan the decrease in the number of traditional family units in our time, I see this as a great time for selecting "relatives" you really wish to be with, relatives who can help your children feel secure in their own situation. In other words, we are now able to elect an extended family. That is just great, and it is going to prove to be a blessing to our future. Regardless of the form, I think we must be careful to call these changing units "families." After all, two people living together can establish family communication and support, even if they are of the same sex. And you are not going to call a divorced mother or father with children to raise anything but a family. I hope that the church and the synagogue will soon recognize the fact that the evening family service must involve all of the above life-styles.

Since everyone is out of the home either at work or at school, what becomes of the American evening meal? I am optimistic, even as I watch the statistics for fast-food joints and prepared foods rise. My mail indicates that many more family units are making an effort to eat two or three evening meals together each week, but it is difficult to prepare fresh meals with only one person in the kitchen, especially if that person just came home at 5:45! The evening meal can become a great time for communication, and so can the preparation time—providing every person in the family unit shares the responsibility for the meal. If we prepare together and cook together and, finally, eat together, we can better keep track of our relationships. After all, the evening meal, even in the midst of our hurried times, is to NURTURE, NOURISH, SUSTAIN, COMFORT, AND CALM US DOWN. It is also the very best means of talking to and getting close to our family members. With a little planning it can be done.

That is what this book is about.

There are options in this volume for every member of the family, including your grandma who lives alone in California, or your two bachelor uncles who live in New Jersey. The kids must get involved in this or we will all starve to death. And we can do this without resorting to take-out, though I would rather eat take-out at my dinner table with my family than eat take-out in the backseat of a car while a plastic clown stares at me.

I have gone through the whole guilt trip about the meaning of the family and how such a definition applies to our own household. We are not Ozzie and Harriet any more than you are. We have our battles and arguments, just as you do. And now that the boys are off to school we do not eat dinner together very often. I lament that fact. I really do. But when they are home we eat. Boy, do we eat! We feast and talk and fill the table with their friends . . . and then spend two days doing the dishes. But it is worth it since you learn something new about those you love each time you eat with them.

What Is Predicted for the American Family Unit?

The sociologists and the demographers paint a really depressing picture. The number of persons involved in a single household will increase during the nineties until the number of people who live alone will outnumber married couples with children. Families, in the traditional sense, will grow smaller and become less involved in the style of the traditional extended family. The young adult population will be smaller in the year 2000 than it is now, though general aging of the population may help to establish a period of comparative stability, perhaps even a light drift back to traditional family orientation. We will hope so. Divorce will probably increase and fewer persons approaching middle age will have an intact marriage. More young adults will continue living with their parents, and as the cost of living increases, more and more extended families will come together under one roof in order to maintain existence.

That is what many of the sociologists predict. If the trend toward single-parent families and just plain singleness continues, the result will be that we will increasingly find ourselves growing old, in semipoverty, alone.

Those are the predictions. I do not believe that I am being naive to think that we can stem at least a part of this movement toward loneliness by bringing one another to table. Such an effort is for the sake of our mental and sociological health, as well as for the sheer joy of the feast.

GLOSSARY

Kitchen Hints from Gus

My name is Gus and I am really quite skilled in the kitchen. I have been asked by Jeff and Craig to add my comments on kitchen safety and creativity to this book. Of course, I am only too happy to do so, but I expect some good things to come from the fact that this book is going to make me famous. All I have to do now is to get rid of Jeff and Craig and then maybe I can have my own show. I look pretty good already, don't you think?

A Kitchen for
the Nineties

Since the definition of the family has changed so much
during the past two or three decades, why has kitchen
design not changed accordingly? We still design cooking
spaces as if there is only one person working within said
space, but we know that two or three, perhaps four, persons
will join in the cooking efforts sometime after 5:45 P.M.
What should be different for this crowd that comes together
to prepare, talk, and finally eat?

In past decades architects designed kitchens using what
was called the "triangle pattern." The kitchen consisted of
one large room to be occupied by one person, and the triangle pattern was a path, a trail, that ran from the stove to
the sink to the refrigerator . . . and then back again. Many
architects are still designing kitchens in this way as if nothing has changed since the 1950s.

A kitchen for the nineties must not be centered around
one person. We assume several people are going to be
cooking at once. Even if you live alone you are going to
have parties in which your friends or adopted (chosen) family will wish to participate. Therefore there must be several
"stations," or cooking positions, within the kitchen. If you
go into a good restaurant you will find that the stations are
very obvious. This is the station for the salad maker, this

one for the dishwasher, this one for the garlic chopper, this one for the main cook.

Arrange your kitchen in such a way that there are two or three chopping boards on the counters so that other people can help in preparation. And clear off those counters of all those electric appliances that you seldom use. Put them in the closet until you need them, as you need counter space more than anything.

Our own kitchen at our home in Tacoma has several stations, since we have always cooked together as a small mob. When the boys were little they called us "The Gang of Four." (I hope you remember enough about the history of China during the past few decades to realize the meaning of this label.) Each night the boys would come in from their paper routes and they would help me cook dinner. Patty was running her bookstore in those days, so when she came home from work I was ready and standing at the front door with a glass of wine for her. And, of course I always wore a clean apron. In any case, when Jason came home from his paper route one night, he immediately went to his station, his cutting board, his own space. His first job was to clean several cloves of garlic, always. I love garlic. On this particular evening he finished cleaning a significant amount of garlic and then he turned to me and said, "Pops, what are we having for dinner?" "Waffles," I replied. He got that Jason-type quizzical look on his face and then mumbled, "Well, why not?"

Channing was making salad at another sink. That is what kitchen stations are for!

If you can afford to put in a bar or salad sink as well as a regular double sink, you will be set. The second sink can function as a salad sink, a bar sink, a last-minute cleaning sink, in short, a serious preparation area.

I do not think that large, square rooms will function as kitchens in our time. Try the galley concept. The name comes from the long and narrow spaces that were used for kitchens in ships, where space was terribly important. I believe that in our time, space is just as important, and if you have a long and narrow kitchen, say with 46-to-

48-inch-wide aisles, several persons can get around but each can have his/her own station. I have designed our home kitchen in this way, as well as both of my television-studio kitchens and our test kitchen at the office. It works.

The Frugal Gourmet
Dream Kitchen

The following design is a very expensive dream, a dream of a kitchen that even I do not own. It is close to my test kitchen in Seattle and has a few favorite characteristics of my studio kitchen and my kitchen at home in Tacoma. You can pick up a few ideas for your own kitchen, perhaps, but this plan will not help much if you live in an apartment in New York City. This dream plan calls for lots of room, and

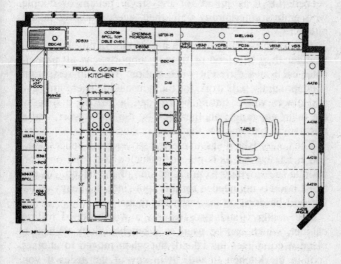

this would be beyond the possibilities of a normal apartment in our largest cities.

Remember that this is a dream kitchen and I have
only parts of it, so far. I designed it for the In-Sink-
Erator Corporation, the people who invented the garbage
disposal and who make the Steamin' Hot water dispenser. It was completely built in a large auditorium and
it was the hit of the Kitchen Show. *Woman's Day* magazine also helped with the presentation. Some of these
concepts will be helpful to you but, remember, this is
still my dream, too.

The concept offered here is based on a revised galley
plan for the kitchen rather than one large kitchen that as-
sumes a sole person is operating the cooking space. The
galley idea of long aisles is much more suited to the nature of the contemporary family, a family in which several people cook at once and therefore several stations are
needed. Or it is suited for the single person or couple
who enjoys entertaining with their guests helping in the
kitchen.

The room is set up in such a way that family members,
whether they be blood or friendly imports, can all participate, each at a different work station. This old restaurant
concept surely will work for the household. There are several places where cutting boards can be placed, a sink by
the main gas range, another sink by the dishwasher, and a
third small bar sink for the salad maker.

The center island has an electric stovetop for sauces, etc.,
and it has burner dials placed in such a way that one can
operate the stovetop from either side of the island. An exhaust hood is not needed for this spot since the heavy cooking will be done on the large gas range.

The center island also features a wood-topped rolling
cabinet, which can be used as a butcher block. When in
place it completes the island, but when moved to another
spot in the kitchen (it will fit in any of the aisles if you
wish to chop beside a stove or counter), the island is
opened up for easy passage from one side of the room to
the other.

The kitchen partially opens through a large pass-through located above the sinks and dishwasher. On the other side is the breakfast nook, which has ample open shelving for the storage and display of those cooking pieces that are used only occasionally.

The kitchen features a full restaurant-style hood and exhaust system above the gas range and the Chinese work.

There is light, light, light, all over the place. I need as many windows as possible and ceiling windows would be ideal.

I have two refrigerator/freezers, and they are placed close enough to the center island to allow for easy unloading. Or you can bring the center-island traveling butcher block to the refrigerators for those big jobs.

A large marble board is placed on top of the counter for the sake of making pasta and pastry.

The stainless draining board next to the gas range functions in conjunction with the pot sink and also acts as a safety area for the person who removes a hot pot from the stove and finds no place to immediately place the pot.

The countertops can be made of the wonderful new products such as Gibraltar or Corian. Plastic laminate material can be used on the dishwashing counter. However, the Gibraltar or Corian, even though they are more expensive, will give you much better service in the long run.

Equipment

I might just as well tell you about my favorite equipment for the kitchen, brand names and all. I must be careful with this since you might think I am getting a little too commercial. I will tell you the truth. Long before I met the In-Sink-Erator people I had their products in my home and my test kitchens. I have had Elkay sinks throughout my home kitchen before I started the shows. I have had a Wolf gas range since my early days, and I have had a KitchenAid food mixer both in my restaurants and in my home, as well as on the set. I always have. Further, this will save me some time since someone is always calling or writing and asking about my favorite kitchen equipment.

So, here is a list of the things that I must have in my dream kitchen.

I would love to have a ISE Steamin' Hot water dispenser at each of the three sinks. These things are lifesavers to a family that is trying to cook good meals in a short time. Craig, my chef and assistant, made a list one afternoon of the uses for this very contemporary device, uses that save a great deal of time in food preparation. Steaming hot water is so essential to the contemporary kitchen that we tend to forget how much time we spend standing around waiting for the teakettle or saucepan to heat up. Who has the time to wait? After I read the list that we made, I realized that I use my Steamin' Hot water dispenser more often than I do my microwave.

Uses for the Steamin' Hot Water Dispenser

BE SURE THAT YOUR HOT WATER DISPENSER IS ADJUSTED TO THE FULL 190° TEMPERATURE WHEN INSTALLED. YOU WANT REALLY HOT WATER WHEN YOU WANT IT!

The uses you have already thought of—tea, instant coffee, instant soups, etc.

Rehydrating Dried Food Products

For dried mushrooms, chile peppers, tomatoes, etc., place in a small bowl and cover with steaming water. Cover bowl with a glass plate and allow to cool on the countertop. Ready for use.

For dried beans, place in a bowl and cover with steaming water. Place a lid on top to trap the steam. Allow to stand for an hour or so. Drain. Ready for cooking.

For parboiling rice, place raw rice in a bowl and cover with ample steaming hot water. Cover with a lid or glass plate and allow to stand for 30 minutes.

Thinning Sauces and Soups at the Last Minute

Soaking Out a Burned Food-Crusted Pan
Add a spoon of baking soda to the steaming hot water.

Coddling an Egg
Have eggs at room temperature. Place 2 whole eggs in a 2-cup measuring glass and cover with steaming water. Let sit for 15 minutes.

Making Simple Syrup
This is used for thinning jams and jellies, making fruit syrups, and adding to puddings and pies. So simple. Place 2 cups of regular sugar in a small saucepan and add 1 cup steaming hot water. Place on a hot burner for a moment and stir to dissolve. Allow to cool.

Cleaning Brass and Copper
If copper and brass are wet and very hot when you clean them, the task is simple. Use the ISE Steamin' Hot water dispenser. Patty, my wife, reminds you to wear heavy rubber gloves when doing this. She is right . . . as always.

Peeling Fruits and Vegetables
Place a peach in a 2-cup measuring glass and cover the fruit with steaming water. Let stand 2 minutes, no more. Remove with a fork and the peel will come right off.

Peel tomatoes just as the peach above.

Blanching Vegetables for Salads
Most vegetables for salads taste better and appear brighter if they are quickly blanched rather than used raw. Use julienne stick slices of carrots, celery, zucchini, and blanch quickly by placing them in steaming hot water along with 1 tablespoon of olive oil to maintain color. Let sit, covered, for 3 minutes and then rinse with cold water.

Onions and frozen pea pods work well when prepared this way for a salad.

Perfect Thin Asparagus

Clean the thin asparagus and rinse in hot water. Drain. Place 2 portions in a bread loaf pan and add 1 tablespoon of olive oil to preserve color. Cover the pan with aluminum foil and set it aside for at least 10 minutes. Drain and serve. The asparagus will still be perfect even if it sits much longer and cools completely.

Melting and Blanching Frozen Vegetables Right out of the Freezer

Frozen corn kernels, peas, beans, etc., can be thawed and blanched all at once using your Steamin' Hot water dispenser. Simply remove the vegetables from the carton and place in a bowl. Cover with steaming hot water and let sit for a few minutes. Perfect for salads.

Quick Corn Salad

Blanch frozen corn kernels as above and drain. Toss with green onions, parsley, fresh dill, and a dressing of olive oil, lemon juice, salt, and pepper.

Remove the Lid from a Jar

Heat the lid quickly with your Steamin' Hot water dispenser and it will come right off.

Sanitize Can Openers After Use

Rinse under steaming water, dry, and put away.

Cleaning Your Good Kitchen Knives

Never throw them in the dishwasher, as it will ruin the edge of the knives. Simply rinse them under steaming hot water, wipe clean, and dry, then carefully and safely store.

Summertime Cooking

When you want to keep the kitchen cool in the summer, remember to rely upon your Steamin' Hot water dispenser as you prepare salads, blanched vegetables, molded salads, etc.

Wintertime in the Kitchen

Don't forget that your Steamin' Hot water dispenser is great for quick tea and coffee, even soups. I use mine for hot buttered rum during the holidays.

Heat Up Those Jams and Jellies

Warm jelly or jam is a delight on a cold morning. So is warm honey, for that matter. Simply place the covered jar in a pan of steaming hot water, about three quarters of the way up the side of the glass. Wait a few minutes while the toast cooks, and enjoy.

Heat Up the Coffee Equipment Before Making Coffee

Every morning I rinse my espresso-maker coffee holder in steaming hot water. The resulting coffee is far superior!

Cleaning a Pastry Brush After Using Oil or Butter

Normally a messy thing to clean up, and one of the reasons that people don't use a pastry brush more often. After using for oil or butter, simply put the brush in a small glass and add a drop or two of dishwashing liquid. Run some steaming hot water into the glass and go on with the rest of your dishwashing. Never put a pastry brush in the dishwasher. Never!

Clean the Border of the Dinner Plate Before Serving

Craig, my assistant and chef, came to this one. It is ingenious. If you ever go into the back of professional kitchens, you will see the line of people using a towel to clean the little messy drops they make on a plate as they dish up the food. They keep the towel over their shoulders and use it for the evening. No! In your kitchen, if a plate does not look perfect just before you serve it, dip a paper towel under the Steamin' Hot water dispenser and wipe the edges of the plate clean. And it will be clean!

You cannot go wrong with ISE garbage disposals. Yes, they have been one of our TV sponsors for years, but please also remember that they invented the garbage disposal. Real quality, along with their dishwashers and trash compactors.

The Wolf gas range people do a fine job. I see no reason to invest in brands that are much more expensive. I have used Wolf ranges in my restaurant and test kitchens for years, and Craig, my chef and assistant, has just installed one in his test kitchen. The cost is quite a bit lower than the more "glamorous" brands, but these Wolfs are built to last. They have been serving the restaurant industry for years, and I am afraid they make no money on replacement parts. You don't need replacement parts!

I cannot cook without my KitchenAid mixers. I have two of Model K5A2 in all of my kitchens. I make everything with mine, including French bread. For the whole family kitchen I think this is the most dependable machine.

KitchenAid makes a fine dishwasher as well.

KitchenAid also makes terrific ovens. I need a set of double electric ovens as well as my gas range, which has a large restaurant oven.

My sinks are all Elkay. Buy the deep models so that you can clean a soup pot without any difficulty. Further, these are good industrial quality so that you don't have to worry about your junior-high kids throwing pots into the sink . . . from halfway across the room. No matter!

Be sure that you have lots of electric outlets throughout the kitchen. Light and outlets. Light and outlets, and then I am happy. I also need a hanging pot rack over the center island. It need not be expensive, as a single pipe of sturdy construction with ample hanging hooks will do nicely.

Finally, please don't assume just because a person is an architect that he/she knows good kitchen design. Find someone to do your kitchen who is a specialist with kitchens for that particularly important part of your home. The fellow who did the drawings, critique, and improvements on my ideal kitchen is a jewel, and he is a certified kitchen designer. This simply means that he is respected in the industry because he knows what he is doing. At first I was amused at the corrections that he made in my original drawings, and then I became embarrassed. He is good. Thanks to Dave Hagerman, C.K.D., of The Kitchen Shop in Lansing, Michigan, for he prevented my dream kitchen from becoming a nightmare.

Find good help. The kitchen can be the most creative room in your house for you and all your family members.

Never store food in aluminum. Aluminum is fine for cooking but not for storage. If you have acids, such as in tomato sauce or eggs or lemon, in your food you can create aluminum oxide when you store those foods in aluminum containers. Use plastic for storage: Aluminum oxide is just as tough on humans as it is on Australian terriers.

Safety in the Kitchen

This is not a chapter written just for children. It is for the whole family.

I have found that older people share with younger people certain dangerous attitudes about the kitchen. Both are a bit forgetful and are easily distracted. Both need to be very careful about climbing up on a step of some sort in order to reach things. Both have a tendency to be a bit careless, the young people because they do not yet know any better, and the older persons because they have spent so many years in that kitchen.

So, this article is for the sake of all members of the family, regardless of their age.

Safety must be an essential part of a kitchen, just as are the stove and the refrigerator. It is not a step, like adding chopped olives to the bowl. It is an attitude you have from the moment you design your kitchen. The section on kitchen design (pages 17 to 19) will help with some safety ideas. Here I have listed some quick tips that will help you remember how you may teach your children or mate to act in the food preparation area.

I offer twenty kitchen safety tips.

1. The Kitchen Is a Place of Fire and Flame.

Let your children know about the possible dangers of the

kitchen, but do it in a nonfrightening way, just as you would tell them about the dangers of street traffic. We are not trying to scare the kids, but we are trying to get them to be attentive when in the kitchen.

2. The Knife Is an Important Tool, and a Dangerous One.

Be sure to keep your knives sharp, as a dull knife takes much pressure when used and therefore it is more likely to slip and cut someone. Sharpen the knives for the children and teach them to use knives properly. My own sons used knives a great deal when they were young, but they were careful. They always placed the knife on the food and then placed one hand on the handle and the other on the back of the knife. Thus, when they put pressure on the knife it could not cut their hand. That is not a bad rule for adults.

Keep your fingers bent under when chopping. (Do I have to say that again?)

3. Cut with One Flat Side of Vegetables.

For instance, cut an onion in half the long way and place the flat side on the board. You will have much better control of the vegetable than if it were still in its rolling, round condition.

4. Keep Your Cutting Board Clear of Things Around It.

This will help prevent accidents.

5. Provide a Safe Box or Stepping Stand for Reaching Things.

Don't ever put your children on a three-legged stool while working at the stove. It is very dangerous for young and old. Instead, get a heavy plastic milk box that will be totally sturdy. Craig suggests that you glue small rubber nonskid pads on all four corners of the plastic box. You might be better off to build a small stepping box of ¾-inch plywood, but even then Craig reminds you that you should use non-skid rubber pads on the box. Or, even better yet, purchase a Kik Step stool. Made in Kansas City, it looks something

If you are short, and some people think I am, then use a step
stool in the kitchen. But be sure
it is safe. I fell off Craig's
plastic milk crate. The
Dog!

like an upside-down metal wastebasket. It is very sturdy
and has wheels underneath that contact the floor when you
step on the stool. The result is a device that will not tip
over or slide when someone is on it. It can be purchased
through an office supply house, but it costs around $60, so
it is not cheap. However, if it prevents your mother from
suffering a broken shoulder or your child from falling and
getting burned at the stove . . . what's $60?

6. Have a Fire Extinguisher Beside the Stove.

This is very important. Do not use water to put out a grease
fire or throw water on an electrical fire. You need a small
Class 1-B fire extinguisher for kitchen fires. You can find
one in a hardware store. Check it every few months to be
sure it will be ready for action.

7. Be Prepared to Smother Grease Fires.

When oil or grease ignites in a frying pan, do not panic.
Simply carefully and slowly cover the pan with a lid. Then,
turn off the burner. You may singe your arm a bit, but this
is minor to the damage that you can cause by picking up
the pan and trying to empty it of the flaming grease. Do
not use water. Be sure to keep a proper lid handy when
pan-frying or wok cooking.

8. Do Not Leave Pan Handles Sticking Out over the Stove.

One careless bump and the pan is spilling on you or someone else.

9. Keep Very Small Children out of the Kitchen When Cooking or Prepare a Safe Place Where They Can Play and Watch You Prepare Dinner.

10. Keep Your Pets out of the Kitchen.

A small animal can cause serious accidents when you are carting about a hot pan.

11. Keep a Marble Board or Cutting Board Next to the Stove.

When you pick up a pan that is too hot to handle, set it on this safety area, not on a counter where it may cause damage.

12. Do Not Use Wet Towels or Wet Potholders for Handling Pan.

The moisture will conduct the heat to your hand immediately.

13. Never Pick Up a Hot Pan Unless You Have Already Decided Where You Can Safely Put It.

14. Be Sure You Are Aware of All Burners That May Be On.

This may sound silly, but my assistant and I did a live television show in Boston one morning and we had what could have been a most serious accident. Someone had left a burner in the on position when the stove was last used on the show. When the stove was hooked up for our segment, I did not check to see whether or not any burners had been left on. I placed a glass plate on a burner that I was not using and it exploded right in front of my audience! Be careful with a stove that does not clearly show you whether or not all burners are on or off.

15. Keep Your Ovens Clean.

This will prevent oven fires.

16. Never Allow a Child to Operate an Electric Mixer or Other Electrical Appliances Without Adult Supervision.

I need not explain the dangers prevented here.

17. Teach Children to Handle the Hot Water Faucet Properly.

Do not stick your whole hand under the water tap to test the temperature. Someone may have just used the faucet and the water will be very hot!

18. Provide Ample Light in Your Kitchen.

A dark or poorly lit kitchen increases dangers at every level.

19. Keep the Floor Clean.

A bit of oil or grease on the floor, or a chunk or two of chopped green onion, and someone is going to fall!

20. Hot! Hot! Behind You!

That is a line you will hear in every good restaurant in this country. When carrying hot food or pans and walking behind someone else in the kitchen, be sure to warn them. Teach your children to yell, "Hot! Hot! Behind you!" They will get a kick out of hollering, and you will prevent some possible burns.

If you take the time to keep your kitchen fairly orderly and safe, you will enjoy yourself when preparing meals. A disorganized kitchen is a center for serious accidents.

Kitchen Equipment

Knives

Knives are the most important pieces of equipment in your kitchen. When purchasing knives you should be mindful of the following points:

1. Please do not buy knives that are cheaply made and designed to go into the dishwasher. (No good knife should ever be put into the dishwasher. Low-quality knives may be made of stainless steel so that they are hard enough to take the dishwasher, but they cannot be sharpened.)
2. I prefer the standard old French chef's knife, not a designer gadget. The old model is hard to improve upon, and I have seen no improvement in function with the new "modern"-looking knives. Form follows function. A knife is for cutting. Buy one that does just that.
3. Buy good-quality knives of high carbon steel. They are now made to be nonstaining but are not stainless steel. Use a sharpening steel on them often to keep a good edge. If a sharpening steel makes you a bit nervous, use a Chantry knife sharpener. It is safe and works very well. Please do not consider buying an electric knife sharpener . . . no matter who tells you to

do so. I find that people who use such devices simply sharpen their knives to death. There is no point in doing such a thing.

4. There is no such thing as a knife that never needs to be sharpened, any more than there is a plate that never needs to be washed. Good knives need sharpening and care, so never just throw them in a drawer. Keep them in a rack, and in good repair. A dull knife is very dangerous since you have to work harder and thus are more apt to let the knife slip and cut yourself.

5. I use the following knives constantly, but you may wish some other sizes. (I have about fifty knives. You don't need that many. Neither do I but I love good knives!)

10-inch-blade chef's knife
8-inch-blade chef's knife
Boning knife
Paring knife
Long slicing knife (thin)
Sharpening steel

Chinese Cleaver:

There are several thicknesses available. A thin one is used for slicing and chopping vegetables and a thicker one for cutting meat and hacking poultry. Do not bother buying a stainless-steel cleaver. You cannot sharpen it.

Pots and Pans

Good pots and pans make good cooking easy. Pans that are thin and flimsy can offer only burning, sticking, and lumps. Buy good equipment that is heavy. You will not be sorry.

Tips for Buying Good Equipment

1. Don't buy pots and pans with wooden or plastic handles. You can't put them in the oven or under a broiler.

2. Buy pans that fit your life-style, that are appropriate for the way you cook. They should be able to perform a variety of purposes in the kitchen. Avoid pans that can be used for only one dish or one particular style of cooking, such as upside-down crepe pans.

3. I do not buy sets of pans but rather a selection of several different materials that work in different ways. Most of my frying pans are heavy stainless steel or aluminum with SilverStone nonstick linings. I have aluminum stockpots and saucepans. No, I do not worry about cooking in aluminum since I never cook acids such as eggs or tomatoes or lemon juice in that metal . . . and I always keep aluminum well cleaned, remembering never to store anything in aluminum pots or pans.

   I have copper saucepans for special sauces and some stainless-steel saucepans as well. These are heavy stainless with plain metal handles, with an aluminum core sandwiched into the bottom. I also have a selection of porcelain-enameled cast-iron pans, Le Creuset being my favorite brand for that type of thing.

4. The pots and pans I use the most:

   20-quart aluminum stockpot with lid
   12-quart aluminum stockpot with lid
   12-quart stainless-steel heavy stockpot with lid
   4-quart aluminum *sauteuse,* with lid
   10-inch aluminum frying pan, lined with SilverStone, with lid
   Several cast-iron porcelain-coated casseroles, with lids
   Copper saucepans in varying sizes, with lids
   Chinese wok—I own six of them. (See page 38 for descriptions.)

Machines and Appliances

Please do not fill your kitchen with appliances that you will rarely use. I do not own an electric deep-fryer or an electric slow-cooking ceramic pot or an electric egg cooker or . . .

you know what I am saying. Other pieces of equipment will work for these jobs, and have other functions as well. But, I do use an electric frying pan often because I can control the surface cooking temperature easily, and it's a versatile appliance.

I also have:

Food mixer:
Choose a heavy machine, one that will sit in one spot and, using the different attachments available, make bread dough, grind meat, and mix cake batters. I prefer the KitchenAid and have the large model with the five-quart bowl. For bread-making, you'll need both the paddle-blade and dough-hook attachments. The meat grinder and sausage attachments make for easy and fun sausage-making.

Food processor:
While I use this machine less than my mixer, it is helpful.

Food blender:
I have a heavy-duty model that will take a beating. Don't skimp on this machine. It should be able to puree solids easily—not make just milk shakes.

Electric coffee grinder, small size:
I use this for grinding herbs and spices, not for coffee. It is from Germany.

Special Equipment

Pick and choose among these. Most of them are just amazingly helpful:

Garlic press:
I cannot abide garlic in any form except fresh. Buy a good garlic press. Be careful in purchase as there are now many cheap ones on the market and they just do not work. I use a Susi.

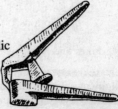

Lemon reamer, wooden:
This is a great device, but since I began using it on television many companies have been producing copies that are just not the right size and shape for proper use. Buy a good one, even if you have seen a cheaper model.

Heat diffuser or tamer:
This is an inexpensive gadget that you place on your gas or electric burner to even out or reduce the heat. It will save you from a lot of burned sauces.

Tomato shark:
This little gadget takes the stem out of the tomato in nothing flat. Be careful—there is a phony one on the market that doesn't work half as well.

Wooden spoons and spatulas:
I never put metal spoons or utensils in my frying pans or saucepans. Metal will scratch the surface, causing food to stick. Buy wooden utensils and avoid that problem. I have grown very fond of tools made from olive wood as it is very hard and will last for years, even with regular use and washing. They cost more to start with but they will outlast the others by three times, at least. I have also found some very durable plastic spoons, spatulas, and gadgets. These are made of an extremely high-heat-resistant plastic. They are the only plastic tools that I have ever found durable. Robison makes them and they are called Ultratemp. Do not bother buying cheap plastic.

Wok:

I use my Chinese wok constantly. It is an ingenious device that is made of steel. Do not buy an aluminum or copper wok. The idea is to have a "hot spot" at the bottom of the wok, thus quickly cooking small amounts of food by moving them about in the pan. Aluminum and copper woks heat too evenly and the advantage of wok cooking is lost. Electric woks do not heat quickly enough, nor do they cool quickly enough. You can use your steel wok on an electric burner, though I prefer gas. If cooking with electricity, simply keep the burner always on high and control the temperature of the wok by moving it off and on the burner.

Small wok:

Single-handled, about 9 inches in diameter with a flat bottom. Ideal for stir-frying for one or two persons, or quickly reheating leftovers. It comes with a nonstick surface for easy cleaning. Find in good cookware shops.

Bamboo steamers:

These stackable steamers, usually three or four in a set, allow you to steam several dishes at once. The advantage that these have over metal steamers stems from the fact  that bamboo will not cause moisture to condense and drip on your food, as metal ones will. I use bamboo steamers for cooking many types of food and for warming up leftovers. I could not run a kitchen without them.

Stove-top smoker:

This is a wonderful device put out by Cameron and it is made entirely of stainless steel. The idea is to place it on top of your stove with a bit of alder or hickory sawdust in the bottom and you can smoke things in just a moment in your kitchen. These are an investment, but you will find yourself smoking all kinds of things. Other sawdusts come with the device and can also be purchased in additional

quantities. I remain partial to alder and hickory.
IMPORTANT: You must have
a strong out-of-the-
house exhaust fan to
use this, or use it outside
directly on the barbecue.

Stove-top grill:
This is great for grilling
peppers, bread, and other
things right on top of the
burner. It is called an
asador, and it works very
well.

Le Creuset stove-top grill:
This device is a rectangular
piece of cast iron with
ridges on the
surface. It
fits directly
on the stove top
across two burners.
Great for grilling indoors if you have an exhaust
fan that draws smoke out of the house.

Grill racks:
Choose one or two sizes of these
racks for grilling on top of a griddle or
on the barbecue. They are
especially helpful in holding
a fish together while
you grill it.

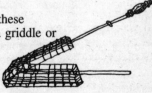

Tortilla press:
This is very helpful in rolling
out dough for dumplings. Buy
a good one that is smoothly
polished and you will have
less trouble with sticking.

Dumpling maker:
This plastic gadget
is cheap but clever. Helps
you make filled dumplings
in nothing flat.

Truffle cutter for cheese:
A very fancy gadget . . . but it
does a great job on slicing
thin bits of hard cheeses.
Great for pasta! I also use
mine for shaving chocolate.

Cheese grater, hand-held:
This little stainless-steel grater is wonderful
for grating cheese on top of
pasta. I use mine right at
the table.

Ginger grater:
This little porcelain piece
works like a scrub board to
grate fresh ginger very
quickly and very fine. From
Japan.

Chopper/noodle cutter/breadstick maker:
An Italian cutting device that I
find just great for making noodles
and breadsticks. It also works well
for cutting fresh herbs such as basil,
parsley, etc.

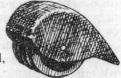

Noodle bird-nest fryer:
This two-basket device presses
the fresh noodles together for
deep-frying. Also used for
grated potatoes. The result is a
fried "bird nest" basket.

Meat skewers:
All kinds are available for
making grilled meat cubes. I
prefer those made of
stainless steel. These
are easily found.

Apple corer/peeler/slicer:
This is a great
device for coring,
peeling, and slicing
apples. I use mine for
making the best thin-cut
potato fries that you can imagine.
Great for shoestring potatoes, as well.

Apple parer/wedger:
This little device cores
and cuts an apple into
wedges. Perfect for
desserts, appetizers, or
baking.

Pepper mill:
The flavor of freshly ground black pepper is
very different from that of the preground.
Find a good mill and grind your own. I have
several mills, but my favorite is a Turkish
coffee grinder. These are expensive, but if
you are a pepper lover you will love this
device. Be careful that the one you buy
comes with a guarantee that it can be
adjusted for pepper.

Meat pounder:
This malletlike
device will flatten out slices of
meat so that they are very thin.
Great for chicken, beef, and
veal dishes.

Plastic sheeting:

Sheeting is very helpful when you are pounding meat thin. It is inexpensive and available in most lumberyards or hardware stores. Ask for clear vinyl sheeting 8 millimeters thick. *Do not store food in this sheeting.*

Fire extinguisher:

A must for your kitchen. Buy one that will work on electrical fires as well as stove fires. Talk to the salesperson. You will sleep better at night.

Marble pastry board:

These can be purchased in several sizes. I could not make pastry, bread, or pasta without one.

Stainless-steel steamer basket:

This is a great help. I have two sizes, and they are adjustable for different pan sizes. Great for steaming vegetables and not expensive.

Steamer stand:

This aluminum stand sits in the bottom of your kettle. A plate of food is placed on top and the pan becomes a steamer. You can also use this as a rack for a double boiler.

Fine strainer for skimming oil:

If you do get into deep-frying, this very thin mesh strainer will help you keep the oil clean. From Japan.

Baking tiles:

These will help you get a good crust on your bread. Whether or not you use a pan the tiles keep your oven temperature even. Salday makes these.

Pasta-rolling machine:

This is the easiest
way to make pasta. I prefer rolled
pasta to extruded, and this machine can
also be used for making other thin
doughs.

Roasting racks, nonstick:

At last a roasting rack for a
serious chicken lover. These work
very well as the bird or roast does
not stick to the rack.

Kitchen scale:

Buy something that is fairly accurate. It will be helpful in
baking perfect breads and in judging the size of roasts.

Mandoline:

This is a wonderful device for
cutting vegetables into thin
slices or into julienne-style
matchstick cuts. Be sure
that you get a good
one and be careful with

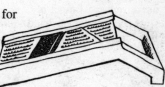

it. You can cut yourself unless you use the guards properly.
You can also cut french fries with this.

Big dinner and serving plates:

A dinner is much more exciting if served on large platters.
Loneoak, in California, makes my favorite large white
plates and serving platters. You can also find wonderful old
serving platters in antique and junk shops.

Big wooden salad bowl:

A good one will cost you some money, but if you like
salad, you know that the greens will just not taste as good
in metal or glass as they will in wood.

Large stainless-steel bowl:

All-purpose mixing bowl 15 inches
in diameter. Ideal for making
bread dough and covering it
while it rises.

Spaetzle maker:

This device rests on top of a
pot of boiling water. The round
hopper is filled with dumpling
batter and slid across the plate
consisting of holes. Dumplings
are cut off and cook when they
fall into the pot. Buy in
gourmet shops.

Sausage funnel:

Some electric mixers
have sausage-making
attachments, or you can
use a sausage funnel to
stuff the casings by hand.
Buy in gourmet shops.

Plastic pouring spouts:

Use in wine bottles for oils,
vinegars, etc. Buy in gourmet
shops or restaurant-supply
stores. I do not use metal
pouring spouts as they corrode
when used with soy sauce,
wine, or vinegar.

Instant response thermometer:

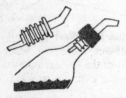

Calibrated from 0 degrees to 220
degrees. Use for making yogurt,
bread yeast, and cheese, and for
testing roasted meats for doneness. These
are not designed to stay in the oven
during cooking. Buy in gourmet shops and restaurant-
supply stores.

Baking sheets:
I think the age of burned rolls and cookies is over, and it is about time. Buy insulated or air-cushioned baking sheets and pans. Wilton has a line called Even-Bake. I have tried them and they work! Bagels, rolls, breads of any kind, turn out much better than you could possibly expect. These are first class!

Individual ovenproof casseroles:
Le Creuset has an elegant line of single-serving casseroles and baking dishes. These are great because you can freeze individual meals in them, then pull one from the freezer and place it right into a conventional oven whenever you like. They are not inexpensive, but they will last. You can also purchase small ovenproof soup crocks and casseroles at restaurant supply stores. These work well; however the dish could crack if you go directly from the freezer to a hot oven with them. These are inexpensive. Just allow thawing time if your individual meal is frozen.

Small loaf pans:
Purchase these in a good cookware shop to make "kid"-size loaves of bread. See page 295.

Anchor Hocking freeze, heat, and serve dishes:
So convenient for people cooking for one or for two. Made of a special plastic that goes right from the freezer into the microwave, or even into a conventional oven up to 400°.

Soda glasses:
Anchor Hocking manufactures replicas of old-time soda fountain glassware. These are lots of fun if you plan on making your own soda fountain classics at home. See pages 371 to 376 for recipes.

Glass baking dishes:
Anchor Hocking offers several shapes and sizes. They are

very inexpensive and durable. Find in good cookware shops and department stores. An absolute must for the kitchen.

Pastry blender:

This gadget is designed to incorporate butter or shortening into flour to make pastry doughs. You simply make short chopping motions into the butter and dry ingredients until a grainy texture is achieved. This procedure is known as "cutting in" the shortening.

Flavor injector:

This plastic device resembles a hypodermic needle and is used for injecting flavors and juices into meats.

Oil can:

Decant your peanut oil or olive oil into this can and keep it by the stove for cooking. The oil is dispensed through a very small spout, which means you'll probably use less oil in your cooking. The can will also protect the oil from sunlight, which could spoil it. Find in good cookware shops.

Large skimmer/strainer:

This has a long handle and an 8-inch-diameter head with holes. The handle allows you to reach into deep kettles, and the large holes in the head strain food quickly. Very versatile and ideal for straining pasta without having to drain the kettle.

Mighty O.J.:
Makes fresh-squeezed
orange juice in a snap.
Perfect for recipes that call
for a large quantity of fresh
citrus juice. If you don't
need a lot of juice at one
time, use a lemon reamer
(page 37).

Poly cutting board:
White plastic cutting board that is soft enough that it won't
damage your good knives. Place this board in the dishwasher for easy cleaning (unlike a wooden cutting board).

Cooking Methods and Terms

Al Dente

This is a wonderful Italian term that means to cook "to the teeth." It means nobody wants soggy pasta. Cook pasta to the teeth or until it is barely tender, still a bit firm. It is much better that way ... and the way Italians intended same to be eaten.

Blanching

Plunging food into boiling water for a very few minutes (the time varies and will be explained in each recipe). The food is then removed and generally placed in cold water to stop the cooking process. The purpose is to loosen the skin of a vegetable or fruit, to set the color of a vegetable, or to cook a food partially in preparation for later completion of the dish.

Browning Meat

When preparing stews and cassoulets, I usually do not flour the meat. You end up with browned flour instead of browning the natural sugars that are in the meat itself. Use a hot pan, and do not crowd the meat or cook it slowly. The meat should be seared or browned very rapidly, thus giving color to the stew and sealing in the meat juices.

Chow (Stir-fry)

A basic cooking method in the Chinese kitchen. Generally a wok is used, but you can also do this in a frying pan. The food is tossed about in a hot pan with very little oil, in a process not unlike sautéing.

Correct the Seasoning

When a dish is completed, a cook should always taste before serving. To correct the seasoning simply means to check for salt, pepper, or herbs to make sure that the dish has turned out as expected. A little correction at the last minute may be necessary.

Dash

Generally means "to taste." Start with less than $1/16$ teaspoon.

Deglazing a Pan

After meats or vegetables have been browned, wine or stock is added to the pan over high heat, and the rich coloring that remains in the pan is gently scraped with a wooden spoon and combined with the wine or stock. If there is excess fat in the pan, you may wish to pour it out before deglazing.

Develop

Developing a food product means that you have allowed it to sit for a time before serving so that the flavors have a chance to blend or brighten.

Dice

This means to cut into small cubes; the size of the cube is generally stated in the recipe. For instance, a $1/4$-inch dice means a cube of that size. It is accomplished very quickly and easily with a good vegetable knife.

Dredging in Flour

Meats or fish, generally sliced thin, are rolled about in flour in preparation for frying or sautéing. The flour is usually seasoned.

Dusting with Flour

Most often a fillet of fish or some type of shellfish (shrimps, scallops, etc.) is rolled in flour, and the excess flour is patted or shaken off. The idea is to have a very light coating on the food.

Grilling

An ancient method whereby the food is cooked on a rack or skewer over hot coals or an open flame.

Hack

When cutting up chicken or thin-boned meats, one "hacks" with a cleaver, thus cutting the meat into large but bite-size pieces and retaining the bone. The presence of the bone will help keep the meat moist during cooking. Do this hacking carefully.

Marinating

Meats or vegetables are soaked for a time in a flavoring liquid, such as soy sauce, wine, oil, or vinegar. The time of the marinating varies with the recipe.

Matchstick or Julienne Cut

Cut vegetables into thin slices, stack the slices, and then cut the slices into thin sticks, like matchsticks.

Mince

A minced vegetable or herb is one that is chopped very fine. It is fine enough to be of a very coarse, granular nature. This pertains especially to garlic, onions, and herbs. The process is done by hand with a knife, or with a food processor.

Pinch of Herbs or Spices

Usually means "to taste." Start with less than $1/16$ teaspoon, and then increase if you wish.

Poaching

Gently cooking fish, meat, or eggs in stock or water at just below a simmer. The liquid should just barely move during the poaching process. When fish or eggs are poached, a little vinegar or lemon juice is added to the liquid to help keep the food firm.

Puree

When you wish to make a sauce or soup that is free of all lumps of any sort, puree the stock. This means that you put it in a food processor and mill it until it is free of all lumps, or run it through a strainer or sieve.

Reducing

Boiling a sauce or liquid over high heat until it decreases in volume, generally by half. The result is a very rich concentration of flavors.

Roux

A blend of oil or butter and flour used to thicken sauces and gravies. The fat and flour are mixed together in equal amounts over heat. If a white *roux* is desired, the melting and blending are done over low heat for a few minutes. If a brown *roux* is desired, the flour is cooked in the fat until it is lightly browned.

Rubbed

When whole-leaf herbs, such as sage or bay leaves, are crushed in the hands so that their oils are released, the herbs are then referred to as having been rubbed.

Sauté

This term comes from a French word that means "to jump." In cooking, sauté means to place food in a very hot pan with a bit of butter or oil and to shake the pan during the cooking process so that the food jumps about. Thus one can cook very quickly over high heat without burning the food. It is not unlike Chinese chowing or stir-frying.

Scalded

Generally this term applies to milk in recipes and it simply means to heat the milk to just under simmering. The milk is scalded when it becomes very hot. It is not a boil at all.

Shot

A liquid measurement that amounts to very little, or "to taste." A shot of wine is about 1 ounce, but a shot of Tabasco is less than $\frac{1}{16}$ teaspoon.

Smoking and Tea Smoking

To cook or flavor food with smoldering wood. This can be done on the stove top with the Cameron Smoker, providing that there is a strong out-of-the-house exhaust system. Chinese black teas such as oolong or po nay can be added to the wood chips to enhance the flavor of the food you are smoking.

Stir-fry

See Chow (page 50).

Sweat

To sauté over low heat with a lid on. This method causes steam and expedites the cooking time.

Velveting

Deep-frying a food in oil at a temperature of about 280° to 300°. This procedure is commonly used for shellfish. The shrimp, etc., is first marinated in a cornstarch and egg white mixture. When deep-fried, a pale, light coating is formed. This process also has a very tenderizing effect.

When chopping, keep your fingers bent under.
Woof! Jeff taught me that one.

Ingredients, Condiments, and Food Definitions

Anchovies (flat, canned)
Used for salads and Italian and French cooking. Buy in cans from Portugal or Spain. Very salty.

Balsamic Vinegar
Italian wine vinegar that has been aged for years. This is wonderful, and no other vinegar can quite compare. From Modena, Italy. Find in any Italian market. The fancy food shops will charge you much too much money for this item.

Bulgur Wheat
Processed wheat for Middle Eastern dishes. Three grinds: fine, medium, and coarse. Find in Middle Eastern stores or in fancy supermarkets or gourmet stores.

Capers
Pickled buds used in salads and dressing. Found in any good supermarket.

Cream

When the term is used in this book, I mean half-and-half or heavy cream. Either may be used, or you may dilute heavy cream with milk.

Dijon Mustard

A style of mustard from France. A good American brand is Grey Poupon.

Dow See

See Fermented Black Beans (below).

Fermented Black Beans

Fermented black beans are a classic condiment in Chinese cuisine. Buy in Oriental markets and keep in tightly sealed glass jars. No need to refrigerate.

Hot Sauce

Tabasco or Trappey's Red Devil will do well. They are found in any supermarket.

Kitchen Bouquet

This is a vegetable extract used for coloring sauces or gravies. It can be found in any supermarket.

Leeks

These look like very large scallions. Wash carefully because they are usually full of mud. Found in the produce section of your supermarket.

Maggi Seasoning

This vegetable extract is used for flavoring soups and gravies. I think it is excellent and buy it in any supermarket.

Matzo Meal

Jewish flat bread that has been ground.

Mortadella
Famous sausage made in Bologna, Italy. Domestic brands can be found in Italian markets and delicatessens.

Mushrooms, Dried European
Cepe, boletus, or porcini. These are delicious but if they come from Europe they will be terribly expensive. Find an Italian market that brings them in from South America, and you will pay only somewhere between $14.00 and $20.00 a pound. The real Italian dried mushrooms will cost you a fortune! You may also find some that are domestic, or go to an Eastern European market and buy dried Polish mushrooms. In any case, keep them in a tightly sealed jar at the back of your refrigerator, where they will keep for a year.

Oils

Butter	Peanut oil
Olive oil	Sesame oil

These are the common oils that I use in my kitchen. I use little butter, but I enjoy the flavor. I dislike margarine.

Orzo
Pasta shaped like rice. Great for pilaf. Find it in Middle Eastern, Italian, or other good delicatessens as well as the supermarket.

Pesto
A sauce of northern Italian origin, made from fresh basil, olive oil, garlic, cheese, and pine nuts. Great for pasta or in soups and sauces. You can purchase this frozen or in glass jars at Italian markets. For a recipe, see page 266.

Pickling salt
Used in pickled meat dishes. Find in any supermarket.

Pine Nuts
Expensive little treasures that actually do come from large Italian pinecones. Find in Italian markets or substitute slivered almonds.

Quick-Rising Yeast

There are a couple of brands on the market now that will cause the dough to rise in half the time. Both Red Star and Fleischmann's manufacture such a thing. You can find these in any supermarket.

Saltpeter

A common kitchen chemical used in preserving meat or preparing corned beef or pork. May be purchased at a drugstore.

Sesame Oil

Used as a flavoring in Oriental cooking, not a cooking oil. Find this at an Oriental market. Used for flavoring a dish at the last minute. The health food store version is not made from toasted sesame seeds, so the flavor will be very bland.

Shallots

A cross between garlic and onion that are a classic ingredient in French cuisine. Find them in the produce section, or substitute a blend of onion and garlic.

Soy Sauce

Light: To be used when you don't want to color a dish with caramel coloring, which is what dark soy sauce contains. Do not confuse this with "Lite" soy sauce, which is lower in salt and flavor. Find in Oriental markets. I prefer Wing Nien brand. It is the very best quality and made by the company founded by my adopted Chinese uncle, Colonel John Young.

Dark: Used in dishes in which you wish to color the meat and sweeten the flavor with caramel sugar. Most common soy sauce. Buy a good quality. I prefer Wing Nien brand. See explanation above.

Tahini

A light paste made of toasted sesame seeds and sesame oil—almost like peanut butter. Used in many Middle Eastern dishes, it is to be found in Middle Eastern delicatessens or fancy supermarkets.

Wines for Cooking

All these wines are readily obtainable. Please do not buy wines that have salt added; they are labeled Cooking Wines but really should not be used at all. My rule is "If you can't drink it, don't cook with it."

Dry sherry
Dry red wine
Dry white wine
Sweet vermouth
Marsala

Herbs and Spices

Buying, Storing, and
Grinding Herbs and Spices

Herbs and spices are some of the most important ingredients in your kitchen. Try to keep them as fresh as possible, so don't buy them in large amounts. Keep them in tightly sealed jars. Try to buy most herbs and spices whole or in whole-leaf form; they have much more flavor that way. Crush the leaves as you add them to the pot. Or use a wooden or porcelain mortar and pestle. For seeds that are hard to grind, I use a small German electric coffee grinder (page 36). I have one that I use just for spices; it works very well.

Try to buy the herbs and spices that you use most frequently in bulk, and then put them in your own spice bottles. The saving realized here is about 70 percent. Hard to believe, but it is true. Find a market that has big jars of spices and you will be amazed at the difference in flavor.

Allspice
Not a blend of spices at all, but a single one. Basic to the kitchen. Buy it ground because it is hard to grind.

Basil

Common in French and Italian cooking. Grow it fresh or buy it dried, whole.

Bay Leaves

Basic to the kitchen for good soups, stews, etc. Buy whole, dried, or if your area is not too cold, grow a bay laurel tree. I have one in Tacoma.

Caraway Seed

This ancient dried seed is excellent for baking fresh breads. In Eastern Europe it is popular in sauerkraut.

Cayenne Pepper

Fine-ground red pepper, very hot.

Cilantro

This fresh form of the coriander plant looks very much like parsley. It can be found in many supermarkets and Oriental groceries.

Cinnamon

Hard to grind your own. Buy it powdered.

Cloves

I use both powdered and whole.

Coriander

The dry, whole seed is common in Mediterranean cooking. The fresh plant, which looks like parsley, is common in Chinese, Indian, and Mexican cuisines. You may see the fresh form in your supermarket listed as cilantro or Chinese parsley.

Cumin

Used in Mexican, Middle Eastern, and Indian cooking a great deal. Buy powdered in the can, or buy the whole seed and grind it. The flavor is much brighter with the whole seed.

Dillweed
Dried, whole. Great for salad dressings and dips. Common in Middle Eastern cuisine.

Fennel
A seed that resembles anise or licorice in flavor. Produces that special flavor in Italian sausage. Buy it whole and grind it as you need it.

Garlic
The bulb, of course. Use only fresh. And buy a good garlic press!

Ginger, Fresh
Very common in Chinese dishes. Buy by the "hand," or whole stem.

MSG
A powder made from seaweed or soybeans. Used as a natural flavor enhancer. Some people seem to be allergic to it and talk about Chinese restaurant syndrome, in which they have a light headache or chest pains after eating food containing too much monosodium glutamate (MSG). Very few people, percentagewise, are bothered by this natural chemical and I use it now and then. *It should be used sparingly, just as you use salt.*

Juniper Berries
These are to be found dried in good spice shops. They will remind you of the flavor of English gin. There is no substitute.

Mint, Fresh
Grow this in the backyard if you can. Great for salads, mint juleps, and Middle Eastern dishes.

Mustard, Dry

Absolute necessity if you love salad dressings. I buy Colman's from Britain.

Nutmeg

Basic to the kitchen. Buy it in bulk, and grate your own with an old-fashioned nutmeg grater.

Oregano

Basic to the kitchen for salads, meats, sauces, etc. You can grow your own, but the best comes from Greece. Buy whole, dried.

Paprika

Light, lovely flavor and color. Buy ground, imported from Hungary.

Parsley, Fresh

Buy in the supermarket produce section, or grow your own. I like the Italian variety, which has flat leaves and bright flavor.

Peppercorns, Black

Buy whole, and always grind fresh.

Red Pepper Flakes, Hot, Crushed

Also labeled "crushed red pepper flakes." Buy in bulk and use sparingly. The seeds make this a very hot product.

Rosemary

Basic to the cooking of Italy and southern France. Grow your own, or buy whole, dried.

Saffron

Real saffron is from Spain and is the dried stamens from the saffron crocus. It costs $2,000 a pound. Buy it by the pinch or use Mexican saffron, which includes the whole flower and is very cheap. Works well, just remember to use much more.

Sage
Basic kitchen herb. Grow your own or buy whole, dried.

Sumac
Herb grown in the Middle East. Burgundy or rust in color and has a wonderful tangy flavor. The Persians sprinkle it on their food and the Lebanese enjoy it as well.

Thyme
Necessary to good French cooking—soups to stews to meat dishes. Buy it whole, dried, or grow your own.

Zartar Blend
From Lebanon. Find in Middle Eastern markets. A blend of *zaatar* (a marjoramlike herb), sumac bark, and chickpeas or sesame seeds. Common in foods from the Middle East.

Television Shows and Recipes

NOTE: Dishes marked with a * were simply displayed and described. A recipe or demonstration was not given for those dishes. However, you will find a full recipe for the dish on the designated page.

SHOW NUMBER AND TITLE

801 BREAD

Jeff opens the new season in his new television kitchen in Seattle.

Offers Basic Bread Dough (page 291) and secrets of easy bread baking (pages 289–90)

Caraway Rye Bread (page 294)

Salami, Olive, and Cheese Bread (page 293)

Rolled Pizza (page 307)

Onion Custard Bread (page 306)

Mincemeat Bread (page 294)

802 PASTA

Pasta is *the* dish for the contemporary kitchen. Jeff prepares a dish for everyone in the family.

Spaghetti with Peanut Butter Sauce (page 217)

Spaghettini with Sand (page 221)

Green Fettuccine with Duck and Porcini Sauce (page 219)

Lidia, chef at Felidia in New York, teaches the kids to make Potato Gnocchi Lidia (page 222)

803 CRUCIFEROUS VEGETABLES

The *Frugal Gourmet Whole Family Kitchen* celebrates what the kids call the "yuck" vegetables. Jeff prepares them in such a way that the kids love them.

Cabbage Sautéed with Caraway (page 241)

Breaded Brussels Sprouts (page 242)

Baked Cauliflower (page 243)

Cauliflower Salad, Russian Style (page 245)

*Mustard Greens Soup (page 101)

*Cabbage Soup with Juniper and Pork (page 103)

804 FRIENDLY FUNGUS

A visit to a mushroom farm gets the kids into "fungus."

Mushrooms and Rice (page 247)

Marinated Button Mushrooms (page 246)

Stuffed Mushrooms (page 248)

*Cream of Mushroom Soup (page 102)

*Mushroom Caviar (page 249)

*Mushrooms on Toast (page 250)

805 THE SALAD BOWL

The Frug offers several salads that will hold for a few days, perfect for the busy cook or the single householder.

One-Week Coleslaw (page 117)

Black-eyed Pea Salad (page 116)

Flank Steak and Lentil Salad (page 119)

*Pasta and Kidney Bean Salad (page 114)

*Patty's Fennel Salad (page 118)
*Red Potato Salad with Bacon (page 121)
*Green Bean Salad, Chinese Style (page 123)
*Artichoke with Egg and Parsley Salad (page 124)

806 RELIGIOUS SIGNIFICANCE OF FOOD

Rabbi Marc Gellman of New York joins Jeff to talk about food in Biblical times and the meaning of the Passover seder.

Honey Whole-Wheat Challah (page 302)
Gefilte Chicken (page 168)
*Challah (page 300)

807 FISH

Jeff offers fish dishes that anyone in the whole family kitchen can appreciate . . . including the kids.

Fish Paste with Cookie Cutters (page 143)
*Fish Dumplings (page 151)
Black Cod, Chinese Style (page 142)
Fish Marinated in Herbed Olive Oil (page 147)
*Seafood in Saffron Cream (page 145)
*Sicilian Tuna (page 144)
*Salmon Salad (page 148)
*Steamed Mussels with Caramelized Onions (page 141)

808 HERBS

The Frugal Gourmet discusses various fresh herbs and their use in healthy and creative cooking.

Pesto Tomato Sauce (page 267)
Minted Peas and Onions (page 267)
Basil, Tomato, and Onion Salad with Cheese (page 268)
*Garlic Herb Soup (page 269)
Herbed Onion Relish (page 271)
Roasted Garlic Butter (page 270)

*Herbed Zucchini Quiche (page 272)
*Herb Bread (page 273)

809 THE GRILL

Jeff talks about the difference between the grill and the griddle and how each can be used in the whole family kitchen.

Grilled vegetables (pages 234 to 235)
Infused oils (pages 152, 197, and 273)
Grilled Pork (page 185)
*Fish Grilled in a Rack (page 151)
Pride of Deer Camp Barbecue Sauce (page 186)
*Grilled Chicken with Rosemary (page 171)

810 CHICKEN

Jeff is still convinced that chicken remains one of the best foods for the modern family unit. Easy to prepare and everybody loves it!

Chicken Patties with Soy and Sweet Vermouth Dip (page 173)
*Chicken Cacciatore (page 172)
*Low-Salt/Low-Fat Chicken Craig (page 174)
Chicken Thighs in Yogurt and Onions (page 175)
Chicken Drumettes for Kids (page 176)

811 DESIGNER IN THE KITCHEN

The Frugal Gourmet shares with us one of his favorite friends, a famous designer, Sara Little. They discuss the kitchen, the meaning of good design, and the nurturing aspects of food.

Chicken in a Nest (page 178)
Peas in Acorn Squash (page 240)
Little Sandwiches (page 328) for after school
    Cucumber with Mayonnaise and Dill (page 328)
    Peanut Butter with Potato Chips (page 328)

Olive Relish on Toast (page 329)
Lettuce Rolls (page 327)
Spaghetti Sauce Bread Dip (page 326)

812   FRUIT

New eating habits point to a wider use of fruit in our diets.
Fruit dishes that are fun for kids is the theme of this show.

Fried Fruit Salad (page 280)
Strawberries with Balsamic Vinegar (page 286)
Baked Apples (page 281)
Broiled Grapefruit (page 284)
*Pear Tart (page 283)
*Peach Cobbler (page 282)
*Blackberry Cobbler (page 282)

813   THE EGG

Jeff takes us to an enormous egg farm and then offers recipes for this versatile food product for the whole family
kitchen.

Eggs Scrambled with Curry and Water Chestnuts (page
202)
Piperade (page 204)
Egg Salad Sandwiches, Old-fashioned Style (page 205)
Omelets (pages 207 to 211)
Soft Eggs and Prawns, Chinese Style (page 206)
*Crustless Green Chile Quiche (page 203)

814   COOKING FOR ONE

Jeff introduces us to several people who live alone, including his mother, Emely. Some dishes and solutions to cooking for one are offered.

Marion's Sugar Cookies (page 315)
Marion's Skokie Casserole (page 225)
Emely's freezer methods (pages 80 to 81)

Tony's Fried Endive (page 235)
Tony's Endive Salad (page 131)

815   FOOD AND COLOR

The Frug visits with a world-famous glassblower and artist,
Dale Chihuly. We watch a glass artisan from Venice make
a beautiful plate and then a discussion is held with our
young friends as to how the color of food on a plate affects
our appetite.

Craig prepares a seafood salad and Jeff serves an entire
buffet of one color, only one (pages 381 to 385).

816   YOUNG PERSON'S DINNER PARTY

Jeff and Craig take some young people to a formal restaurant, where they discuss table manners. Then, back to the
kitchen, where they prepare dishes that young people really
enjoy.

Karen's Meat Loaf (page 188)
    with Porcini Gravy (page 189)
Lettuce Rolls with cold meats (page 327)
Lettuce Rolls with scrambled eggs (page 327)
New York Onion Sauce for Hot Dogs (page 330)
*Peas and Lentils (page 256)
*Corn Salad (page 132)
*Private Loaf Pans (page 295)
*Pita Bread Pizzas (page 332)
*First-Class Toasted Cheese (page 332)
*Rice Timbales (page 257)

817   COOKING WITH ELMO, PART 1

The Frugal Gourmet invites his young friend Elmo, from
Sesame Street, to cook. Kitchen safety for a young person
is discussed as well as the wonders of the stove, the fire,
and flame.

Pork and Black Pepper, Chowed (page 192)
Steamed Shrimp with Sesame Oil (page 154)

818   COOKING WITH ELMO, PART 2

Sesame Street's Elmo returns to the whole family kitchen to cook again with Jeff. More on kitchen safety for young and old alike. Sautéed and smoked foods are celebrated.

Chicken Smoked with Olive Oil (page 177)
Lamb with Green Peppers and Carrots (page 190)

819   THE AMERICAN SODA FOUNTAIN, PART 1

Jeff has located a real soda fountain from the 1920s. He takes some young people through the history of ice cream and soda water and then prepares treats from the old days.

Sodas (page 372)
Milk Shakes (page 372)
Frappes (page 373)
Malted Milk Shakes (page 373)
Sundaes (page 373)
Black and Whites (page 374)
Purple Cows (page 374)
Dusty Millers (page 374)
Phosphates (page 375)
Floats (page 375)
Banana Splits (page 375)
Brooklyn Egg Creams (page 375)

820   THE AMERICAN SODA FOUNTAIN, PART 2

Jeff is amused with the language of the old-fashioned soda fountain clerks called Jerks! He explains the language used in a luncheonette during the forties and fifties and offers some quick examples of the foods offered there.

Egg Salad Sandwiches, Old-fashioned Style (page 205)
Tuna Salad Sandwich (page 331)
Toasted Cheese Sandwich (page 332)
Date-Nut Bread with Cream Cheese and Walnuts (page 333)

If I skid on the kitchen floor, you can be sure that someone else is going to skid as well. Keep the floor clean and use rugs that won't slip or turn up if you have short people like me about.

COOKING FOR ONE

I do not do loneliness. I cannot take it, and it seems to be one of the most rapidly growing social realities in our culture. In the beginning of the nineties we discovered that 23 million Americans live alone. That, according to *The New York Times,* is one quarter of all American households, and twice the number of single households reported in the 1970 census.

What is different about living alone?

Some people really seem to enjoy solitude. No one else is in the bathroom . . . there are no phone calls for someone else . . . no one is watching TV when you want to read. Other than those luxuries, living alone each day is a little too quiet for me. But some like it.

When I told my mother, Emely, who has lived by herself for about thirty years, that I was writing an article about the problems of loneliness in a single household, she immediately tried to set me straight. She always has! She points to the fact that she is not lonely at all when eating. She has the newspaper, the television, and now and then a neighbor's cat stops by to chat and mooch a meal. She has friends down the hall and she goes out for lunch now and then with two girlfriends that she has known since I was in Cub Scouts. But she is different from many who suddenly find themselves living alone in our time. The difference is that she has been living like this for years, and she is a survivor . . . and a stubborn Norwegian on top of it!

I think my mother's secret to living alone and enjoying it centers around the fact that she has disciplined herself always to eat very well. She loves to cook and to eat, and she is in great shape. For most people, living alone is very depressing and thus they tend to eat poorly. The most accepted solution to solitary diets seems to center around frozen and prepared foods.

The frozen TV dinner tray offers an out, I suppose, but it is still a very lonely meal. We thought for a while that privately prepared foods would be a great blessing for the whole culture, but we now seem to be realizing that the great blessing of privateness also comes with the burden of loneliness.

I cannot eat privately. It just kills me. I have to be with someone when I am eating, even though they are not with me at table. For me the table is the proper place for communication and I need to be in the presence of other people when I eat. When I am on the road I cannot eat in my room. I go to a restaurant and sit by myself . . . but even then people wave and come over to me to say hello and to tell me that the shows are helpful. I feel better. Right away! It took me a long time on the road to learn to eat alone in a decent place without dying from guilt over the fact that my wife, Patty, and the boys were not with me. I can do it now, as I have accepted the fact that I am who I am. And my feeling of loneliness while on the road is a great luxury since I am able to get up and fly home. Many people who live alone do not have that wonderful possibility.

For many singles in our culture, loneliness is a sign of rejection, particularly among the elderly. The family, if there is one, does not call often enough and when they do they always tell the person living alone that they are "so proud of you since you live all by yourself. You are so wonderfully independent!" So many of our older citizens live by themselves simply because they do not want to be a burden of any sort on the family. If you have an older relative who lives alone, and of whom you are justly proud, I think you had best go visit to find out if your relative really enjoys living alone or if he/she is suffering from the loneliness of independence.

Loneliness often results in a lowering of self-esteem, of self-worth. Why am I by myself? Why do I feel of so little value? If you have lived with someone for years and that precious person dies, you may well feel this lack of personal value. Something that has gone on for years has been taken from you and you must learn to adapt to a whole new life-style. You must learn to enter that fraternity of those who live alone, and this is really tough on widows and widowers. And I have met many bachelors and single women who feel the same loneliness.

What are the problems that come from eating alone? Most people, unless you are as tough as my mother, suffer from any or all of the following:

Problems

Poor diet.
They don't take the time to prepare nutritious meals.

Little variety in food.
They get into ruts and eat the same thing too often.

Frozen-food syndrome.
They rely too much on prepared frozen meals, which may be convenient but they offer too much salt and fat and too little in the way of flavor and nourishment.

Eating too much due to loneliness.
They fall back on memories of their childhood when eating was a sign of affection, and thus eat too much due to loneliness.

Eating too little due to loneliness.
Loneliness causes many to feel that they are not worth the effort involved in preparing a good meal . . . so they do not eat well. "I'm just not worth it!" It is a matter of integrity.

I can only suggest a few solutions to the truly difficult problems that I have listed above.

Solutions

If you live alone, eat with someone else at least three times a week.

When someone is sitting across the table, you are less likely to eat too much or too little. Learn to watch out for one another.

Cook full meals several times a week and freeze them.

You will find marvelous new plastic freezer containers on the market that will go from the freezer into the microwave. Anchor Hocking has a new line of Pop-Top containers that are great for any kitchen, but particularly helpful to people with arthritis of the hands.

Anchor Hocking has also been thinking about the growing number of single persons living alone, and they make a whole line of oven- and microwave-proof glassware for cooking and freezing in small amounts. These items are well made but not expensive.

Schiller and Asmus, the makers of porcelain-covered heavy cast-iron metalware from France, have put a line of small frying pans, casseroles, and oval baking dishes on the market. They are colorful and work very well, though they tend to be expensive. These may be great gifts for your relatives who live by themselves . . . whether widow, widower, bachelor, or single woman. Hey, don't forget the young kids who live by themselves!

You might go to a local restaurant supply house and purchase some individual ovenproof porcelain casseroles with lids. You can freeze food in these or use them in the oven, though after taking them from the freezer, you must bring them to room temperature before putting them in the oven. These are great for freezing meals. Just label them and stuff the freezer.

Look around the department stores for a small Chinese wok for just one or two. I have several of these and love them. You can find them with a nonstick surface and they are just great for cooking for one or two or for heating things up in a hurry. I sent Jason and Channing, my sons in college, several of these and they love them.

Prepare your own frozen dinners. If you cook one day a week, you can put dinners, sauces, vegetables, casseroles together and freeze them in small containers. When you are ready to eat, the freezer is ready for you. My mother is so involved in such preparation that her freezer is stuffed all of the time. The other day I walked by the thing and it burped at me!

Prepare good meals for yourself.
If you can get into thinking about meals for a few weeks instead of a single meal for a single night, you will eat much better.

Prepare ahead of time and freeze:

Sauces (spaghetti, omelet, gravy, etc.)
Chili
Baked pasta
Meat loaf
Casseroles
Omelet fillings
Soups

All of these freeze well. In addition, see the section on salads to make ahead. These will hold for a few days.

Keep powdered milk about.
New versions are much better than those you remember from years ago, and such milk is easy to store and use . . . and a very necessary source of calcium and vitamins A and D. But no fat! Use in cooking and, when you are in a pinch, for fresh nonfat milk.

Avoid canned food as much as possible.
Fresh is best. Please see to it that you get the food you deserve. I know that sometimes you may have to rely on

canned food, but please do it as seldom as possible. Fresh foods are much better for you, and they are certainly more enjoyable at table.

I have told you nothing that you did not already know. However, I hope that I am giving you that extra push so that you will feed yourself well.

Finally, if you always have something ready in your refrigerator or freezer, you are ready to invite someone over for a meal. It will be no chore for you, and that person should invite you back within a few days.

If someone is kind enough to feed you, be sure to say, "Thank you," even if it is a dish that you don't like. I know, as I have eaten a lot of dog food!

I know some friends who prepare food and place it in small containers and then trade with other friends who live alone. Further, you know me well enough to realize that I would prefer to trade and thus increase the variety of my diet. I think you and I are together on this one!

Our friend and studio helper Marion suffered the loss of her husband a few years ago. In order to fight her sense of loneliness, she prepares casseroles and delivers them to sick or lonely friends. What a great way to still feel useful and good about yourself. But then, that is Marion, a grandma's grandma.

HEALTHY EATING

Salt and fat, along with Big Macs and Sugar Smacks, have become new words for sin in our time. The problem is our health, and the question is, can we eat our way to health? Are there certain food products that we need to avoid in order to become a healthier person, a person more in charge of his/her own existence? I do not believe that we can label one or two food products as the sources of our heart and obesity problems, but many in our culture seem to feel that abstaining from this or that will actually solve the problem. Further, many of the professionals in the health field have played into this very American game of seeking a few items on which we can pin our health difficulties. So many nutritional reports have come out during the last few years, reports that claim that this food product or that food product is bad for us, that the American public is becoming fearful of enjoying a real meal. Then, a few months after the first terrifying article, another appears that claims the first article was false. I talk with people every day who really no longer have any idea as to what healthy eating is. That is how confused we are. Maybe there's more confusion than fear.

I don't really believe that there is one single solution to our dilemma. We seem to have reacted to the current new information on food and health in the same way that we react to most things in our time. Instant gratification means that if we have a pain we take a pill. If we are bored . . . well, we have a pill for that, too. We seem to think that problems of health should also have quick solutions. "Cut down on this and eat more of that!" The relationship between eating and physical health is not that simple.

Let me point to some of the more confusing areas.

Salt is a major concern in our time. I have cut down on salt since I had an artificial valve placed in my heart, and the dietician told me that I must avoid salt as it would raise my blood pressure. I have since learned that only 20 percent of the persons in our culture are affected in this way by salt, and even those studies are now in question. Many doctors are now looking at the possibility of a lack of calcium being an issue in hypertension, or high blood pressure, and they are urging us to cut down on salt all right, but to drink plenty of milk for calcium.

Meanwhile, in France a scientist asks why the French can eat so much salt and butterfat, primarily in the form of wonderful cheeses, and not have heart problems similar to those found in America. While he has not yet totally finished his experiments, he believes that fresh milk is a critical factor here, in that milk fat, in the fresh form, will adhere to the walls of our arteries while fermented milk, in the form of cheese, will be much less likely to do so. But with our hamburger and french fries, we often have a milkshake, possibly compounding our fat intake problem. Further, many dieticians feel that our children drink milk long after it is needed in their diet, thus possibly giving rise to a lifetime of high blood pressure and heart problems. Certainly calcium is needed regularly for our entire lives, but perhaps we might consider other sources than just milk. However, here again is confusion, since milk and milk fat are tolerated very well by some people.

A possible solution to the problem of milk in our diet and hypertension may be found in the fact that the French drink so much more red wine with their meals than we do. I know, just a short time ago we were told to cut back on alcohol for the sake of our hearts. Then some other authorities decided that a little wine in moderation, such as two or three glasses a day with meals, would be helpful to the heart. There also seems to be some evidence for the claim that wine helps in breaking down fatty substances that build up in our arteries. And wine certainly helps relieve stress.

Since the French drink on the average of ten times more wine each year per person than we do and have fewer heart problems, perhaps we should listen to this French doctor. But we must also point out the fact that the French have more liver problems.

This sounds like dangerous talk if you or someone in your family is addicted to alcohol. Everything in this article is intended to point to moderation in all things. That is just a good basic rule!

Since I have long advocated cooking with wine, I must respond to another study that I believe frightened many American cooks in a most irresponsible way. Many newspapers recently reported the findings of a study that claimed that all of the alcohol does not cook out when you cook with wine. The authors stated that 5 percent of the alcohol remains in the cooked food. Since I was a chemistry major in my early days, I must dispute the study on purely scientific terms. Alcohol cooks out at 160°, and water does not even boil until 212°. Thus, if alcohol is placed in a boiling stew or soup, it evaporates before the meal is served. However, even if these people are right in claiming a bit of the alcohol remains, what is the point in making such a claim that is not fully explained? The alcohol that could remain in the stewing pot is so minimal that it is inconsequential. For instance 2 cups of wine, containing 12 percent alcohol, are placed in a chicken or beef stew for 8 persons. When the cooking is completed and the dish is served, there could remain in the pot only a tiny bit more than ½ *teaspoon* of alcohol for the entire 8 people! Now, that bit is certainly not even going to be noticed and it is physically impossible to be affected by so little a thing. According to this study, even a lemon pound cake, flavored with vanilla and lemon extracts, should have more alcohol in it than the stew! We seem so prone to exaggerate these studies when seeking healthy eating habits. Maybe it is just the American press, since the actual study did talk about the fact that the final alcohol content in a dish had a great deal to do with the nature of the food itself and the length of time that it was cooked. The newspapers should bring the whole story, not just some new and amazing fact that sounds incomprehensible.

We are told to avoid nitrates in our foods. However, if we really do not understand what nitrates are, then we are duped into avoiding the wrong foods. We run to the health food store and order organically grown carrots, rather than commercially grown carrots, in order to avoid nitrates. Catch this! A pound of organically grown carrots contains more nitrates than a pound of commercially grown carrots, and more nitrates than a pound of bologna.

Fat is another product that has been given so much press lately that we are reluctant to enjoy good cooking. No, I am not calling for gross use of butter in the frying pan, though you will never find me using margarine. I am convinced that hydrogenating vegetable oils in order to make them firm produces something that is even harder to digest than butter. Many dieticians agree. What is it then about fat that causes such concern?

The major concern is cholesterol, which builds up on the walls of our arteries and thus blood cannot flow freely, hence high blood pressure. Our heart has to work too hard to pump blood through this tightened system.

All fats, whether animal or vegetable, contain the same calorie count and all cause the liver to produce cholesterol, but animal fats cause the liver to become much more active in this production than do vegetable fats. So, when you read a label that says the product is "lower in cholesterol," you must check to see what kind of oil the manufacturer is talking about, and how much of that oil the product actually contains. Of course, there is no cholesterol in vegetable oils; only fats that come from animals that have livers contain cholesterol. But *all* fats and oils cause the human liver to produce cholesterol, so the solution is to cut down on all fats of any and every kind.

A completely fat-free diet is very dangerous since fat is necessary to our bodily functions. The question is whether or not you can digest the fats that you take in. In my kitchen I stick to olive oil, peanut oil, and small amounts of butter for flavoring. The new word on olive oil is that it is good for your system since it is of the unsaturated fatty acid family and it actually helps break down cholesterol that has built up in your system. Peanut oil is in this same helpful group. So I use these two oils in cooking. I do not use lighter oils in cooking, oils such as cottonseed or soybean, since they have a tendency to burn at cooking temperatures, thus producing peroxides that many feel are even more dangerous to our systems. These lighter oils are fine for salads.

I have tried to cut down on animal fat of every form, but I still enjoy meat. I love pork and beef and I simply choose lean cuts, trim most of the fat away, though I eat more stews than I do steaks. Pork spareribs, a favorite at our house, are celebrated now and then. Moderation remains the key.

Please do not think that chicken or poultry fat is better for you than beef or pork fat. The qualities are similar, though poultry fat is easier to remove since most of the fat is in the skin. Pull off the skin and go at it!

Some other factors concerning our new knowledge of fats will help to confuse you further. We were told a few years ago to avoid fatty fish such as black cod and my beloved salmon. Now we are told that these fish fats are actually good for us . . . but again, moderation is the key.

I read a wonderful article in *The New York Times* the other day in which some French doctors claim that the reason that people in southern France, where goose and duck fat is popular, do not have serious heart ailments is because goose and duck fat is closer to olive oil than to butter. Further, the French always consume a bit of red wine with the fat, and thus it is better digested. I will be waiting to hear from our American authorities on this one. I love duck fat.

Finally, we should admit that no single diet is right for everyone. Our body chemistries are different, and we have different needs.

From my own study of American eating habits I have come up with the following suggestions. Again, moderation is, as far as I am concerned, the key to proper eating.

1. Don't binge.

Running from one diet to another will never really help your system, and in the long run you will probably gain back any weight that you may have lost. Dieting seems to lead to bingeing, and bingeing back to dieting . . . so it is hard to win.

2. Eat a variety of fresh foods. Avoid processed or fast foods as much as possible.

Some experts feel that the four food groups should be changed from dairy, meat, vegetables and fruit, and grains to a new emphasis on grains, fruit, vegetables, and beans. We do need to cut down on meat and animal fat, but we certainly do not need to eliminate it entirely. Don't take away my beloved cheese! While I could never be a complete vegetarian, I have cut down on animal fat intake. I do believe that one is not going to eat a healthy diet if the diet is boring. There is no way to get around that fact. A boring diet will simply cause you to cheat . . . and that is no way to maintain one's sanity. Cut down on meat and eat more beans and grains. Eat fresh vegetables and enjoy a good salad. Keep cruciferous vegetables in your diet as many authorities believe that these vegetables (cabbage, kale, broccoli, Brussels sprouts) inhibit certain forms of cancer. In short, eat what your great-grandmother called a good diet. It is true that we have gone overboard on meat, but I see no need to give it up entirely if we return to a balanced diet. It is not difficult to do.

3. Cut down on fat intake but do not eliminate it.

Olive oil is great on bread, so you can cut down on butter. Trim your favorite meat cuts and *never* buy hamburger from a butcher. Buy a pot or chuck roast, or a beef round, trim it well, and grind your own hamburger. You will be startled by the increase in flavor. You might also try very lean cuts of meat, such as Select. It is less expensive than Prime or Choice since the fat is not marbled but, rather, in chunks on the side that are easy to remove. Grind the meat and add a little olive oil to replace the fat content. Great flavor!

4. Cut down on fresh milk fat but get that calcium.

I think we keep fatty milk in our diet much longer than we need to. Our bodies do not need much regular milk as long as we get enough calcium in the rest of our diet. Milk is just one of those favorite foods from our youth that make us feel like Mom is still there with the cookies. Try replacing your love for milk with the wonderful cheeses offered us by our American cheese makers. Some studies indicate that fermented milk, or cheese, is much easier to digest than fresh milk. And there are low-fat cheeses, though I dislike most of them. Further, there are many other foods that are high in calcium, such as clams, oysters, canned salmon with the bones, sardines, herring, almonds, and collard, turnip, and mustard greens. Cabbage as well. And don't forget that nonfat fresh milk! You might even consider nonfat or low-fat yogurt, along with frozen yogurt.

5. Add dinner wine to your menu.

Wine in moderation seems to be one of the best things that we can do for ourselves. Not only will it get us off coffee and soda pop but it will help us relax at dinnertime. Further, it helps in digestion and appetite, and many studies indicate that it is good for the heart. Red wine seems to be best here.

6. Snack only on healthy foods.

We have gotten into the habit of having a big greasy jelly donut at 10:00 A.M., then lunch, then some kind of pastry with coffee in the afternoon, then dinner. I am sure it is just habit, and a comforting habit at that, but we certainly don't need it. I think we will feel better if we take in more moderate amounts of food and enjoy it more. Avoid sugar and fat, and if you feel the need to snack, then choose fruit. And a friend who is really in the know in this field tells

me that many times we snack when we are only thirsty.
Try drinking more water each day.

7. Try to eat often with others.

You will eat a much healthier diet, and less in terms of
amounts, if someone you like is sitting across the table from
you. Dr. Evette Hackman, a nutritionist and a charming
person, claims that she has a dietician friend who says,
"Reach for your mate, instead of your plate!"

8. Get rid of the guilt of eating in our time.

Now and then you are going to want to go for the pork
spareribs. Do so for your own sanity and desires, but balance off the old piggy with some low-fat grain dishes and
lots of vegetables. Nothing to feel guilty about . . . now and
then.

9. Maintain moderate weight.

If that is not for you, okay. But do not binge out on sweet
and fatty snack foods and then wonder why you keep gain-
ing. Make a change to healthier eating habits slowly, but
make it, especially for the sake of your life.

I hope that in offering you this information I have not
come off as if I think I am an authority on health and diet.
I am not. However, since my artificial heart valve was im-
planted within me, I have been so thankful to be alive that
I have tried very hard to pay attention to what is going on
in the food world and to the new dieticians and food professionals . . . people who really care. (No, I did not need a
valve replacement due to bad eating habits. I had rheumatic
fever when I was a child and I blew out my aortic valve.)
The new foodies who care, at least in the professional field,
are a good lot, but since we have so much information
coming at us all at once, we really need to listen very carefully. There is no simple solution to healthy eating in our
time. Every one of us is different, and each of us needs to
develop eating habits that work for us. Cutting down on
salt or fat is only a part.

No diet is going to work if the diet does not also include

an evaluation of the way you live. Do you get enough rest? Do you drink too much alcohol? Do you allow yourself to be put under heavy stress while working? Do you take enough time off from work so that you can remember who you are? Do you relax and have fun? Do you take prescription drugs to alleviate symptoms that could be better dealt with by a change in life-style? The term "body," meaning yours and mine, refers to a package deal. That is what the body means. A thousand forces can influence our bodies every day, and we have to take charge. A change in diet will probably not do a complete job, but coupled with a good understanding of ourselves and those around us, the diet will certainly help.

(I can see it coming. Patty, my wife, always edits my remarks and I know what she is going to say about the above paragraph. "Jeffrey, did you write that for your readers or for yourself?")

What's the difference?

Now, go to the table and do what your Greek grandma used to tell you to do. "Be quiet, and eat your broccoli!"

RECIPES

Soups

During the nineties I expect to see the American household return to the enjoyment of beautiful soup. I say "return" because a generation ago soup was an expected part of the meal. Now we claim that we don't have time to make such a treasure, and I think that is just a shame.

We bring back the soup pot with relish . . . and for two reasons. First, soup is delicious, absolutely grand, when made from the beginning. Second, soup is frugal, as nothing is wasted, nothing! We are going to learn a great deal about "waste not, want not" during the nineties.

When I was a child during the Second World War, I remember my mother making vegetable soup, and it was during difficult times. How she loved soup, and as my interest in cooking increased, I began to pay more attention to what she put in the pot. I finally realized that what she was serving was "Synopsis Soup," a brief synopsis of the past week. Nothing was wasted, nor was it a leftover for long. Eventually, it wound up in the soup pot. I still love that kind of thing, and the thicker the better. I love soups so thick that you have to push on the spoon to get it to sink!

I have always made similar soups for my family, but I was not aware of the fact that the boys were on to me.

When Jason was quite young, he helped me with a live television show in Chicago. While his brother, Channing, was demonstrating wok cooking, the audience howled when poor Channing's potholder caught on fire. Not to be outdone, for Jason is an actor and loves an audience, he turned to me and told me about leftovers. He came up with a great line. "Dad, you know how I feel about leftovers. If I don't like something that you cook then you mix it with something else and if I don't like that then you mix it with something else and if I don't like that then you put it on a sandwich and if I don't like that then you put it in a salad and if all else fails you make soup out of it!"

You are right, Jason. That is what leftovers are for.

Now, let's get out the soup pot and get frugal!

MUSTARD GREENS SOUP
SERVES 6 TO 8

My real love for mustard greens soup began when I was a kid spending my allowance at a Chinese restaurant. This soup is a snap to make at the last minute, providing you have prepared the soup stock a few days before. It has a very clean flavor that all members of your family crowd will enjoy.

2 quarts Chicken Stock (page 109) or use canned
½ cup dry white wine
3 tablespoons olive oil
2 cloves garlic, peeled and crushed

1 cup peeled and thinly sliced yellow onion
1½ bunches mustard greens, washed and chopped
2 eggs, beaten
Salt and freshly ground black pepper to taste

In a 4-quart pot, bring the stock and wine to a simmer. Heat a large frying pan and add 2 tablespoons of the oil, the garlic, and onion. Sauté until the onion just becomes tender, and add to the pot of simmering stock. Heat the frying pan again and add the remaining tablespoon of oil. Sauté the mustard greens a few minutes until they collapse. Add to the pot. Cover and simmer 5 minutes or until the mustard greens and onion are tender. Pour the beaten eggs slowly over the top of the soup and gently stir in. Salt and pepper to taste.

CREAM OF MUSHROOM SOUP
SERVES 8 TO 10

This is a classic opener for a dinner party. And you and the crowd that you call your family in our time should have more dinner parties. Made ahead, it only improves in flavor, but be careful when heating it up before dinner, as you do not want to burn it or curdle it. Just be gentle with low heat.

1 ounce dried mushrooms (Italian porcini or the South American variety, which cost much less, see page 57)

2 quarts Chicken Stock (page 109) or use canned

¾ cup butter

¾ cup all-purpose flour

½ cup dry white wine

2 tablespoons olive oil

3 cloves garlic, peeled and crushed

1 pound fresh mushrooms, sliced

1 cup heavy cream

½ teaspoon Worcestershire sauce

2 tablespoons dry sherry

Salt and freshly ground black pepper to taste

GARNISH

Fresh chopped chives

Place the dried mushrooms in a small bowl and add 1 cup of hot water. Allow to soak for 45 minutes. Bring the stock to a simmer in a 4-quart pot. In a small frying pan, melt the butter. Add the flour to the butter and cook together to form a *roux* but do not brown. Using a wire whisk, whisk the *roux* into the hot stock. Continue whisking until smooth and lump free. Stir the wine into the pot, cover, and simmer gently. Heat a large frying pan and add the oil and garlic

and sauté a few seconds (be careful not to burn the garlic).
Add the fresh mushrooms and sauté until just tender. Strain
the liquid from the dried mushrooms into the thickened
stock. Chop the soaked mushrooms coarsely and add to the
frying pan. Sauté a few minutes more. Add the contents of
the frying pan to the pot along with the cream and the
Worcestershire sauce. Simmer for 5 minutes more. Add the
sherry, salt and pepper to taste, and garnish with chives.

CABBAGE SOUP WITH
JUNIPER AND PORK
SERVES 8 TO 10

This is a most hearty soup and it really is much better after
cooking and then sitting in the refrigerator for a few days.
It is typical of the soups that are celebrated in Eastern Europe and it is a whole meal in itself. Serve with very dark
bread and lots of beer.

3 quarts Chicken
   Stock (page
   109) or use
   canned
3 tablespoons olive
   oil
3 cloves garlic,
   peeled and
   crushed
1 medium yellow
   onion, peeled
   and sliced
3 pounds green
   cabbage, cored
   and shredded

1 pound pork steak,
   deboned and
   julienned
1½ teaspoons juniper
   berries
½ cup dry white
   wine
Salt and freshly
   ground black
   pepper to taste

Heat the stock in an 8-quart stainless-steel soup pot. Heat a large frying pan and add 2 tablespoons of the oil, the garlic, and onion. Sauté until the onion is clear. Add the cabbage and sauté 5 minutes more. Add to the pot of stock. Heat the frying pan again and add the remaining tablespoon of oil. Add the julienned pork and brown the meat. Add the pork to the pot. Crush the juniper berries, using the side of your knife, and add to the pot along with the wine. Cover and simmer 1½ hours. Add salt and pepper to taste.

CHICKEN BROTH WITH CUSTARDS
(From The Frugal Gourmet's Culinary Handbook)
SERVES 6 TO 8

This soup will be fun for the kids and yet very lovely for a late-night dinner party. The recipe comes from the turn of the century, when people in this country thought soup to be a necessity, not an addition.

If you use a small cookie cutter to cut the custards, you can make some funny shapes for the younger members of your clan.

8 eggs, beaten
¾ cup milk
1 teaspoon salt
 Pinch of cayenne pepper
2½ quarts Chicken Stock (page 109) or use canned
2 bay leaves
¼ cup cornstarch
¼ cup cold water
2 teaspoons Worcestershire sauce

Salt and freshly ground white pepper to taste
2 carrots, peeled and julienned
2 stalks celery, julienned
1 medium yellow onion, peeled and julienned

GARNISH
Chopped parsley

In a mixing bowl, combine the beaten eggs with the milk, salt, and cayenne pepper. Pour the mixture into a greased

8×8-inch baking dish and cover with aluminum foil. Bake at 375° for 20 to 25 minutes, or until set. Set aside to cool.

In a 6-quart pot, heat the Chicken Stock and the bay leaves. Mix together the cornstarch and the water until smooth. Stir the cornstarch mixture into the pot and bring it all to a boil. Simmer for 5 minutes, stirring until smooth and lump free. Add the Worcestershire sauce, salt, and white pepper. Stir in the carrots, celery, and onion and simmer, covered, for 20 minutes. Remove the bay leaves.

Remove the cooked egg mixture from the baking dish. Cut into fancy shapes with a small cookie cutter or cut into squares with a knife. Add to the soup and heat for a minute or two. Serve with parsley garnish.

POTATO PEEL SOUP

This one is really for the kids. Well, then again, maybe not. I have always felt bad about throwing out potato peelings since I enjoy them so. I make potato salad without even peeling the potatoes! Try this trick for using the peelings, but you understand that the peels must be placed in the soup stock just after you wash and peel the potatoes. Otherwise the peels will begin to discolor.

Save the peels from washed potatoes and simmer in Chicken Stock (page 109) along with chopped carrots, onions, and celery. Simmer until all is tender, about 30 minutes. Add fresh herbs and spices to your liking. Add some milk or half-and-half, and then salt and pepper to taste. This is really a very good soup, especially if you add fresh dill and parsley.

COLD ZUCCHINI SOUP
SERVES 4

Cold soups are great for the frugal family in our time. This is easy to make and it keeps for a few days in the refrigerator. Your kids, and friends, will be surprised at how they enjoy cold soup. Do not serve this to your children when they come in after making snowmen.

1¾ pounds green
     zucchini,
     trimmed and
     sliced
½ cup peeled and
     chopped yellow
     onion
3 cups Chicken
     Stock (page
     109) or use
     canned
¼ cup yogurt

¼ cup sour cream
½ teaspoon grated
     fresh ginger
Salt and freshly
     ground white
     pepper to taste

GARNISH
Chopped scallions

Place the sliced zucchini in a 4-quart pot along with the onion and stock. Cover and simmer for 15 minutes. Drain, reserving the stock. Puree the zucchini and onion, but do not let them get too mushy. Return to the pot along with the reserved stock. Stir in the yogurt and sour cream until smooth. Add the ginger and the salt and white pepper. Cover and refrigerate until very cold, about 6 to 8 hours. Garnish with scallions.

BEEF STOCK
MAKES 5 QUARTS

This recipe may cause you to think that I am being a bit inconsistent in that you must cook this stuff for hours. Doesn't sound very frugal, I know. However, this will prove to be a blessing in your kitchen, as it will turn out to be the basis of many gravies, soups, and stews. You cannot buy this stuff, but it keeps very well either in the refrigerator or the freezer.

Bare rendering bones, sawed into 2-inch pieces

Carrots, unpeeled and chopped

Yellow onions, unpeeled and chopped

Celery, chopped

Tell your butcher that you need bare rendering bones. They should not have any meat on them at all, so they should be cheap. Have him saw them up into 2-inch pieces.

Roast the bones in an uncovered pan at 400° for 2 hours. Be careful with this because your oven may be a bit too hot. Watch the bones, which you want to be toasty brown, not black.

Place the roasted bones in a soup pot and add 1 quart water for each pound of bones. For 5 pounds of bones, add 1 bunch of carrots, 1 head of celery, and 3 yellow onions, chopped with peel and all. (The peel will give a lovely color to the stock.)

Bring to a simmer, uncovered, and cook for 12 hours. You may need to add water to keep the soup up to the same level. Do not salt the stock.

Strain the stock and store in the refrigerator. Allow the fat to stay on top of the stock when you refrigerate it; the fat will seal the stock and allow you to keep it for several days.

CHICKEN STOCK
MAKES ABOUT 4 QUARTS

I love chicken soup. The world loves chicken soup. There is no such thing as a good chicken bouillon, and you should stoop to using canned chicken broth only during times of dire emergency. This is so easy to make and it freezes well, though the fresh version is always the best, of course. This stock should become basic in your frugal kitchen, and when you have some in storage you will be amazed at the clever things that you think up in terms of making good soup from some strange leftovers. But you have got to have the stock.

3 pounds of chicken
   necks and backs
   (Buy in bulk at
   the supermarket;
   they're cheaper
   that way. But be
   sure that they
   smell fresh.)
4 stalks celery,
   chopped into
   large pieces

6 carrots, peeled and
   chopped into
   large pieces
2 large yellow onions,
   peeled and
   chopped into
   large pieces
Salt and freshly
   ground black
   pepper to taste

Rinse the chicken parts in hot water from the tap and then drain them for a moment. In a large pot, place the chicken necks and backs in water to cover. Bring to a boil, uncovered. Add the celery, carrots, and onions. Add salt and pepper to taste. Reduce heat and simmer, uncovered, for 2 hours. Strain and refrigerate.

Salads

The consideration of a good salad in our time shows no green in judgment, not at all. For the contemporary living unit, a good salad for dinner is one of the best things that we can do for ourselves. And I don't mean stopping at a salad bar on the way home from work, although many of my friends do such a thing. I mean the preparation of salads that will hold up for a few days, salads that can be served one day and changed for the next. No green in judgment here. As a matter of fact, one of the ways to keep a salad for a few days is to eliminate the greens. It is still a salad.

Salads that hold up are particularly helpful to those who live alone. It is boring to make a salad for oneself and then watch the leftovers die right in front of you. These recipes are to be made for several persons, with leftovers being no problem at all. So a family of several can enjoy a quick evening meal from this section, and a bachelor can have dinner in the refrigerator when he returns home from work, dinner guest in hand.

If you have not gotten into the habit of making salads out of just about anything, you might want to reconsider. A simple salad of tuna, olives, onions, hard-boiled eggs, and a little celery, along with a good olive-oil-and-lemon-juice dressing, can be heaven.

113

Further, the "get frugal" theme of this book urges you to open the refrigerator and think about what you have in the way of leftovers that would go great in a heavy salad, devoid of the greens that collapse. Green in judgment, indeed!

PASTA AND KIDNEY BEAN SALAD
SERVES 4 TO 6

This is the kind of cold refrigerated salad that I really love. No, it is nothing new, but I wanted to remind you of something that you really used to like and somehow forgot about. This is one of those dishes. Easy to prepare, and it keeps for a few days in the refrigerator.

1 cup dried red
    kidney beans
½ pound small
    pasta shells
1½ cups sliced
    radishes
2 bunches scallions,
    chopped
1 cup sour cream
1 cup mayonnaise

Juice of ½ lemon
⅓ cup olive oil
Salt and freshly
    ground black
    pepper to taste

GARNISH
Additional freshly
    ground black
    pepper to taste

Place the beans in a 4-quart pot and add 2 cups of cold water. Bring the beans to a boil, cover, and turn off the heat. Allow to stand for 1 hour. Drain and return the beans to the pot. Cover the beans with plenty of fresh cold water and bring to a boil. Cover and simmer gently for 25 minutes or until tender. Drain and cool.

Bring a pot with 4 quarts of water to a boil. Add a pinch of salt and boil the pasta until al dente. Drain and rinse with cold water; drain well.

Place the beans and the pasta in a large bowl along with the radishes and scallions. In a small bowl, combine the remaining ingredients. Whisk until smooth and add to the pasta mixture. Fold all together, cover, and refrigerate for 4 to 6 hours. Fold the salad a couple of times while chilling. Serve with additional freshly ground black pepper.

I have never approved of mothers telling their children that they should be members of the clean plate club. Nobody ever had to tell me to clean my plate!

BLACK-EYED PEA SALAD
SERVES 6 TO 8

Black-eyed peas are really not peas at all but beans. They have a sort of subtle smokey flavor and for that reason they make a great salad. What with the new emphasis on eating more beans, this is a jewel for your crowd. It keeps for a few days, and you can add some other things to it as you go along. Try adding tuna, leftover cold fish, leftover chicken . . . etc.

¾ pound dried black-eyed peas
1 medium yellow onion, peeled and chopped
1 teaspoon salt
¼ teaspoon ground allspice
3 cloves garlic, peeled and crushed
¼ teaspoon freshly ground black pepper
¼ pound bacon, chopped
2 tablespoons olive oil
1 cup diced ham
2 stalks celery, sliced
1 medium red bell pepper, cored, seeded, and diced

2 bunches scallions, sliced
¼ cup chopped parsley

DRESSING

1 teaspoon dry mustard (I like Colman's best)
⅔ cup olive oil
1 tablespoon lemon juice
1 tablespoon white wine vinegar
Salt and freshly ground black pepper to taste
Lettuce cups for serving (optional)

Place the peas in 4-quart pot and add twice as much cold water. Add the onion, salt, allspice, garlic, and pepper.

Bring to a boil, cover, and simmer until tender, about 30 to 35 minutes. Test the peas while cooking so that you don't overcook them. Drain and spread out on a sheet pan to cool.

Heat a medium-sized frying pan and add the bacon. Cook the bacon until almost crisp. Drain the fat, remove the bacon, and set aside. Heat the frying pan again and add the 2 tablespoons of oil. Add the ham, celery, and red bell pepper. Sauté for about 3 minutes and allow to cool. Place in a large bowl along with the cooled peas, reserved bacon, scallions, and parsley.

Place the dry mustard for the dressing in a small bowl. Add 1 tablespoon of the oil and mix together until lump free. Add the rest of the oil and the remaining ingredients. Blend together and add the black-eyed pea mixture. Fold the salad together, cover, and refrigerate for 4 to 6 hours. Fold the salad a couple of times while chilling. Serve in optional lettuce cups.

ONE-WEEK COLESLAW
SERVES 8 TO 10

I really cannot clearly remember the night when I first tasted this dish. It was in a United Methodist Church in Washington State, Centralia, I believe, and we were having a potluck supper prior to my preaching at the evening service. This charming older woman came to me and told me of the ingredients for this salad. I hate normal sweet coleslaw, but I loved this one. "It will keep for a week," she proudly exclaimed. Perfect for the frugal kitchen!

1 2½-pound head green cabbage, cored and sliced for coleslaw

2 medium green bell peppers, cored, seeded, and julienned

2 medium yellow onions, peeled and sliced

¼ cup plus 2 tablespoons sugar

⅔ cup cider vinegar

2 teaspoons celery seed, whole

2 teaspoons dry mustard (I like Colman's best)

2 teaspoons salt

¾ cup olive oil

Salt and freshly ground black pepper to taste

Place the sliced cabbage in a large bowl with the bell peppers, onion, and ¼ cup of the sugar. Toss together and set aside.

In a small stainless-steel saucepan, add the remaining 2 tablespoons of sugar, the vinegar, celery seed, dry mustard, and salt. Heat to a boil and simmer for 2 minutes. Allow to cool. Pour over the vegetables along with the olive oil and salt and pepper to taste. Toss together well, cover, and refrigerate for several hours. Toss a few times while chilling.

PATTY'S FENNEL SALAD
SERVES 4 TO 6

The inspiration for this totally delicious salad stems from my wife's complete hang-up on Italy. Several months ago she announced that she was taking a walking tour of northern Italy but that she would call whenever she had a good meal. Well, I got some great calls . . . and some good recipes. When I married this woman she cooked coffee . . . and that too long. Today she is a fine cook, and this is a variation on one of her recent party recipes.

2 pounds fresh
  fennel
3 tablespoons olive
  oil
2 cloves garlic,
  peeled and
  crushed
¾ cup cored, seeded,
  and julienned
  red bell pepper
½ cup cored, seeded,
  and julienned
  green bell
  pepper
1 cup peeled and
  sliced white
  onion

1 bunch scallions,
  chopped
2 tablespoons
  chopped parsley

DRESSING
½ cup olive oil
1 tablespoon lemon
  juice
1 tablespoon white
  wine vinegar
Salt and freshly
  ground pepper
  to taste

Trim off the top stalks of the fennel and save for another use. Cut the bulb in half lengthwise and trim out the core. Cut the fennel into ⅜-inch strips. Heat a large frying pan and add the 3 tablespoons of oil. Add the garlic and fennel, and sauté over medium-low heat for 2 minutes. Do not brown the garlic. Add both bell peppers and sauté 2 minutes more. Add the onion and sauté 1 minute more. Remove from the frying pan to a bowl and allow to cool. Add the scallions and parsley. Blend together the ingredients for the dressing. Add to the bowl of vegetables. Toss together, cover, and chill.

FLANK STEAK
AND LENTIL SALAD
SERVES 6 TO 8 AS A SIDE SALAD, 4 AS A MAIN DISH

I really enjoy lentils, and since the new call is for more beans and legumes and a cutting down on just meat for dinner, I offer this dish. The meat flavors the salad, and the lentils have a bit of that smokey flavor that is so delicious. I described this dish to Craig and this is what he came up with. It is better than my original and it will be even better if you serve it the second day after making it.

1¼ cups lentils
6 cups cold water
¼ cup chopped parsley
1½ cups peeled and thinly sliced white onion
1 cup cored, seeded, and julienned red bell pepper

1 tablespoon white wine vinegar
Salt and freshly ground black pepper to taste

1 pound flank steak
Salt and freshly ground black pepper to taste
Olive oil for grilling

DRESSING
¾ cup olive oil
2 tablespoons lemon juice

Place the lentils in a 4-quart pot and add 6 cups of cold water. Bring to a boil, cover, and simmer 15 minutes or until just tender. Drain and cool.

Place the drained lentils in a mixing bowl. Add the parsley, onion, and bell pepper. Blend together the ingredients for the dressing and add to the lentils and vegetables. Toss together, cover, and marinate in the refrigerator for 4 hours. Toss the lentils a couple of times while chilling.

Season the steak with salt and pepper to taste, and brush the meat with olive oil. Grill over high heat just until rare, about 2 minutes per side (do not overcook). Remove and allow to cool. When the lentils have marinated for 4 hours, slice the steak thinly across the grain. Toss with the lentil and vegetable mixture. Adjust the salt and pepper if needed.

RED POTATO SALAD
WITH BACON
SERVES 4 TO 6

This is a fine variation on regular potato salad in that it
keeps a day or two longer and the flavor is really very rich.
We tasted this in Wisconsin when we were visiting with
our friends at the In-Sink-Erator Corporation. They had a
big lunch for us on the day that they announced they were
going to sponsor our shows, and I was touched by this
particular dish prepared by a good Wisconsin woman.
There is a little touch of Germany here as well as America.
That's Wisconsin!

2 pounds small red
    potatoes
⅓ pound bacon,
    diced
1 cup peeled and
    thinly sliced
    yellow onion
4 scallions, chopped
¼ cup mayonnaise
½ teaspoon dry
    mustard (I like
    Colman's best)

1 tablespoon white
    wine vinegar
½ cup olive oil
Salt and freshly
    ground black
    pepper to taste
2 hard-boiled eggs,
    peeled and
    chopped

Wash the potatoes and drain. Using a paring knife, trim a
band of the peel about ½ inch wide (depending on the size
of the potatoes) around the circumference of each potato.
This will form an attractive "belt." Boil the trimmed potatoes gently in ample, lightly salted water until just tender.
The potatoes are done as soon as they pierce easily with a
sharp knife. Carefully drain, spread on a tray, and allow to
cool.

Cook the bacon in a medium-sized frying pan until almost crisp. Add the onion and cook until limp. Drain off
any excess fat. Place the cooled potatoes in a bowl along
with the cooked bacon and onion, and the scallions. In an-

other bowl, blend together the mayonnaise, dry mustard, vinegar, oil, and salt and pepper to taste. Add to the bowl of potatoes and toss together. Fold in the hard-boiled eggs. Cover and refrigerate.

When the kitchen is crowded and you are short, as I am, it is best to leave and go take a nap.

COLD GREEN BEAN AND BACON SALAD
SERVES 6 TO 8 AS A SALAD, 4 TO 6 AS A MAIN COURSE

This just sounded good to me, and it certainly qualifies as a salad that can be made ahead of time and enjoyed when you are good and ready. It will hold up for a couple of days, though it is best served on the same day of preparation.

2 10-ounce boxes frozen cut green beans, thawed
½ pound bacon, diced
1 bunch scallions, chopped
2 tablespoons chopped parsley
⅓ cup olive oil
1 tablespoon lemon juice
2 tablespoons white wine vinegar
Salt and freshly ground black pepper to taste

Blanch the green beans in boiling water for 1 minute. Drain
well and rinse in cold water to cool. Drain well again. Cook
the bacon until it is almost crisp. Drain the fat. Combine
the beans, bacon, scallions, and parsley in a bowl. Mix
together the oil, lemon juice, and vinegar. Add to the bowl
of beans and toss together. Add salt and pepper to taste.
Refrigerate for 2 to 3 hours. Toss the salad a couple of
times while chilling.

GREEN BEAN SALAD,
CHINESE STYLE
SERVES 6 AS A GOOD HEARTY SALAD

This is the kind of thing that all of us should try often. Pick
out a favorite cuisine and think up a salad based on our
favorite flavors of that cuisine. Simple! Just remember that
we want it to keep for a couple of days. I offer this one.

- 2 tablespoons peanut oil
- 2 10-ounce boxes frozen cut green beans, thawed
- 2 tablespoons light soy sauce (page 58)
- 1 tablespoon rice wine vinegar (find in Oriental markets)
- 1 teaspoon grated fresh ginger
- 1 clove fresh garlic, peeled and crushed
- 2 tablespoons sesame oil
- ½ teaspoon sugar
- 6 scallions, chopped
- 2 tablespoons chopped fresh coriander

Bring 1 quart of water to a boil and add the peanut oil.
Add the thawed green beans and let sit for 1 minute. Drain
and rinse in cold water to cool. Place in a colander and
drain well.

Mix all remaining ingredients as for a salad dressing.
Toss with the drained beans and enjoy. Keeps for 2 days
in the refrigerator.

ARTICHOKE WITH EGG
AND PARSLEY SALAD
SERVES 6 TO 8

This is one of my favorite "quickies," though it is best marinated for a couple of hours. For a variation you might want to add a small shot of curry powder. Please don't mix the eggs with the salad until just before serving, as they will discolor the whole dish. As long as you keep the eggs separate from the salad you can make preparations a day or two in advance and then throw this together at the last minute.

2 14- to 15-ounce cans artichoke halves or quarters, drained	1 tablespoon lemon juice
	Salt and freshly ground black pepper to taste
1 cup peeled and sliced white onion	5 hard-boiled eggs, peeled and quartered
½ cup chopped parsley	Lettuce cups for serving
½ cup olive oil	

Place the drained artichokes in a bowl with everything but the eggs. Toss well and allow to marinate for 2 hours. Just before serving, add the hard-boiled eggs. Serve at once in lettuce cups.

RICE SALAD
SERVES 8 TO 10

This dish reminds me of my childhood. Now and then my mother would prepare a rice salad, but I think this version is even better than hers. Yes, it is rich, but it will serve a good group and it keeps well for a few days.

2 cups raw Uncle
  Ben's
  Converted Rice
  (regular, not
  instant)
1½ cups thinly sliced
  celery
¾ cup peeled and
  thinly sliced
  white onion
1 large bunch
  scallions,
  chopped
½ cup cored,
  seeded, and
  julienned red
  bell pepper
¼ cup chopped
  parsley

2 tablespoons
  chopped fresh
  mint

DRESSING
1 tablespoon white
  wine vinegar
2 tablespoons lemon
  juice
½ cup mayonnaise
½ cup sour cream
¾ cup olive oil
  Salt and freshly
  ground black
  pepper to taste

Lettuce cups for
  serving

Cook the rice as per the instructions on the box. Pour onto a sheet pan and allow to cool. Remove to a large bowl and add the celery, white onion, scallions, red bell pepper, parsley, and mint. Fold all together.

In a small bowl blend the vinegar, lemon juice, mayonnaise, and sour cream. Slowly whisk in the olive oil until smooth. Salt and pepper to taste. Toss the dressing with the rice and vegetables. Cover and refrigerate at least 4 hours. Toss a couple of times while chilling. Serve in lettuce cups.

ONION AND
COTTAGE CHEESE SALAD
SERVES 8

I love onions with cottage cheese. If you prepare this ahead of time, and it will keep for a few days, use very mild onions or the flavor may grow to be a bit strong for you. Be sure and remember not to put this on the torn greens until time to serve.

3 medium yellow
  onions

DRESSING
½ cup white wine
  vinegar
½ cup olive oil
  Juice of 1 lemon
  Salt and freshly
  ground black
  pepper to taste

1½ pints small-curd
  cottage cheese
⅓ cup chopped
  parsley

1 head romaine
  lettuce, washed
  and torn, for
  serving

Cut off the ends of the onions. Peel the onions whole and slice into rings about ⅛ inch thick. Place in a large stainless-steel or porcelain bowl. Combine the ingredients for the dressing and toss with the sliced onions. Cover and refrigerate for 2 days. Toss a couple of times while refrigerating.

Drain the onions, reserving the dressing. Toss the cottage cheese with the drained onions and the parsley. Arrange the torn greens on plates and drizzle with a little reserved dressing. Top with the cottage cheese mixture.

TANGY HOMMUS DRESSING
MAKES 1½ CUPS

Hommus is a paste made of sesame seeds, almost like a thin peanut butter. It is an ancient flavor going back to biblical times, and it is just smashing on almost everything. Try this on cold potatoes, cold vegetables, leftover cold meats. Anything. It keeps well, so make a whole batch.

- 1 cup hommus (find in Middle Eastern markets)
- ¼ cup olive oil
- 1 tablespoon lemon juice
- 1 tablespoon lime juice
- 2 tablespoons water
- Salt and freshly ground black pepper to taste

Blend all together until smooth. I use my food blender. Toss with greens or pour over greens or other cold vegetables and meats.

CELERY SLAW
SERVES 6

I do not like cabbage coleslaw. I know that this sounds like some sort of heresy, but I dislike that sweet dressing on cabbage. This celery slaw is not sweet at all, though it is rich enough to simply add to other chopped greens.

1 1 ¾-pound head celery, cleaned and julienned
1 large white onion, peeled and thinly sliced
¼ cup chopped parsley

DRESSING
½ cup olive oil
1 cup mayonnaise
¼ cup sour cream
3 tablespoons white wine vinegar
1 tablespoon fresh lemon juice
1 teaspoon celery seeds, whole
½ teaspoon Colman's dry mustard
Salt and freshly ground black pepper to taste

Combine the celery, onion, and parsley in a large stainless-steel bowl. Blend together the ingredients for the dressing. Toss with the vegetables, cover, and refrigerate for 6 to 8 hours or overnight. Toss a few times while refrigerating.

GARDENER'S SALAD
(from The Frugal Gourmet's Culinary Handbook)
SERVES 6

This is a fresh and crunchy salad of vegetable sticks, and it holds up for a couple of days. This is typical of a salad served in New York and Chicago at the turn of the century. It looks very up-to-date, but it is quite old.

1 cup peeled and
   julienned carrots
1 cup julienned
   green beans
½ cup frozen peas
1 cup julienned
   green zucchini
1 cup julienned
   yellow zucchini
½ cup peeled and
   chopped white
   onion
½ cup cored, seeded,
   and julienned
   red bell pepper

DRESSING

2 tablespoons
   chopped parsley
¾ cup olive oil
2 tablespoons white
   wine vinegar
Juice of 1 lemon
Salt and freshly
   ground black
   pepper to taste
Lettuce cups for
   serving

In a large pot of simmering water, blanch the carrots, beans, and peas for a few minutes and drain. Rinse in cold water to stop the cooking process and drain again.

In a large bowl, toss the blanched vegetables with the zucchini, onion, and bell pepper. Mix together the ingredients for the dressing, add to the vegetables, and toss well. Refrigerate. Serve in lettuce cups.

CHOPPED OLIVE DRESSING
MAKES 3½ CUPS DRESSING

This is quite unusual for a salad dressing in that it is absolutely heavy with olives and garlic. Make a batch of this and keep it in the refrigerator. It will keep for a good week or more and can be used on all sorts of salads that you can throw together at the last minute.

1 cup pimiento-stuffed green olives, drained	1 tablespoon white wine vinegar
1 cup pitted black California olives, drained	Freshly ground black pepper to taste
2 cloves garlic, peeled and crushed	Salt to taste (not too much, as the olives are salty!)
2 tablespoons chopped parsley	GARNISH
1¼ cups olive oil	Freshly grated
2 tablespoons lemon juice	Parmesan cheese (optional)

Chop the drained olives coarsely and place in a bowl. Add the garlic and the parsley. In another bowl, mix the remaining ingredients together. Stir into the olive mixture and allow to marinate on the counter for 2 hours. Stir the dressing occasionally. Toss with salad greens.

OPTIONAL: Garnish the tossed salad with grated Parmesan cheese.

ORZO SALAD
WITH PESTO MAYONNAISE
SERVES 8

Orzo is simply rice-shaped pasta. It works great in such a salad because it will not get soggy even after a couple of days.

I know that you have heard from some very fine Italian cooks that pasta should not be used in salads, but I have had great pasta salads in Rome, Milan, and Bologna. So, go to it. You will like this one.

1 pound orzo pasta
(find in Italian
markets)
2 bunches scallions,
chopped
1 medium red bell
pepper, cored,
seeded, and
finely chopped
1½ cups thinly sliced
celery

DRESSING
2 tablespoons white
wine vinegar
Juice of 1 lemon
⅓ cup Pesto Sauce
(page 266)
1 cup mayonnaise
1 cup olive oil
Salt and freshly
ground black
pepper to taste

Cook the pasta in lightly salted water until al dente. Drain
and rinse with cold water; drain well. Combine the drained
pasta in a large bowl along with the scallions, bell pepper,
and celery. Mix the ingredients for the dressing until
smooth. Add to the pasta and vegetables and fold together
until all is combined. Salt and pepper to taste. Refrigerate.
Toss a couple of times while chilling.

TONY'S ENDIVE SALAD
SERVES 4

This salad is so simple that it is deceiving. Tony Scoccolo,
an Italian friend in Seattle, brought this dish to us when we
did a show on cooking for one. Tony's wife died a few
months before the show, so he told us about how he was
doing. He makes a simple salad out of the heart of the
endive and then cooks the outer leaves for a vegetable dish.
Such Italian ingenuity.

2 large heads endive
½ cup olive oil
1 tablespoon lemon
    juice
1 tablespoon white
    wine vinegar

Salt and freshly
    ground black
    pepper to taste

Remove dark green outer leaves from the endive and save for Tony's Fried Endive (page 235). Use only the pale-colored, less bitter inside leaves for the salad. Tear into bite-sized pieces. Mix the remaining ingredients until smooth. Toss with endive.

CORN SALAD
SERVES 8 TO 10

Please think about making quick salads from frozen vegetables. Nothing could be more convenient or more versatile. This one is a good example. You will think up many more, I am sure.

3 10-ounce boxes
    frozen corn
    kernels, thawed
½ cup chopped
    parsley
2 bunches scallions,
    sliced
½ cup olive oil

1 tablespoon lemon
    juice
1 tablespoon white
    wine vinegar
Salt and freshly
    ground pepper to
    taste

Blanch the thawed corn in boiling water for 1 minute and drain well. Rinse quickly in cold water to stop the cooking and drain well again. Combine with the parsley and scallions. Mix the remaining ingredients together and toss with the corn. Serve right away or chilled.

ASPARAGUS AND MORTADELLA SALAD
SERVES 4

This recipe is the result of a very creative argument. I love cold asparagus, and Craig, my chef, and I were trying to work out an Italian asparagus salad. Mine was terrific, but then he yelled, ''Mortadella!'' Here is proof of the profound nature of the argument, and we both won. I love this stuff, but don't keep it for more than two days.

1 pound fresh
    asparagus spears
2 tablespoons olive
    oil
⅓ pound mortadella
    (find in a good
    delicatessen)
1 tablespoon
    chopped parsley
½ cup peeled and
    sliced white
    onion

DRESSING
½ cup olive oil
2 tablespoons lemon
    juice
Salt and freshly
    ground black
    pepper to taste

Lettuce leaves for
    serving

Break the tough ends off the asparagus and discard. Cut the spears into 2-inch pieces. Place the 2 tablespoons of olive oil in boiling water and blanch the asparagus quickly. Do not overcook! Drain the asparagus and rinse with cold water to stop the cooking. Drain again and place in a medium-sized bowl. Cut the mortadella into ⅛-inch by 2-

inch-long pieces. Add the mortadella and parsley to the asparagus along with the onion.

Mix the ingredients for the dressing and toss with the asparagus mixture. Allow to marinate in the refrigerator for 2 hours. Toss a couple of times while marinating. Serve on beds of lettuce.

CHICKEN AND TUNA SAUCE SALAD
SERVES 8 AS AN ENTRÉE SALAD

This sounds so strange to some people, but this blending of flavors is common in Italy. Blending fish with pork or chicken is also common in China, so we might as well get with it. Further, this salad is just fine for the next few days, so you can be ready for a dinner party on very short notice.

2 pounds cooked chicken meat, diced (the meat should not be dry)
1 cup thinly sliced celery
1 cup peeled and thinly sliced white onion
1 medium red bell pepper, cored, seeded, and chopped small

¼ cup chopped parsley

1 recipe Tuna Sauce (opposite) (omit the capers)
½ cup mayonnaise

Lettuce leaves for serving

Combine the chicken, celery, onion, red bell pepper, and parsley in a bowl. Mix the Tuna Sauce and mayonnaise together until smooth. Toss all together except the lettuce. Cover and refrigerate 2 to 4 hours. Toss a couple of times while chilling. Serve on lettuce leaves.

TUNA SAUCE
(From The Frugal Gourmet Cooks Three Ancient Cuisines)
MAKES 1½ CUPS

The Italians call this sauce *tonnato,* and it can be served over cold tomatoes, hard-boiled eggs, cold pasta salad, or on freshly cooked chicken. You think up the other variations!

1 6½- or 7-ounce can of tuna packed in water, drained
8 flat anchovies, drained on a paper towel
¼ cup fresh lemon juice
2 tablespoons brandy
¾ cup olive oil, at room temperature
1 tablespoon chopped capers

Place the tuna, anchovies, and lemon juice in a food blender. Blend for a few moments and add the brandy. Slowly pour in the olive oil as the machine runs. Remove the sauce from the container and stir in the capers.

Serve over meats and salads. Traditionally this is served with cold veal, but I love it over chicken.

BLEU CHEESE DRESSING
(From The Frugal Gourmet Cooks with Wine*)*
MAKES 6½ CUPS

I know I should not eat much of this dressing, but it is my favorite salad dressing . . . though I am trying to get along on olive oil and wine vinegar, with a shot of fresh lemon juice. Every once in a while I have to make a batch of this, and I put it on everything from salads to chicken to French dip hamburgers. It will hold up well in the refrigerator, so a fresh salad with this very rich dressing should be no problem . . . now and then.

2 cups buttermilk
4 ounces bleu cheese
1 quart Best Foods or Hellmann's mayonnaise
2 garlic cloves, peeled and crushed
1 dash Worcestershire sauce

1 tablespoon dried parsley flakes (Do not use fresh parsley as the leaves will spoil. The dry parsley will last much longer in the dressing.)

For the dressing use a fork to mix a bit of the buttermilk with the cheese until the cheese is soft but not smooth. Stir in the remaining ingredients. Do not use a food blender or a food processor. Refrigerate. Stir before each use.

Fish

> *Fish is held out to be one of the*
> *greatest luxuries of the table and not only*
> *necessary, but even indispensable at*
> *all dinners where there is any*
> *pretence to excellence*
> *or fashion.*

Isabella Beeton, *The Book of Household Management,* 1861

I am a child of the Pacific Northwest, born and raised in Seattle. The idea of living without fish has never occurred to me, nor do I expect such a thought will occur to me in the future.

Here in Seattle we have perhaps the best selection of fresh fish that you can find anywhere in the nation, and we do eat plenty of the fruits from the sea.

I remember eating seafood from the time I was very little, though this was just after the Second World War and the family was short on money. So, off we would go to the ocean beach for razor clams or to the inland bay for clams and oysters. Sometimes my mother would dig up a geoduck and then we were ready for a feast. The geoduck is the largest bivalve (two shells) in the mollusk family, and it has a neck that is so long that the poor creature cannot pull this appendage into its shell. Mom would make steaks out of these necks and then fry them in flour and butter. Such a sweet memory of my early days at table.

These days I walk through the Pike Place Farmer's Market and talk with the crew at any one of four major fish stalls. Fresh salmon, sea bass, black cod, true cod, ling cod, tuna, octopus, halibut, sole, mussels, clams, Dungeness

139

crab, and more. We are lucky that fish is so prevalent and popular here that it is always fresh. If you live in an inland area, please be sure to check for freshness in all seafoods.

How Do I Know the Seafood Is Fresh?

1. It should smell fresh, like the sea, not like an old fishing dock. As a matter of fact, the shop should not smell fishy.
2. The fish should be bright in color, with clear eyes and bright red gills. Don't be reluctant to pull back the gill and see that the inside is brightly colored.
3. Poke the fish. The flesh should be firm. Your finger indentation should not remain more than a few seconds. If a dent does remain, it means that the fish is deteriorating.
4. Check the inside of the belly and be sure that it is fresh and bright in color. You will often see Craig, my chef, marching through the fish stalls picking up everything in sight and sniffing and poking. The fishmonger is not bothered by this since he knows a wise cook when he sees one.
5. Keep your fish very cold, in the coldest part of your refrigerator. I find that the biggest problem with fish from the local supermarket is that it has not been properly cared for. Find a good fish merchant or check very carefully when in a supermarket.

The following collection of seafood recipes should delight all of the members of your clan. Teach your children to taste all fish dishes so that they realize that there is a great difference between the flavor of canned salmon (ugh!) and fresh.

STEAMED MUSSELS WITH CARAMELIZED ONIONS
SERVES 4 TO 6 AS AN APPETIZER

When I was a child we did not eat mussels. People in the Seattle area simply preferred clams. Much less work to eat. When I began dating Patty, my wife, we would go into Greenwich Village in New York and eat mussels in red sauce at a great Italian restaurant. Now mussels are very "in" in Seattle, and I think it is largely due to that blessed Italian influence.

Craig developed this for Patty. It is both Italian and Northwest, and it is really quite simple.

3 tablespoons butter	Freshly ground black pepper to taste
2 medium yellow onions, peeled and thinly sliced	⅓ cup dry white wine
2 pounds Penn Cove mussels	1½ tablespoons balsamic vinegar
2 tablespoons olive oil	⅓ cup heavy cream
2 cloves garlic, peeled and chopped	**GARNISH** Chopped parsley

Heat a large frying pan and add the butter and onion. Sauté over medium heat for 5 minutes. Cover and "sweat" the onion down over low heat. Cook until the onion becomes golden brown and caramelized, about 20 minutes. Be sure to stir the onion often. Set aside.

Trim the fuzzy beards off the mussels and wash and drain. Heat a 6- to 8-quart pot and add the oil, garlic, and black pepper to taste. Sauté for 15 seconds and add the drained mussels and wine, and bring to a boil. Stir the mussels, cover, and reduce the heat to a simmer. Steam the mussels open, stirring once, about 5 to 7 minutes. Drain the mussels into a colander, reserving the broth or ''nectar.''

Heat the frying pan with the onion again and strain in the reserved nectar. Add the balsamic vinegar and cream, and simmer a few minutes to reduce and thicken slightly. Add the opened mussels in their shells and toss until all is hot and coated with the onion sauce. Serve immediately with parsley garnish.

BLACK COD, CHINESE STYLE
SERVES 4 TO 6 AS A COURSE FOR A CHINESE DINNER

My dear friend and adopted Chinese auntie, Mary Young, took me to a restaurant just outside San Francisco, in Emeryville. It is called Hong Kong East Ocean, and it is a seafood house. They served this dish, and I was just astounded at the richness and clarity of flavor. This recipe is as close as I can come to theirs.

Black cod is very rich and, I am afraid, rather expensive. On the East Coast it is called sablefish. Please try this one, as it is one of the most delectable fish dishes I know.

4 tablespoons dark soy sauce (page 58)
2 tablespoons honey
3 tablespoons dry sherry
2 teaspoons sesame oil
2 to 3 pounds fresh black cod roast

Mix together the soy sauce, honey, sherry, and sesame oil in a bowl. Add the fish and allow to marinate several hours, turning occasionally.

Bake at 350° for about 20 minutes, depending on thickness. Baste the roast with the marinade once or twice during cooking. The secret to this dish involves your not overcooking it.

FISH PASTE
WITH COOKIE CUTTERS
DINNER FOR 4 TO 5 KIDS

This is not just a gag for the kids. These fish paste cookies really are quite good.

Children seem to be bothered more by the color and texture of fish than they are by the flavor. Here the texture and color are changed and the sherry and ginger help get rid of any strong fishy taste.

1 pound boneless
    cod
2 egg whites
1 tablespoon light
    soy sauce (page
    58)
1 tablespoon dry
    sherry
½ teaspoon grated
    fresh ginger

3 tablespoons
    cornstarch
Additional
    cornstarch for
    dusting
Peanut oil for pan-
    frying

Cut the fish into small pieces and place in a food processor with the egg whites, soy sauce, sherry, ginger, and 3 tablespoons cornstarch. Chop the fish finely until you have a smooth paste. Scrape down the sides of the processor a couple of times while chopping.

Place a sheet of waxed paper on the counter and dust it liberally with cornstarch. Place some of the fish paste on top and pat it down. Dust with more cornstarch and place another sheet of waxed paper on top. Using a rolling pin, roll on top of the waxed paper to flatten out the paste to about ¼ inch. Use cornstarch as necessary to prevent sticking. Remove the top layer of waxed paper and cut out figures with your favorite cookie cutters.

Heat a large frying pan and add a couple of tablespoons of peanut oil. Pan-fry the ''fish cookies'' until slightly brown on both sides. Remove to drain on paper towels. Repeat with remaining fish paste. The number of cookies you'll get depends on the size of the cutters.

SICILIAN TUNA
SERVES 4

Your children should taste the difference between fresh tuna and canned. This dish is easy to prepare, honest in terms of its history, and simply delicious. But the tuna must be fresh. Be sure that it is and then you will be in heaven!

Do I need to tell you that you do not want to overcook tuna? The center should be soft and moist, not dry and firm.

4 6-ounce fresh
    tuna steaks
½ cup all-purpose
    flour for
    dredging
½ cup olive oil for
    pan-frying
1 medium red
    onion, peeled
    and thinly
    sliced
¼ cup Chicken
    Stock (page
    109) or use
    canned

1½ tablespoons white
    wine vinegar
Freshly ground
    black pepper to
    taste
1 tablespoon
    chopped
    parsley
Salt to taste

Roll the tuna steaks in flour and pat off the excess. Heat a large frying pan and add the oil. Pan-fry the fish over medium heat, about 1 to 2 minutes per side, and remove to a warm plate. Do not overcook. Discard half the oil and return the pan to the heat. Add the onion, Chicken Stock, vinegar, and black pepper. Sauté for about 5 minutes until the onion just becomes tender and the sauce reduces a bit. Add the parsley and salt to taste. Spoon the sauce over the warm fish and serve.

SEAFOOD IN SAFFRON CREAM
SERVES 4 TO 6

I cannot remember where I first tasted this dish. I do remember describing it to Craig, my chef and assistant. He nodded, said nothing, turned his back on me, and I left the kitchen. Soon I heard the clanking and banging of pots and knives on the chopping board. He presented me with this dish and simply said, "Close?" No, Craig, it is better than the dish that I remembered. That is the mark of a true chef,

I suppose. You describe a dish to him and he says nothing. He just cooks it beautifully.

This is one of the richest seafood dishes that you will ever eat. Yes, it is great on linguine. Just forget about the rice.

1 pound Manila or butter clams
½ pound Penn Cove mussels, beards removed
2 tablespoons olive oil
½ cup dry white wine
1 cup raw Uncle Ben's Converted Rice (cook per instructions on the box)
½ pound large sea scallops

½ pound medium shrimp, peeled
1 cup all-purpose flour for dredging
2 tablespoons butter
1 cup heavy cream
Pinch of good saffron
Salt and freshly ground white pepper to taste

GARNISH
Chopped parsley

Rinse the clams and place in a small bowl. Cover with cold water and allow them to sit for 1 hour. Do the same with the mussels. Drain the clams and the mussels. Heat a medium-sized pot and add 1 tablespoon of the oil. Add the drained clams and ¼ cup of the wine. Bring to a boil, cover, and simmer about 8 minutes until the clams open. Drain into a colander, reserving the broth or "nectar." Heat the pot again and cook the mussels as above, using the remaining oil and wine, but only for about 5 minutes or until opened. (Discard mussels that have not opened.) Drain into a colander, reserving the nectar. Remove the clam and mussel meat from their shells and set aside, covered. Discard the shells. Pour the two nectars through a strainer into one bowl and set aside.

Prepare the rice and set aside to keep warm.

Roll the scallops and shrimp in the flour and pat off the excess flour. Melt the butter in a large frying pan and briefly sauté the scallops and shrimp for 1 minute. Remove to cool. Add the reserved nectar to the frying pan along with the cream and the saffron. Bring to a simmer and cook, uncovered, to reduce and thicken slightly, about 5 minutes. Return all the seafood to the pan and simmer 1 to 2 minutes more. Do not overcook the seafood! Salt and white pepper to taste. Serve over the rice with parsley garnish.

FISH MARINATED IN HERBED OLIVE OIL

This is just an ingenious recipe. No, it is not mine. A wonderful Italian woman operates a restaurant in Seattle called Mamma Melina. She is a strong-willed but gracious and creative person, and she shared this secret for the most tender and moist fish that you can imagine. Save the oil marinade and use it for more fish. Just great! Further, it is perfect for our time, because this dish sitting in your refrigerator was prepared during usual dinner preparations the night before.

4 cloves garlic, peeled and crushed
Handful of fresh rosemary, removed from stems
Handful of fresh oregano, removed from stems
Handful of Italian parsley
Freshly ground black pepper to taste

Fresh fish fillets or steaks (thick halibut or salmon is best)
2 cups olive oil
Salt to taste

GARNISH
Lemon wedges

Place the garlic, rosemary, oregano, parsley, and black pepper in a food processor and chop coarsely. Rub on both sides of desired fish and place in a glass baking dish. (Do not add any salt or acids such as lemon juice or vinegar at this time!) Add the oil and turn the fish a couple of times. The fish should be nearly or completely submerged in the oil. For best results, the fish should be covered and refrigerated overnight. You may also marinate it for just a few hours.

To cook, pat off the excess oil and lightly salt to taste. Grill, broil, or bake to your liking. Do not overcook! Serve with lemon wedges. The leftover herbed oil can be refrigerated for a few days and reused *only* for other fresh *seafood* preparations.

SALMON SALAD
(From **The Frugal Gourmet's Culinary Handbook***)*
SERVES 4 TO 6 AS A FIRST COURSE OR SALAD COURSE

This dish comes from a cookbook first published in 1904. The ingredients are fresh and carefully presented, and the resulting dish is very refreshing. Do not overcook the salmon steaks.

2¼ pounds fresh
    salmon steaks
    (thick steaks
    are best)
Salt and freshly
    ground black
    pepper to taste
  2 tablespoons
    chopped fresh
    dill
  1 cup thinly sliced
    celery
 ½ cup peeled and
    sliced white
    onion
  1 cup canned beets,
    well drained
    and cut in ⅛-
    inch dice (buy
    beets packed in
    glass with
    water, not
    pickled)

 ¾ cup olive oil
  3 tablespoons lemon
    juice
  1 tablespoon white
    wine vinegar
Lettuce leaves for
    serving

GARNISH
  3 hard-boiled eggs,
    peeled and sliced

Preheat the oven to 350°. Season the salmon with salt and pepper (easy on the salt). Place the salmon in a 13×9-inch baking dish and cover with aluminum foil. Bake for 25 minutes. Remove the foil, cool, and debone and skin the salmon. Discard the bones and skin. Tear the salmon into large flakes, but do not shred it. Combine the cooked salmon, dill, celery, onion, and drained beets in a large bowl. In another bowl, mix the oil, lemon juice, and vinegar. Add to the salmon mixture and fold it in gently. Try not to break up the salmon too much. Serve in lettuce leaves with sliced egg garnish.

SALMON PUTTANESCA
SERVES 4

Usually puttanesca sauce is reserved for pasta. The dish supposedly was developed by ladies of the night who offered a short pasta meal when "entertaining." Mamma Melina, who runs a fine Italian restaurant in Seattle, offered me a similar sauce on salmon. I was surprised at the wonderful results, and I expect you will be as well.

6 tablespoons olive oil
2 cloves garlic, peeled and minced
2 ounces or more black kalamata olives, pitted and chopped
1 teaspoon coarsely chopped capers
1 large fresh tomato, peeled and coarsely chopped
4 or 5 anchovy fillets, chopped
4 6-ounce salmon fillets

Freshly ground black pepper to taste
1 cup all-purpose flour for dredging

GARNISHES
Salt and freshly ground black pepper to taste
Chopped parsley
1 teaspoon crushed red pepper flakes (optional)

Heat a large frying pan and add 3 tablespoons of the oil and the garlic. Sauté the garlic until golden brown. Add the olives, capers, tomato, and anchovy fillets. Stir well and heat through for about 6 minutes.

Season the salmon with black pepper. Roll each fillet in flour and pat off the excess flour. Heat another large frying pan and add the remaining 3 tablespoons of oil. Sauté the fish over medium heat about 2 minutes on each side. The fish should be lightly browned but not overcooked! Top the fish with the sauce, season to taste, and garnish with chopped parsley and optional red pepper flakes.

FISH DUMPLINGS

We are talking simple here . . . but the fish must be fresh. Further, the flavor is so light, due to the ginger and sherry, that every member of your crowd will enjoy these.

Prepare the fish paste from Fish Paste with Cookie Cutters (page 143) using only 1 tablespoon of the cornstarch. Mix the paste well and simply spoon walnut-sized balls of the paste into boiling Chicken Stock (page 109) or fish stock. The fish dumplings will poach in the hot stock in just a few minutes. Season the stock to your liking before you add the dumplings. Fresh chopped coriander makes a great garnish for this dish.

You might also wish to throw in some torn-up iceberg lettuce. Toss it right into the soup, and when all is reheated, serve. Very Hong Kong!

FISH GRILLED IN A RACK
SERVES 4 TO 6 AS A FISH COURSE

This is an easy way of preparing a fine fish meal, and in no time at all, after work, providing you have marinated the fish the night before.

This method of grilling keeps the fish very moist, and it does not allow the outside of the fish to become overly dry while the center remains raw.

You will need a 1½- to 2-pound whole fish, such as a snapper or rock cod. Marinate the fish as you would for Fish Marinated in Herbed Olive Oil (page 147). Rub off the excess oil and place the fish in a fish grilling rack (page 39). Grill the fish on both sides over a hot fire. The fish is done when the thickest part of it springs back slightly when touched. The fish should become quite brown by the time it is done. Place the whole fish on a platter and serve with lemon wedges. This can also be cooked with the fish rack directly on a hot griddle. Be careful of flareups from the dripping oil.

INFUSED OIL FOR GRILLING FISH

Infused oils for cooking and grilling are very "in" at the moment. This one is from one of the young chefs at Kaspar's by the Bay, a fine restaurant in Seattle. The chef, Steve Miller, helped us with this "whole family" series of shows. He is diligent and well trained, insightful and hardworking. And why not? His boss, Chef Kaspar, is Swiss. He is good!

You can use this refreshing oil just as a dip for your French bread or as a topping for your baked potato. You will think up other uses, I am sure.

2 cups olive oil
¼ of 1 lemon peel only, coarsely chopped
½ cup coarsely chopped basil leaves
¼ cup coarsely chopped parsley
3 cloves garlic, peeled and crushed

Combine all ingredients in a small bowl or jar and allow to stand at room temperature for 2 hours. Brush fish with the oil when grilling. The oil will keep for several days in the refrigerator.

SEAFOOD SALAD
SERVES 6 AS A SALAD OR FISH COURSE

This is straightforward, fresh, and just delicious. It takes some time to prepare and it must be made on the same day as the meal, but you can prepare a good bit of the seafood the day before. Then finish and throw this together. Very rich and tasty. If you wish to stretch it out, add some cold cooked leftover fish such as boneless salmon or cod.

1 **pound fresh mussels**	2 **tablespoons sour cream**
4 **tablespoons olive oil**	2 **tablespoons lemon juice**
¼ **cup dry white wine**	½ **cup olive oil**
1 **pound sea scallops**	**Salt and freshly ground black pepper to taste**
¾ **pound medium shrimp, peeled**	1 **cup peeled and sliced white onion**
1 **pound squid with heads, cleaned and cut into rings**	1½ **cups sliced celery**
	3 **tablespoons chopped parsley**
DRESSING	
1 **cup good mayonnaise (not salad dressing!)**	**Lettuce leaves for serving**

Trim the fuzzy beards off the mussels. Rinse and drain. Heat a 4- to 6-quart saucepan and add 1 tablespoon of the oil, the drained mussels, and the wine. Bring to a boil, cover, and simmer about 5 to 7 minutes, until the mussels open. Stir them once while cooking. Drain the mussels and save the broth or "nectar" for another use. Remove the mussels from their shells and set aside.

Heat a medium-sized frying pan and add another 1 tablespoon of oil. Add the scallops and sauté briefly until just cooked. Remove and cool. Heat the pan again and add another 1 tablespoon of oil. Add the shrimp and sauté until just barely cooked and pink. Remove and set aside to cool. Heat the pan again and add the remaining 1 tablespoon of oil. Add the squid and sauté about 30 seconds until the rings curl up slightly. Remove and allow to cool.

Place the ingredients for the dressing in a large bowl and whisk together until smooth. Add the cooked and cooled seafood. Add the white onion, celery, and parsley. Toss together and serve in lettuce leaves.

Always wash your hands before cooking. You may need help with this. I do!

STEAMED SHRIMP WITH SESAME OIL
SERVES 4 AS A FISH COURSE

I demonstrated this dish to Elmo, the cute fuzzy little red monster from *Sesame Street*. He proved to be a prize student and a great help in keeping the kitchen safe. He claims that he loves steamed shrimp, or at least his "worker" made such a claim. I thought I knew what these puppeteers go through in bringing life to their little creatures, but I was very wrong. The work is more strenuous than you can believe, and the actors more skilled than I ever understood.

In any case, here is a fine steamed dish that takes only a few minutes to prepare. You really should buy a Chinese bamboo steamer set, as the metal steamers will drip water on your food and thus dilute the flavors.

1 pound medium shrimp, shells on	1 tablespoon dry sherry
2 scallions, chopped	½ tablespoon sesame oil
½ teaspoon grated fresh ginger	
1 tablespoon light soy sauce (page 58)	

Place the shrimp, shells on, in a shallow porcelain bowl. Add the remaining ingredients and toss about. Place the bowl in a hot bamboo steamer (page 38) and steam about 5 to 7 minutes, until the shrimp are pink and barely firm. Stir the shrimp once during cooking to make sure they cook evenly. Peel and eat, or eat the shell and all.

SCALLOPS WITH VEGETABLES, CHINESE STYLE
SERVES 4 TO 6 AS PART OF A CHINESE MEAL

This is another dish that we showed to Elmo of *Sesame Street* fame. Actually, the dish was demonstrated for us by the chefs at my favorite Chinese restaurant in Seattle. Phil and Alice Chan run the Sea Garden Seafood Restaurant, and this is one of their fine offerings. Wei Chin showed us how to prepare this on our Fire and Flame special show.

If you love to cook in our time, you simply must have a wok!

SAUCE	1 egg white
2 teaspoons cornstarch	1 tablespoon cornstarch
½ cup Chicken Stock (page 109) or use canned	Pinch of salt
	2 cups peanut oil for deep-frying
1 tablespoon light soy sauce (page 58)	½ cup peeled and sliced carrots
Pinch of salt	1 cup baby corn, drained (a canned product found in any Chinatown)
Pinch of sugar	
Pinch of MSG (optional)	
	1 cup snow peas
½ pound sea scallops	¼ cup dry sherry

Place the ingredients for the sauce in a small bowl and stir together until smooth. Set aside.

Place the scallops in another small bowl and add the egg white, cornstarch, and pinch of salt. Stir together with your hands until coated.

Heat the oil in a wok to about 300° and add the scallops. The oil is not very hot, as we want to cook very lightly or "velvet" the seafood. Deep-fry for 10 seconds and remove to drain. Add the vegetables to the hot oil and fry for 10 seconds. Remove to drain. Discard all but 1 tablespoon of the oil in the wok (saving the oil, of course). Heat the wok until very hot and return the scallops and vegetables. Stir-fry along with the sherry. Stir the sauce together again and add to the wok. Toss and stir-fry until all is hot and slightly thickened.

STEAMED WHOLE FISH, CHINESE STYLE
SERVES 4 TO 6 AS A COURSE IN A CHINESE MEAL

I am always amazed at the simplicity of really fine Chinese cooking, and then I am amazed a second time at the results! The following very simple dish was demonstrated to us by Ahn Wong, one of the staff at the wonderful Sea Garden Seafood Restaurant in Seattle. You have to have a good-sized steamer for a good-sized fish, but a 12-inch bamboo steamer (page 38) should do well for most of your steaming needs.

4 4-inch pieces of scallion (white part only)

1 whole snapper or rock cod, about 1½ pounds (cleaned and scaled)

1½ tablespoons very thinly julienned fresh ginger

Salt to taste

6 sprigs Chinese parsley or cilantro

Freshly ground white pepper to taste

¼ cup peanut oil

2 tablespoons light soy sauce (page 58)

GARNISHES

½ cup julienned scallions (use the tops from the scallions above)

On an oval platter, place the 4-inch pieces of scallion a couple inches apart crosswise on the plate. Place the whole fish on top of the scallion "logs." This will allow the heat to pass underneath the fish while it is steaming. Top with the ginger and salt to taste. Place the entire plate in an active steamer and cook for 20 to 25 minutes or until the fish does not spring back when touched. Do not overcook!

Remove the plate from the steamer and top the fish with the garnishes except for the peanut oil and soy sauce. Carefully heat the oil in a small frying pan until it just begins to smoke. Carefully pour the hot oil over the garnished fish. Drizzle a puddle of soy sauce on the plate around the fish and serve.

STEAMED MUSTARD SHRIMP
SERVES 4 AS AN APPETIZER

I thought he was crazy. No, I do not know him, but he is a fan of mine so I am a fan of his. He sent me this recipe, a recipe from his father, and I read it. I always read recipes that my friends send to me, but this one sounded a bit strange. Bob Johnson, somewhere in Pennsylvania, insisted that I try this. Use a metal steamer rather than a bamboo one and you will be set. Bob is right. This is messy. You need lots of beer. Do not invite your mother-in-law. Eat off papers on the table. Do not feed the scraps to the cat. The cat will die . . . tonight. Otherwise, enjoy a really fine shrimp dish.

I have changed his recipe only a bit by adding thyme. I need all the thyme I can get.

1 pound medium shrimp, shells on (26 to 30 per pound)	½ teaspoon dried thyme, whole Salt to taste (very little)
3 tablespoons Colman's dry mustard	**GARNISH** Chopped parsley

Place half the shrimp in the bottom of a metal steamer rack.
Sprinkle with half the mustard, half the thyme, and a tiny
bit of salt. Top with the remaining shrimp, mustard, thyme,
and salt. Steam the shrimp until just firm, about 7 minutes.
Move the shrimp around halfway through the cooking time.
Garnish with chopped parsley. Peel and eat directly out of
the steamer basket. Be sure to lick your fingers.

STEAMED SHRIMP GOLDFISH
SERVES 4 AS A MAIN COURSE ACCOMPANIED WITH RICE

This clever trick comes to us from Hong Kong. I am very
worried about what Hong Kong is going to become after
the big change of 1997 . . . but in the meantime I will claim
that it is the greatest food city in the world.

Now, to the recipe below. Fresh shrimp paste is molded
into Chinese porcelain soup spoons and garnished to look
like goldfish. These are then steamed. Who would go to
such work for a meal except the Chinese? Now and then
you need to do this with your kids or clan or family or
friends, whoever these people are, those with whom you
celebrate the table. In the end, however, it is the kids who
think this is a gas . . . and they can form them and cook
them. Get the kids into the kitchen.

**FOR THE FRESH
SHRIMP PASTE**

1 pound medium
  shrimp, shells on
  (26 to 30 per
  pound)
⅛ teaspoon grated
  fresh ginger, or
  less to taste
1 tablespoon light
  soy sauce (page
  58)
1 egg white
  Pinch of freshly
  ground white
  pepper
  Pinch of salt (not
  much)
2 teaspoons
  cornstarch
1 medium carrot,
  peeled and sliced
  into ¹⁄₁₆-inch
  pieces

1 10-ounce box frozen
  peas

SAUCE

2 cups Chicken Stock
  (page 109) or use
  canned
1 tablespoon
  cornstarch
2 tablespoons cold
  water
  Salt to taste
  Pinch of freshly
  ground white
  pepper
2 egg whites, beaten

Steamed rice for
  serving

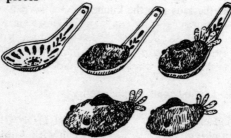

Peel the shrimp, saving the shells. Place the shrimp in a
food processor along with the remaining ingredients for the
shrimp paste except for the carrot and the peas. Puree until
smooth, scraping down the sides a couple of times. Form

an oblong mound of the paste in a lightly oiled Chinese porcelain soup spoon. Cut a slice of carrot in half and stick it in the top of the molded fish paste; this will represent the goldfish's dorsal fin. Stick in two peas for eyes. Snip off the tails of the reserved shrimp shells and stick them into the formed paste to represent a tail. Continue with the remaining paste, oiling each spoon as you go (see illustration). Set aside.

Bring the Chicken Stock to a simmer in a small pot. Mix the cornstarch and water together until smooth. Whisk the cornstarch mixture into the stock and simmer until smooth, whisking the whole time. Add salt and white pepper to taste. Stir in the egg whites so that they cook and form strands. Set aside, covered.

Place the filled spoons in a bamboo steamer rack (page 38) and steam for about 6 minutes or until pink and firm.

To serve, put a pool of the sauce on a plate and push the cooked goldfish out of its spoon directly into the sauce.

SMOKED WHOLE SHRIMP
SERVES 4 AS AN APPETIZER

I have more fun with my Cameron Smoker (page 38). It allows you to smoke all kinds of fresh meats and seafood right on the top of your stove. You must have a kitchen fan that vents the smoke outside of the house, not one of those fans that simply circulates the fumes through an inside filter.

This is delicious and simple eating.

Wood chips for
  smoking
1 pound medium
  shrimp, shells on
  (26 to 30 per
  pound)

OPTIONAL
Serve with Annie's
Extra-Special
Tartar Sauce
(page 162)

Sprinkle about 2 or 3 tablespoons of wood chips in the bottom of a Cameron Smoker. Place the drip pan on top of the chips and the cooking rack on top of the drip pan. Arrange the shrimp on the rack and place the smoker over medium heat. As soon as smoke begins to rise, slide the lid into place. Turn the heat to low and smoke the shrimp for 5 to 10 minutes, or until just firm. Remove the shrimp and peel and eat. Serve with optional sauce.

ANNIE'S EXTRA-SPECIAL
TARTAR SAUCE
SERVES 4 AS AN APPETIZER

There is only one thing wrong with having a popular television show. I have a lot of friends that I have never met, and Annie is one of those friends. She lives on the Upper West Side of New York, and at seven years old she is quite a cook, and a young woman of considerable chutzpah! She sent me this recipe, claiming that even her mother, who is always on a diet, enjoys this. I admit it is an excellent tartar sauce, and I submit it to you with appreciation to Annie in Manhattan. Hey, Annie, we have got to meet!

Craig and I decided that we would prefer fresh garlic rather than the garlic powder that Annie uses. I am sure that she will understand.

1 teaspoon Colman's
    dry mustard
2 teaspoons cold
    water
½ cup mayonnaise
3 tablespoons sour
    cream
2 teaspoons lemon
    juice
  Freshly ground
    black pepper to
    taste
2 tablespoons
    chopped parsley
1 small clove garlic,
    peeled and
    crushed
2 tablespoons
    chopped fresh
    dill
1 teaspoon
    Worcestershire
    sauce

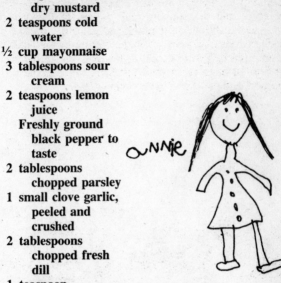

In a small bowl, mix the dry mustard and the water. Add the remaining ingredients and stir until smooth. Refrigerate. Serve with seafood or use as a sandwich spread.

Chicken

Chicken has always been a favorite of mine. When I was a little kid in Tacoma, during the Second World War, my mother raised chickens in our garage, thus assuring us of good meals no matter how bad the market or the economy became. So clever, that woman. But I had to feed the messy little rascals, so we were not fond of one another. I was fond of the chicken once it was on my plate. Oh, my mom's chicken and dumplings. As you say in Brooklyn, "To die for!"

When I was a kid, chicken was comfort food. Fried chicken on Sundays, chicken and dumplings or chicken and noodles during the week. Today chicken is called a health food.

In all fairness to the beef, lamb, and pork growers, I must tell you that there is no difference, in terms of your health, between chicken fat and the fat of other creatures. It is true that most of the fat on a chicken is to be found in the skin, so if you want to cut down on fat, simply remove the chicken skin before cooking . . . and remove much of the flavor along with it. I am torn on this issue, so I simply cut down on all fat, but I have trouble cooking a skinless chicken. He looks so undressed!

The chicken dishes in this section are just fine for the nineties-style family. Most of these dishes do not take long to prepare, nor are they expensive. Further, there are some fun dishes that young people can prepare.

GEFILTE CHICKEN
SERVES 8 TO 10, AND LEFTOVERS ARE DELICIOUS

If you are Jewish you might laugh at this recipe since normally it is fish that is used for "gefilte." My new friend Rabbi Marc Gellman from New York did this recipe for us on one of our shows and explained that the term "gefilte" actually refers to the filling, such as matzo meal, that is added to the meat mixture. This dish is just wonderful and you can tell from the recipe that the Rabbi is no right-winger. I love the guy!

He credits Grandma Sarah with the original.

CHICKEN MIXTURE
- 1 large onion, peeled and chopped
- 2 tablespoons peanut oil
- 6 boneless, skinless chicken breasts (Each chicken has two breasts. Right? Right!)
- ½ cup peeled and diced carrot
- ¼ cup coarsely chopped parsley
- Juice of 1 lemon
- 2 packets G Washington's Golden Seasoning and Broth (Find in any fancy supermarket. Be sure to get the Golden, not the Rich Brown.)
- 1¼ cups matzo meal
- 4 large eggs

½ cup cold water
   Salt and freshly
      ground black
      pepper to taste
      (easy on the
      salt)
   SOUP
2 tablespoons
      peanut oil
1 large yellow
      onion, peeled
      and sliced
1 large carrot,
      peeled and
      diced

5 cups hot water
1 tablespoon mild
      paprika
   Juice of 1 lemon
2 tablespoons
      coarsely chopped
      parsley
2 packets of G
      Washington's
      Golden Seasoning
      and Broth
   Salt and freshly
      ground black
      pepper to taste

Heat a frying pan and sauté the chopped onion in 2 table-spoons of oil until clear. Set aside to cool. Remove any cartilage, bone, or tendons from each chicken breast and cut the chicken breasts into small pieces.

Place the ½ cup carrot and ¼ cup parsley in a food processor and chop coarsely. Add the cooled onion, the pieces of chicken, and the remaining ingredients for the chicken mixture (you may have to do this in batches). Chop together into a coarse paste, scraping down the sides of the food processor as you go. Refrigerate for 1 hour.

Heat a 4-quart pot for the soup and add the oil and sliced onion and sauté until just tender. Add the remaining ingredients except the salt and pepper to taste. Turn off the heat until the chicken mixture has refrigerated for 1 hour.

Form the chicken paste into balls slightly smaller than golf balls. Keep your hands damp with water to prevent the balls from sticking to your hands. Place the formed balls on a sheet of oiled waxed paper.

Bring the pot of soup to a gentle boil. Drop the balls one at a time into the hot soup pot. Keep the temperature up and carefully shake the pot as you add the chicken balls so they don't stick together. Cover the pot and cook over low heat for 40 minutes. Salt and pepper to taste. Allow to cool a bit, but serve warm.

GRILLED CHICKEN WITH PRIDE OF DEER CAMP BARBECUE SAUCE
SERVES 4

I think this is real family eating, regardless of whom you claim as your family on that cooking night. This is so simple that you will make it often, I am sure, but it is only simple if you bother to make the Pride of Deer Camp Sauce ahead of time. Make a full batch and seal it up in quart jars. It does not have to be refrigerated if used within 3 months.

**4 chicken quarters
(legs and thighs)**

**1 cup Pride of Deer
Camp Barbecue
Sauce (page 186)**

Place the chicken in a large bowl and add the barbecue sauce. Toss about and marinate for 1 hour, turning the chicken a couple times while marinating.

Grill the chicken on a barbecue over medium-low heat. Cook about 25 minutes per side, basting with the remaining marinade while grilling. The chicken is done when you pierce the bottom of the thighs and the juices run clear.

GRILLED CHICKEN
WITH ROSEMARY
SERVES 2 TO 3

I do not know whether you can grow fresh rosemary in your yard year-round. In Seattle and Tacoma it is simple, but only the Greeks and the Italians seem to bother growing it. I could not run a kitchen without fresh rosemary and I do not intend to pay $1.50 for a tiny bunch from the supermarket.

This dish is Italian in flavor and easy to prepare. Yes, you can use dried rosemary in a pinch but soak it in a few tablespoons of warm water for 1 hour before using.

1 3½-pound chicken, cut in half	Juice of 1 lemon
2 tablespoons fresh rosemary	¼ cup olive oil
3 cloves garlic, peeled and crushed	Salt and freshly ground black pepper to taste

Place the chicken in a large bowl with the remaining ingredients. Toss together until all is coated. Allow to marinate for 1 hour. Grill the chicken over medium-low heat, about 25 minutes per side. Brush the chicken with the remaining marinade while grilling. The chicken is done when you pierce the bottom of a thigh and the juices run clear.

CHICKEN CACCIATORE
SERVES 3 TO 4

Now do not jump to conclusions. This is not a complicated recipe and it is not supposed to be. I just happen to think that chicken cooked in good spaghetti sauce is a great thing for our time and I want you to remember it in your daily meal planning.

If you have prepared the good Italian Tomato Sauce and keep it in your refrigerator, you are set for this one. If you are in a real pinch, you can use a commercial sauce. There are some good ones on the shelves these days. Choose those that are packed in glass, not cans.

1 3½-pound chicken, cut into eighths Salt and freshly ground black pepper to taste (easy on the salt) 2 tablespoons olive oil	½ cup dry red wine 2 cups Italian Tomato Sauce (page 216) GARNISH Chopped parsley

Season the chicken with salt and pepper to taste. Heat a large frying pan and add 1 tablespoon of the oil. Brown half of the chicken and remove it to a 4- to 6-quart stove-top casserole. Brown the rest of the chicken in the remaining oil and add to the pot. Add the red wine and tomato sauce. Bring to simmer, cover, and simmer gently for 40 minutes. Stir the chicken occasionally. Garnish with parsley.

NOTE: You can serve this with pasta or rice on the side.

CHICKEN PATTIES WITH SOY
AND SWEET VERMOUTH DIP
MAKES ABOUT 3 DOZEN

Some of the new processed food products that are on the market these days are just too good to miss. Ground chicken is one of those products. Check several brands in your area or talk with your merchants. You want a brand that has a lower fat content than the cheapest brand.

I enjoy this dish, and the kids can help in the cooking process. Then they will enjoy the dinner even more.

1 tablespoon peanut oil	**Salt and freshly ground black pepper to taste**
1 medium yellow onion, peeled and chopped	
2 pounds ground chicken (buy frozen or grind your own)	**DIP**
	¼ cup light soy sauce (page 58)
1 cup plain bread crumbs	1 tablespoon sweet vermouth
1 egg, beaten	2 scallions, chopped
½ cup chopped parsley	**Flour for dredging the patties**
	Peanut oil for panfrying

Heat a frying pan and add the oil and onion. Sauté the onion until tender and set aside to cool.

In a large bowl, combine the ground chicken, bread crumbs, egg, parsley, sautéed onion, and salt and pepper to taste. Mix together until all is incorporated.

Prepare the dip and set aside.

Form the chicken mixture into balls about the size of walnuts. Pat the balls into little pancakes between sheets of lightly floured waxed paper. Dredge the patties in flour and shake off excess. Pan-fry the patties on both sides in peanut oil until golden brown. Drain on paper towels. Serve with the dip.

LOW-SALT/LOW-FAT
CHICKEN CRAIG
SERVES 3 TO 4

Craig thinks like I think. When he says "low-fat" he means low animal fat. The amount of olive oil in this dish does not bother either of us since olive oil is one of the helpful rather than hurtful oils. Besides, most of the marinade is drained from the chicken before cooking.

This dish has a bright and herby flavor, a flavor that all in your clan will enjoy.

1 3-pound chicken, cut into eighths	½ teaspoon freshly ground black pepper
1 tablespoon fresh sage	1 cup olive oil
1 tablespoon fresh rosemary	½ cup dry white wine
1 tablespoon fresh oregano	1 tablespoon fresh lemon juice
4 cloves garlic, peeled	

Cut the wings off the breast and pull all the skin off the chicken pieces. Save the wings and skin to make stock at another time.

Chop the sage, rosemary, oregano, garlic, and black pepper together to make an herb paste. Rub the chicken well with the paste and place in a bowl. Add the oil and toss so that everything is coated. It is best to marinate this, covered, in the refrigerator overnight, but 2 hours of marinating will work fine. Drain most of the marinade before cooking.

Heat a large nonstick frying pan and sauté the chicken about 10 minutes per side. No additional oil will be needed because of the marinade. The chicken is done if the juices run clear when pierced with a knife. Add the wine and lemon juice to the hot pan of chicken and simmer a couple minutes to reduce the liquid and form a sauce. Serve the chicken with the sauce spooned over the top.

NOTE: The remaining marinade can be refrigerated for several days and reused to prepare another chicken dish.

CHICKEN THIGHS IN YOGURT AND ONIONS
SERVES 4

This dish is very Middle Eastern in flavor. While it is terribly easy and quick to prepare, it has enough depth of flavor for a fine dinner party. Don't kill yourself cooking for a dinner party in our time. You should enjoy the party just as much as your guests do!

3 tablespoons olive oil
2 cloves garlic, peeled
  and crushed
2 medium yellow
  onions, peeled
  and sliced
8 chicken thighs
  Salt and freshly
  ground black
  pepper to taste

2 cups plain yogurt
1 tablespoon chopped
  parsley

GARNISH
Sumac (page 65) or
zartar (page 65)

Heat a large frying pan and add 2 tablespoons of the oil. Add the garlic and onion and sauté until the onion is tender. Do not brown.

Season the chicken with salt and pepper to taste. Heat another frying pan and add the remaining 1 tablespoon of oil. Brown the chicken on both sides and remove to a 13×9-inch glass baking dish. When the onions are tender, stir in the yogurt and parsley off the heat. Salt and pepper to taste. Pour the yogurt mixture over the chicken thighs and bake at 375° for 35 minutes. Garnish with sumac or zartar.

CHICKEN DRUMETTES FOR KIDS
MAKES 24 PIECES, OR SERVINGS FOR 3 YOUNGSTERS

This one is such fun to prepare, but it takes some time and your kids must know how to deal with a sharp paring knife. I suggest that you do the cutting and let the kids prepare the little drumsticks by pulling the meat down on the bone. They will need some help, but dinner will be terrific!

12 chicken wings
2 tablespoons olive oil
2 cloves garlic, peeled and crushed
1 teaspoon dried oregano, whole

Juice of 1 lemon
Salt and freshly ground black pepper to taste
2 tablespoons grated Parmesan cheese

Cut each wing into 3 pieces at each of the two joints (see the illustration), and you wind up with the wing tip (which I generally set aside and use for soup), the middle portion, and finally, the thickest part of the wing, that part that is closest to the bird, literally the upper arm of the bird. The upper arms make marvelous little drumsticks. Use the middle portions of the wings for this recipe as well.

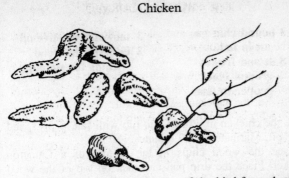

Cut the meat of the upper arm of the bird from the bone at the smallest end. Then push the meat down to the largest end, thus forming a small drumstick, very rich in flavor.

Place the cut-up wings in a bowl and add everything but the Parmesan cheese. Toss and allow to marinate for 30 minutes.

Place the chicken pieces on a broiler pan. Broil in the top part of the oven on high broil. Turn and baste the chicken pieces with the remaining marinade every few minutes. When they are browned nicely, sprinkle with Parmesan cheese and allow the cheese to melt and brown. Watch closely so that the cheese doesn't burn.

CHICKEN SMOKED WITH OLIVE OIL
SERVES 3 TO 4

I did this dish for Elmo, the little fuzzy red monster from *Sesame Street*. He could not believe that it was so simple ... and I eventually sent the actor behind Elmo, Kevin Clash, a Cameron Smoker (page 38). This is one of the most valuable devices in my kitchen, and certainly one of the most helpful for the kitchen of the nineties.

1 3-pound chicken,	3 tablespoons olive oil
cut in half	2 tablespoons wood
Salt and freshly	chips for smoking
ground black	
pepper to taste	

Place the chicken in a bowl and rub with salt, pepper, and olive oil. Marinate for 30 minutes.

Place the wood chips in the bottom of a Cameron Smoker. Place the drip pan and rack on top of the wood chips. Arrange the chicken on the rack and slide the lid in place. Heat the unit over medium fire until it begins to smoke. Reduce the heat to low and smoke the chicken for 15 minutes. Place the whole unit in a preheated 375° oven and bake for 35 to 40 minutes. The chicken is done if the juices run clear when the bottom of the thighs is pierced.

CHICKEN IN A NEST
MAKES 8 BASKETS

Sara Little, a dear friend and a highly respected food designer, told me that food served in its own edible container will prove helpful to the family units of the nineties. Thus this dish. The potato basket holds the creamed chicken and the whole thing works together to offer the kids a dish that can be entirely eaten . . . and I mean entirely.

POTATO NESTS

5 potatoes
4 cups peanut oil for
    deep frying

CHICKEN FILLING

3 tablespoons butter
6 tablespoons all-
    purpose flour
1 cup Chicken Stock
    (page 109) or
    used canned

1 cup half-and-half
¾ pound cooked
    chicken meat,
    diced
Salt and freshly
    ground black
    pepper to taste

GARNISH

Chopped parsley

Peel the potatoes and grate them coarsely. As you do this, keep the grated potato in lightly salted water so that it will not discolor. Press the grated potatoes dry on paper towels.

Heat the oil in a wok to 380°. Dip the bird's-nest frying basket (page 40) into the pan to oil it. Take the baskets apart and fill the bottom basket with the dried grated potatoes, forming a basket of potato within the wire basket. Replace the smaller basket within the larger, and clamp shut. Deep-fry until golden brown, about 3 minutes. To remove, gently take out the smaller basket. Knock out the potato basket by gently tapping the wire frame upside down on the counter. The potato basket will fall out. Drain on paper towels.

In a small saucepan, melt the butter. Add the flour and cook together to form a *roux*. Do not brown! Whisk in the Chicken Stock and half-and-half. Bring to a simmer, whisking until smooth and lump-free. Stir in the cooked chicken meat and increase the heat. Salt and pepper to taste. When the chicken filling is cooked through, arrange the potato baskets on a platter and fill them with the hot chicken filling. Garnish with chopped parsley.

Red Meat

Red Meat

*I am a great eater of beef, and I believe
that does harm to my wit.*

Shakespeare, *Twelfth Night*

I am also a great eater of beef, and I do not believe that
it does harm to my wit. Too much meat may be harmful
to my health, but not to my wit.

Concern over red meat in our time seems to have grown
all out of proportion. It is true that I have tried to cut down
on animal fat during the last few years, but that does not
mean that I must eliminate my beloved red meat from my
diet. I trim the fat carefully and I never buy hamburger
from a butcher. I buy a chuck roast, trim the fat, and grind
my own. Once in a while I have to have pork spareribs. I
don't do it often, but when I do I am in pig heaven. Well,
heaven for me, perhaps not for the pig.

Vegetarians in our time seem to have an evangelistic cry
that claims that red meat eaters are violent while vegetarians are gracious of heart. Lord, when the vegetarians start
screaming at me in public and the red meat eaters are quiet
and kind, then I have to wonder about the logic behind this
argument. I do eat lots of vegetable dishes and I really do
believe that we have all eaten too much red meat in our
culture. Perhaps we should think as do the Chinese. They
claim that meat, especially red meat, is to be used for flavoring a vegetable dish. Our dear Thomas Jefferson made
the same claim, and that is how he cooked and ate.

Jefferson is a good example for all of us, but do not

deprive me of my spareribs. Now and then they are just right for me.

You will notice that this section on red meats is smaller than that for vegetables. So be it, but you will find some of my favorite dishes here. Pride of Deer Camp Barbecue Sauce may just change your life and Karen's Meat Loaf makes the best sandwich that I know. Chef Andy's recipe for Beef Chow Fun (Chinese rice noodles) causes me great hunger even as I write, and my favorite hamburger is here for all to see. It is really not just a hamburger but rather a Chopped Sirloin French Dip in Heat!

Enjoy! Please stay away from the hamburger drive-ins as they offer too much fat and too little flavor. You can feed your chosen family much better hamburgers if you grind your own beef and cook at home. I promise you that this is true!

GRILLED PORK
SERVES 4 TO 6 AS A MEAT COURSE

This is so good and I love pork so much! You can use pork steaks for this dish but you should trim them well if you are cutting down on fat intake. If you use pork chops, which contain less animal fat, be sure not to overcook them or they will be very dry.

The cumin and garlic give this dish a sort of South of the Border flavor. It is a favorite of mine.

1 teaspoon ground cumin	Salt and freshly ground black pepper to taste
Juice of 1 lemon	
¼ cup olive oil	6 boneless pork steaks or pork chops
2 tablespoons dry white wine	
2 cloves garlic, peeled and crushed	

Combine everything but the pork in a small bowl. Stir well, pour over the pork, and marinate for 1 hour. Turn the pork a few times while marinating.

Grill over medium heat, turning once and basting with the leftover marinade. Grill to desired doneness.

GRILLED PORK RIBS WITH PRIDE OF DEER CAMP BARBECUE SAUCE
SERVES 4 TO 5

Now it is time for the proof! If you have made a batch of Pride of Deer Camp Barbecue Sauce, you are set for some time. Try this dish and see what happens to your family. If you have little ones about I hope that you did not make it too spicy. When you eat this stuff you know you are eating!

4 pounds pork spareribs	**1 cup Pride of Deer Camp Barbecue Sauce (below)**

Marinate the ribs in whole pieces in the sauce for ½ hour. Place the ribs on a broiler pan and bake at 375° for 1 hour. Baste them with the sauce while baking. Remove from the oven and finish off on the barbecue or grill to your liking. Baste again while grilling.

PRIDE OF DEER CAMP BARBECUE SAUCE
MAKES 8 QUARTS

This product is hard to explain, but if you make it no explanation will be necessary. In the Carolinas and in the hills of Arkansas barbecue sauces contain much less tomato than those found in the rest of the country . . . and they contain more vinegar and spice. The result is fantastic.

This one is from Arkansas and is the gift of a dear friend

of ours, Ms. Sarah Lea, general manager of the Lenox House Hotel in Chicago. We stay there often when we are in the Windy City and Sarah's hospitality is as fine as her barbecue sauce.

Sarah makes a jug of this stuff and stores it under the kitchen sink. That is how you do it in Arkansas. I prefer to store it in quart canning jars in the refrigerator. This way I can share a jar with a friend anytime I wish. Don't worry about the amount that this recipe produces. You will find lots of uses for it and you will also be able to give away a few quarts.

1½ cups dark brown sugar	½ cup crushed red pepper flakes (or a little less if you do not like a spicy hot sauce)
1½ cups Worcestershire sauce	
1½ cups prepared mustard	3 quarts red wine vinegar
1 quart ketchup	2 quarts water
½ cup freshly ground black pepper	1 quart white wine
	1½ cups salt

Place all the ingredients in a 12-quart stainless steel pot and bring to a boil. Reduce the heat to a low simmer, cover, and cook for 30 minutes. Store, covered, in glass canning jars in the refrigerator.

NOTE: Suggested uses include a marinade sauce and a barbecue sauce. Also good in Bloody Marys.

KAREN'S MEAT LOAF
WITH PORCINI GRAVY
MAKES 2 MEAT LOAVES

Both Craig, my chef, and I were brought to the stove by our mothers. I rarely meet a chef who does not make the same claim. "My mother is an excellent cook," Craig claims, "and she was always taking dishes the extra mile. She still does. And even her meat loaf is superb!"

Craig served this to my mother one evening and she claimed that it is the best meat loaf she has ever eaten. Can you imagine? Such a remark from *my* mother?

1 recipe Porcini
    Gravy
    (opposite)
3 tablespoons olive
    oil
3 cloves garlic,
    peeled and
    crushed
1 medium yellow
    onion, peeled
    and minced
1 cup minced celery
1 cup peeled and
    minced carrots
½ pound
    mushrooms,
    minced
½ cup chopped
    parsley
½ cup dry red wine

1 cup fine bread
    crumbs,
    preferably
    freshly ground
1 cup milk
1½ pounds lean
    ground beef
1 pound boneless
    pork roast,
    trimmed and
    finely ground
½ pound mild
    Italian sausage
2 eggs, beaten
2 teaspoons sweet
    paprika
Salt and freshly
    ground black
    pepper to taste

Prepare the Porcini Gravy and set aside.

Heat a large frying pan. Add the oil, garlic, and onion and sauté. Cook for 1 minute and add the celery, carrots, mushrooms, and parsley and sauté until lightly browned.

Add the red wine and simmer a few minutes until the liquid is evaporated. Set aside and cool.

Soak the bread crumbs in the milk for 10 minutes. In a large bowl, mix together the ground beef, pork, and sausage with the soaked bread crumbs. Add the cooled vegetable mixture along with the beaten eggs, paprika, and salt and pepper. Work together well with your hands until all is incorporated. Cook a tiny portion of the mixture in a small frying pan and taste. Adjust the salt and pepper if needed.

Pack the meat mixture into two nonstick loaf pans and cover with parchment paper and foil. Bake in a preheated 350° oven for 30 minutes. Reduce the oven temperature to 300° and bake for an additional 30 minutes. Remove from the oven and allow to stand for 10 minutes. Serve with the Porcini Gravy.

NOTE: When chilled, this makes a wonderful sandwich, just wonderful. A little mayonnaise, Dijon mustard, lettuce, and caraway rye bread and you are set!

PORCINI GRAVY
MAKES ABOUT 3½ CUPS

I know of no one who does not just love a good brown gravy. Craig developed this one because we both love mushrooms and because he was trying to impress my mother one night when he served meat loaf. This is great with meat loaf, but it is so rich that you can get away with serving it with toast—toast with gravy, a great staple from the Depression. Your kids may wonder when you serve them a plate of toast covered with gravy, but I bet you that they will love it.

1½ ounces dried porcini mushrooms (or the South American variety that cost much less, page 57)

¾ cup hot water

2 tablespoons butter

5 tablespoons all-purpose flour

2 cups Beef Stock (page 108) or use canned

¼ cup dry vermouth

¼ cup milk

½ teaspoon Maggi liquid seasoning

Salt and freshly ground black pepper to taste

Soak the porcini in ¾ cup hot water in a small bowl for 45 minutes.

In a 4-quart pot, melt the butter. Add the flour and cook together to form a *roux*. Do not brown! Whisk in the Beef Stock until smooth. Bring the sauce to a simmer and whisk until thickened and lump-free. Strain the liquid from the soaked porcini into the sauce. Chop the porcini coarsely and add to the pot along with the vermouth, milk, and Maggi. Simmer gently, uncovered, for 20 to 30 minutes. Salt and pepper to taste.

LAMB WITH GREEN PEPPERS AND CARROTS
SERVES 4 TO 6

Lamb has got to be the most misunderstood red meat of our time. When I was a child we were told to cook old lamb until it became even older, and the results were disastrous and distasteful. In our time young lamb is probably one of the best food values on the market since so little lamb is needed to flavor a fine dish.

I cooked this dish on a show with Elmo, the little red monster from *Sesame Street*. He decided that he loved lamb. So do I, and so will the young people in your clan if you just do not overcook it. Not in our time!

1 cup peeled and julienned carrots	1 medium green bell pepper, cored, seeded, and julienned
2 tablespoons olive oil	
2 cloves garlic, peeled and chopped	Salt and freshly ground black pepper to taste
¾ pound boneless lamb, trimmed of fat and julienned	½ teaspoon freshly ground coriander seeds

Blanch the carrots. (I use my ISE Steamin' Hot water dispenser. Place the carrots in a small bowl and cover with the steaming water. Cover the bowl with a plate and let stand a few minutes.)

Heat a wok or frying pan and add the oil and garlic along with the lamb. Stir-fry the lamb briefly until browned. Drain the balanced carrots and add to the pan along with the bell pepper. Stir-fry a couple minutes until all is hot and tender. Add the salt and pepper to taste and the coriander. Toss about and serve.

PORK AND BLACK PEPPER, CHOWED
SERVES 4 TO 6 AS PART OF A CHINESE MEAL

If you are short on time when it comes to cooking in the evening, then you simply must get a Chinese wok. Everything goes into the wok and cooks quickly, and I mean everything. In order to make my point I want you to try this very delicious and very quick pork dish.

¾ pound boneless pork butt, fairly thinly sliced

2 tablespoons light soy sauce (page 58)

½ teaspoon grated fresh ginger

1 tablespoon dry sherry

2 tablespoons peanut oil

2 cloves garlic, peeled and chopped

Pinch of salt

Plenty of freshly ground black pepper

GARNISH

Chopped fresh coriander leaves

Steamed rice for serving

Cut the sliced pork into bite-size pieces and place in a small bowl with the light soy sauce, ginger, and sherry. Marinate for 15 minutes.

Heat a wok and add the oil, garlic, and salt. Add the marinated pork and stir-fry for a few minutes until the pork is just cooked. Add plenty of black pepper to taste and toss about. Garnish with coriander and serve with steamed rice.

BEEF CHOW FUN
(From Sea Garden Seafood Restaurant)
SERVES 4 TO 6

I still remember the first time that I tasted this dish in San Francisco's wonderful Chinatown. I was with my beloved adopted Chinese auntie, Mary Young, and each time I would visit San Francisco she would tell me that she had found a new place for chow fun. In those days I could not get the fresh thick rice noodles in any other city but San Francisco. Now you can purchase these noodles fresh in any Chinatown. Just look for a noodle shop.

We owe this great recipe to Chef Andy Wong of the Sea Garden Seafood Restaurant in Seattle. Andy is just great, and you can always tell when he is in the kitchen.

This will take some doing for the beginning cook, but if you are comfortable with a wok you are all set!

½ pound beef flank steak
1 egg white
1 tablespoon cornstarch
Pinch of salt
2 cups peanut oil for deep-frying
1 tablespoon fermented black beans (*dow see*) (find in any Chinese market)

1 tablespoon dry sherry
¾ pound fresh fun (fresh rice noodles) (find in Chinatown)
½ tablespoon dark soy sauce (page 58)
1 cup fresh bean sprouts
4 scallions, chopped

Slice the beef thinly across the grain and place in a small bowl. Add the egg white, cornstarch, and salt. Mix together until smooth and all is coated. Marinate for 15 minutes.

Heat the oil in a wok to 300°. Add the beef and deep-fry for 30 seconds. This is not really deep-frying but rather light frying, what the Chinese call "velveting." Remove the beef with a strainer and allow to drain. Remove all but 2 tablespoons of the oil from the wok.

Rinse and drain the black beans. In a small bowl, mash together the black beans and sherry into a paste. Cut the fresh fun into ½-inch-wide strips.

Heat the wok and the 2 tablespoons of oil again until very hot. Add the fresh fun, black bean paste, dark soy sauce, and the reserved beef. Stir-fry for 20 seconds. Add the bean sprouts and scallions and quickly stir-fry for 30 to 45 seconds more, until the dish is colored a light brown and all is hot.

SPARERIBS WITH BLACK BEAN SAUCE
(From Sea Garden Seafood Restaurant)
SERVES 4 AS PART OF A CHINESE MEAL

This is another dish that I have loved since my first visit to San Francisco, one of the great restaurant cities in America.

This version has been given to us by Chef Wai Chin of the Sea Garden Seafood Restaurant in Seattle's Chinatown. I think it is the garnishes that make this dish so totally delectable.

2 tablespoons fermented black beans (*dow see*) (find in Chinatown)

1 tablespoon peanut oil

1 pound pork spareribs (have the butcher saw the ribs into 1-inch strips and cut them into single-bone pieces)

2 cloves garlic, peeled and crushed

Pinch of salt
Pinch of sugar
Pinch of MSG (optional)

GARNISHES

2 teaspoons dark soy sauce (page 58)

3 scallions, chopped

4 sprigs fresh coriander

2 teaspoons sesame oil

1 tablespoon peanut oil

Rinse and drain the black beans. Combine with the oil in a small bowl and mash together into a coarse paste.

Place the ribs in a bowl and combine with the bean paste, garlic, salt, sugar, and optional MSG. Mix together with your hands until all is coated.

Spread the ribs out on a porcelain platter and place it in an active bamboo steamer (page 38). Steam the ribs for 15 to 20 minutes, then remove from the steamer. Garnish with soy sauce, scallions, coriander, and sesame oil.

Heat the peanut oil until very hot. Pour over the top of the garnishes.

JEFF'S FAVORITE HAMBURGER

This is not a normal hamburger at all, though I love those, too, if made at home. I got into the habit of eating this dish at the Harbor Lights, a seafood restaurant that has held on to the Tacoma waterfront for three generations.

This makes a quick and wonderful meal when served with a tossed salad. Grill an oblong-shaped ground sirloin patty and place it on a grilled Poor Boy roll. Don't overcook the meat. Serve with a ramekin each of Quick Au Jus (below) and Bleu Cheese Dressing (page 136). Dip the sandwich in the Au Jus and then into the dressing. Delicious!

QUICK AU JUS
MAKES ABOUT 1¼ CUPS

1 teaspoon olive oil
1 clove garlic, peeled and crushed
1 10½-ounce can Campbell's Beef Broth (not bouillon cubes!)

1 tablespoon dry sherry
Pinch of freshly ground black pepper to taste

Heat the oil in a small saucepan and sauté the garlic a few seconds. Do not burn the garlic. Add the beef broth straight out of the can (no water). Add the remaining ingredients and simmer 2 minutes.

Remember that people become confused when they are all cooking together and having a good time. Just stand by the kitchen door and watch. They will feed you sooner or later.

INFUSED OIL FOR GRILLING MEAT
(From Kaspar's by the Bay)
MAKES 2¼ CUPS

This is another gift from Kaspar's by the Bay restaurant, one of my favorite places in Seattle. It is not gimmicky, though everyone is using infused oils these days. Read the list of ingredients and you will immediately see that the oil will impart a wonderful flavor to any meats that you might be grilling or broiling. There is no salt in this recipe.

2 cups olive oil
1½ teaspoons coarsely cracked black pepper
2 tablespoons fresh rosemary needles, removed from the stem, pounded just a bit

¼ cup coarsely chopped parsley
3 cloves garlic, peeled and crushed

Combine all the ingredients in a small bowl or jar and allow to stand at room temperature for 2 hours. Brush meat with the oil when grilling. The oil will keep for several days.

Eggs

Recipe cooking is to
real cooking as painting by number is
to real painting: just pretend.

John Thorne, *Simple Cooking*

The idea of giving a recipe for cooking an egg bothers me. I would think that all of us would know how to cook an egg properly since the egg is one of Mother Nature's most perfect foods, though in our time Mother Nature is being blamed for all kinds of dietary sins, including the sin of the egg.

According to the authorities that I most respect, eggs are not serious villains in our diet. They contain a good deal of lecithin, which helps in their digestion . . . and which means that eggs are really quite good for us. However, eating eggs every morning for breakfast makes no sense to me, any more than does eating beans every night for dinner. Variety is the key to health in our time. I am convinced of that.

We ate eggs long before we ate the chickens. How many chickens did we have to have before we decided we could eat not only the gift but the gift giver? This eating of the giver probably first occurred in China, where chickens were first domesticated. I expect that in our time we would just as soon have the eggs as the chickens. So, the following egg dishes should be helpful to your modern family unit. Just don't overdo on eggs, or on anything else for that matter.

201

A warning is offered in our time concerning salmonella, a bacteria that chickens can pass on through their eggs. Be sure to cook your eggs to 140°, which means a soft-boiled egg is all right, but a raw egg in a salad dressing is not. This warning should be heeded most by those people who live east of the Mississippi. My egg farmer, Barry Wilcox of Wilcox Farms in Washington State, claims that to date we have not seen a case of salmonella west of the Mississippi. While he has no explanation for that, he does urge all of us to watch the quality of the eggs that we buy.

EGGS SCRAMBLED WITH
CURRY AND WATER CHESTNUTS
SERVES 3 TO 4

I am embarrassed about this one. I receive many letters and recipes from fans and I try to answer each letter. This is, in my opinion, a very good egg dish and I have only the recipe, as the author wrote it on a small piece of paper. I do not have a name or an address! If this is your dish, then let me know so that I can credit you eventually.

What a great life! More recipes than I can use . . . and I lose the addresses. Forgive me and let me know who you are . . . and to you people who are sending me recipes, be sure to put your name and address on your letters! Please. . . .

6 eggs
  Dash of
    Worcestershire
    sauce
  Salt and freshly
    ground white
    pepper to taste
1 tablespoon chopped
    parsley

2 teaspoons curry
    powder
1 tablespoon peanut
    oil
1 clove garlic, peeled
    and crushed
1 cup sliced water
    chestnuts,
    drained

Beat the eggs together in a small bowl and stir in the remaining ingredients except the oil, garlic, and water chestnuts.

Heat a frying pan or wok and add the peanut oil and garlic. Add the egg mixture and allow the eggs to set slightly. Add the water chestnuts and scramble together over medium heat until cooked to taste.

CRUSTLESS GREEN CHILE QUICHE
SERVES 8 TO 10

I love quiche but I do not always have time to make a crust. This dish is perfect for the harried cook in our time. If you do not like green chiles, then substitute something else like garlic, zucchini, and oregano. Or perhaps chunks of tomato. Change nothing in the basic mixture and think up anything you like. Asparagus would be terrific!

10 eggs
½ cup butter, melted
½ cup all-purpose
    flour
1 teaspoon baking
    powder
¼ teaspoon salt
1 pound large-curd
    cottage cheese

2 4-ounce cans diced
    green chiles (I
    like Ortega
    brand)
  Freshly ground
    black pepper to
    taste
1 pound mozzarella
    cheese, grated

Whip the eggs in a mixing bowl until fluffy. Whisk in the melted butter, flour, baking powder, and salt. Stir in the cottage cheese, chiles, black pepper, and half the mozzarella.

Place the mixture in a greased 13×9-inch glass baking dish. Top with the remaining cheese. Bake in a preheated 400° oven for 15 minutes. Then reduce the temperature to 350° and continue to bake for 35 to 40 minutes, or until the eggs are set and the top is lightly browned. Allow to cool a bit and cut into squares.

NOTE: You can also bake the egg mixture in oiled ramekins to make individual little casseroles for a first course. Watch these closely, though, as the quiche will cook more quickly in them than it will in the larger baking dish.

PIPERADE
SERVES 4

This wonderful dish of vegetables and eggs is of Basque origin, the Basques being that nationality of people who live in the Pyrenees mountains between northern Spain and southern France. They have a fierce sense of national pride, and yet they have no officially recognized nation. They must declare themselves to be Spanish or French.

In this dish you will see the flavors of both Spain and France put together with a Basco touch.

2 tablespoons olive
    oil
2 tablespoons butter
2 cloves garlic,
    peeled and
    crushed
1 medium yellow
    onion, peeled
    and sliced
1 medium green bell
    pepper, cored,
    seeded, and
    sliced
1 medium red bell
    pepper, cored,
    seeded, and
    sliced

3 tablespoons
    chopped parsley
¾ cup coarsely
    chopped ripe
    tomato
    Salt to taste
8 eggs, beaten
4 scallions, chopped
    Freshly ground
    black pepper to
    taste

Heat the oil and butter in a large frying pan and sauté the garlic, onion, and bell pepper slices. Sauté until just tender. Add the parsley and tomato. Cook a few minutes more over medium-high heat to evaporate any excess liquid. Add the salt to taste, beaten eggs, and scallions. Scramble everything together and top with plenty of freshly ground black pepper.

EGG SALAD SANDWICHES, OLD-FASHIONED STYLE
MAKES 4 SANDWICHES

During the taping of our *Whole Family Kitchen* series I ran across several youngsters who had never tasted an egg salad sandwich. I could not believe it. So I offer this dish because it was a favorite of mine when I was a child, and while I know you have a similar recipe, you may have forgotten to make it for your kids. Cook the eggs a day ahead when preparing dinner and refrigerate. Then mix everything together on the day of serving.

8 hard-boiled eggs, peeled	Salt and freshly ground black pepper to taste
2 tablespoons peeled and minced yellow onion	
2 tablespoons chopped fresh chives	4 iceberg lettuce leaves
½ cup mayonnaise	8 slices caraway rye bread

Coarsely chop the eggs and place them in a bowl with the remaining ingredients. Stir together. Spread equal amounts of egg salad on 4 slices of caraway rye bread. Top each with a lettuce leaf and another slice of bread.

SOFT EGGS AND PRAWNS, CHINESE STYLE
SERVES 4 AS PART OF A CHINESE MEAL

This is real foo young as it is done in Canton and Hong Kong. Those deep-fried egg patties are a San Francisco invention, and the Chinese are not fond of them at all.

This dish is cooked just until the eggs are set, so it is very moist. I like mine to be just a tad runny.

½ pound medium
   prawns, peeled
1 egg white
1 tablespoon
   cornstarch
Pinch of salt
2 cups peanut oil for
   cooking the
   prawns
2 cloves garlic,
   peeled and
   chopped

½ cup frozen peas,
   thawed
6 eggs, beaten
Salt and freshly
   ground white
   pepper to taste

GARNISH
Fresh coriander

Butterfly the prawns by making a slit with a paring knife down the backs of the prawns. Place the prawns in a small bowl and stir in the egg white, cornstarch, and pinch of salt. Mix all together with your hands until smooth and coated. Marinate for 15 minutes.

Heat the oil in a wok to 300° and deep-fry the prawns for 1 minute. This is not really deep frying but rather light frying, what the Chinese call "velveting." Remove the prawns and drain. Remove all but 1 tablespoon of the oil from the wok.

Heat the wok again and add the garlic, peas, and prawns. Stir-fry for 1 minute and add the beaten eggs. Salt and white pepper to taste. Scramble together until the eggs are barely set. They must not be hard, but rather soft and a bit runny if you wish. Garnish with chopped coriander.

THE CLASSIC OMELET
SERVES 1

It seems to be time to get back to basics, basics for the frugal nineties. I showed omelet cooking on my very first shows some ten years ago and now I want you to reconsider omelets. They are quick to prepare, totally versatile, and everyone in your clan will love them. So here is the easy method of preparation. There should be no secrets to good omelets.

HINT: THE OMELET PAN. Please do not buy a fold-over pan, hinged in the center so that you can layer rather than fold the omelet. Choose an aluminum pan with sloping sides, preferably covered with SilverStone. The pan should have a metal handle so that it can be put under a broiler if you wish. Any good restaurant supply house or gourmet shop will have one of these. Use it for nothing but omelets and once you have cured it, don't ever wash it with soap. Just swish it out with hot water and put it away. The recipe here calls for a 10-inch pan. You can use this size pan for 2- or 3-egg omelets.

THE BASIC RULES
FOR A GOOD OMELET.

1. Use butter and peanut oil in your cooking. The blend of the two will prevent the butter from burning and will give the eggs a fine flavor and color.
2. Have the eggs at room temperature. I always have a few eggs sitting in a bowl on the counter to use for cooking. They keep fine for 2 weeks in the refrigerator, but you must bring them to room temperature before creating an omelet.
3. Never put salt in the egg mixture. It toughens the eggs. Add the salt just before folding.
4. Never use milk in the egg mixture. Use only water. Milk makes your omelet watery since it will not blend with the eggs. Water blends and helps keep the omelet high.
5. Heat the pan before you put in the peanut oil and butter. When the butter stops foaming, add the eggs.

BASIC OMELET
SERVES 1

3 eggs, at room temperature	Salt and freshly ground black pepper to taste
1 tablespoon water	
½ tablespoon peanut oil	
½ tablespoon butter	**GARNISH**
	Chopped parsley

Heat the pan over medium-high heat. Whip the eggs with a table fork in a small bowl. Add the water and whip again.

Place the oil and butter in the heated pan at the same time. When the butter stops foaming, whisk the eggs a couple of times, and pour them into the pan. When the omelet begins to set, you may have to lift the edge with a wooden spatula and allow the wet portion of the mixture to run under the omelet. Add salt and pepper if you wish.*

Slide the omelet onto a plate and, holding the handle backhand, fold the omelet over in half, using the pan. Garnish with parsley or some of the filling you have used and serve hot.

FILLINGS FOR OMELETS

Spaghetti Sauce.
I know that this sounds a bit weird, but Channing, my oldest son, claims this is just great. I agree.

*Before salt and pepper are added, any filling may be added. Place it on the front half of the omelet (the handle side of the pan is considered the back portion).

Vegetables.
Any precooked or leftover vegetables are delicious with eggs.

Swiss Cheese.

Ham and Onion.
Sauté them a bit first.

Green Peppers and Fresh Herbs.
Sauté them a bit first.

Kosher Salami and Onions.
Sauté them a bit first.

Onions and Pesto Sauce (page 266).
Sauté them a bit first.

Tomato and Cheddar Cheese.
Sauté them a bit first.

Sour Cream and Pepperoni.

Tomato with Pride of Deer Camp Barbecue Sauce (page 186).

Chili.
Sounds a bit weird again, eh? Try a red bean omelet, so popular in New Orleans.

Pasta

The angels in Paradise eat nothing but
vermicelli al pomidoro.

Duke of Bovino, Mayor of Naples, 1930

There is no other food product, I am sure, that brings more contentment and satisfaction to more people than pasta.

When I was a child we had pasta in two forms. Spaghetti and macaroni. That was it. Today the number of shapes and flavors that are available provide an incredible list of possibilities for the frugal and harried cook. Further, with a growing emphasis on the necessity of our eating more grains, pasta is perfect. Just perfect!

We can credit Thomas Jefferson as being the first person to serve pasta at a formal dinner party in the Colonies. He called it "Macaroni Pie," a dish that he brought with him following his travels in Italy. Today we call it macaroni and cheese . . . à la Tom Jefferson.

Interesting to note, is it not, that the Italians make pasta from one product, wheat, but they shape it into a thousand different forms? The Chinese, on the other hand, make pasta from at least a dozen different grains and beans but make it into only one shape, noodles.

Pasta is quick and fulfilling. No, I do not think that you have to make your own pasta from scratch, though that is great for a special party. Buy good-quality dried pasta and you will be just fine. Stay away from cheap supermarket brands and purchase pasta that is 100 percent pure semolina wheat. It will not go soggy on you while you are preparing dinner.

ITALIAN TOMATO SAUCE
(From The Frugal Gourmet Cooks Three Ancient Cuisines*)*
MAKES 3 QUARTS

You know I want you to cook at least one day a week. If you really mess up the kitchen during that one day, who cares? It is better than starting from scratch each night.

You need to keep this sauce on hand. Make it some night while you are cooking the evening meal and have someone else do the chopping. Store it in plastic containers in the refrigerator for 1 week or in the freezer for 1 month. Since it has no meat it is very versatile.

2 28-ounce cans tomato puree
1 6-ounce can tomato paste
1 quart Chicken Stock (page 109) or Beef Stock (page 108) or use canned
2 cups dry red wine
¼ cup olive oil
2 yellow onions, peeled and minced
6 cloves garlic, peeled and finely chopped
2 ribs of celery with leaves, minced
1 carrot, unpeeled and grated
½ cup chopped parsley
½ pound fresh mushrooms, chopped
½ teaspoon crushed red pepper flakes
1 tablespoon dried oregano, whole
1 teaspoon dried rosemary, whole

2 bay leaves, whole
1 tablespoon dried
   basil, whole, or
   2 tablespoons
   chopped fresh
   basil
2 cloves, whole

½ tablespoon freshly
   ground black
   pepper
2 tablespoons salt or
   to taste
1 teaspoon sugar

Place the tomato puree, tomato paste, chicken or beef stock, and red wine in a large pot.

Heat a frying pan and add the olive oil. Sauté the onion, garlic, celery, and carrot until they just begin to brown a bit.

Add to the pot along with the remaining ingredients. Bring to a light boil, then turn down to a simmer. Simmer for 2 hours, partly covered. Store in the refrigerator in plastic, glass, or stainless-steel containers . . . never aluminum, as the acid in the tomato will "eat" the aluminum. This sauce will keep for 1 week in the refrigerator or 1 month in the freezer.

SPAGHETTI WITH
PEANUT BUTTER SAUCE
SERVES 4 TO 6 AS A PASTA COURSE

I included this dish not just for the sake of the kids, though they will love it. Anybody in your family group that remembers peanut butter from their childhood will get into this one. It is so simple that it is embarrassing, but the flavors are from the Far East and you need not be embarrassed at all!

½ cup creamy peanut
    butter
⅓ cup hot water
1 tablespoon light
    soy sauce (page
    58)
1 clove garlic, peeled
    and crushed
⅓ cup heavy cream

1 teaspoon sesame
    oil
2 shots Tabasco
    (optional)
¾ pound spaghetti

GARNISH
Fresh coriander

Place the peanut butter in a small glass and add the hot water. Stir with a fork until smooth. Add the remaining ingredients except the pasta and coriander. Stir together until smooth and set aside.

Cook the pasta and drain well. Place the drained pasta in a bowl. Stir the reserved peanut butter mixture together again and add to the cooked pasta. Toss all together and garnish with coriander.

PESTO PRIMAVERA
SERVES 6 TO 8

Primavera, in Italian, refers to the springtime, and thus to fresh vegetables. While you have probably had primavera sauce before, at least I hope you have, you will like the variation in this one since we have added Pesto Sauce, that wonderful blend of garlic and fresh basil.

You can make up this whole thing a day ahead if you wish, and then cook the pasta on the night of the meal. Best made the same day, it is still terrific if you make it ahead.

2 cloves garlic,
  peeled and finely
  minced
1 tablespoon olive oil
1 small yellow onion,
  peeled and sliced
2 medium ripe
  tomatoes,
  chopped
Salt and freshly
  ground black
  pepper to taste
½ teaspoon dried
  basil, whole

½ teaspoon dried
  oregano, whole
2 medium zucchini,
  coarsely grated
½ cup dry red wine
2 tablespoons Pesto
  Sauce (page 266)
  or to taste
1 egg
¼ cup grated
  Parmesan cheese
1 pound penne or
  linguine

In a large frying pan, sauté the garlic in the oil until it is
lightly browned. Add the onion and sauté until it is clear.
Add the tomatoes, salt and pepper, basil, and oregano. Simmer for a few minutes, and add the zucchini. Cook for
about 5 minutes over high heat or until the moisture is
almost gone. Add the red wine and the Pesto Sauce and
simmer to reduce the moisture; set aside.

Beat the egg and Parmesan cheese together; set aside.

Cook the pasta in lightly salted water until al dente and
drain.

Heat the sauce again and stir in the beaten egg and
cheese. Pour over the cooked pasta and serve.

GREEN FETTUCCINE WITH DUCK
AND PORCINI SAUCE
SERVES 6 TO 8 AS A PASTA COURSE

No duck is safe if Craig, my chef, is around. While this
dish is inspired by the wonderful cooking of Lidia, from
the restaurant Felidia in New York, it was Craig who developed this version.

Yes, this is an involved dish that you would make for a

very nice dinner party, but it qualifies for this book of frugal cooking for the nineties because the entire sauce, and thus every bit of work of the dish, can be made ahead of time. All you need to do is warm up the sauce and cook the pasta on the night of the blessed duck event.

This is a great and grand dish. Truly fine eating!

½ ounce dried porcini mushrooms (or the less expensive South American type, page 57)
Salt and freshly ground black pepper to taste
1 3¼-pound duck, quartered
1¼ cups Chicken Stock (page 109) or use canned
1 cup dry white wine
2 tablespoons olive oil

3 cloves garlic, peeled and crushed
1 medium yellow onion, peeled and thinly sliced
¼ pound fresh mushrooms, chopped
1 cup heavy cream
1 pound spinach fettuccine

GARNISHES
Grated Parmesan cheese
Chopped parsley

Soak the dried porcini in ½ cup hot water for 1 hour.

Salt and pepper the duck quarters to taste. Heat a large nonstick frying pan and brown the duck pieces. Remove the browned pieces to a large stove-top casserole, discarding any fat in the pan. Add the Chicken Stock and ½ cup of the wine. Cover and simmer gently for 1½ hours. You may have to add some water to the pot if it begins to dry out.

Allow the duck to cool, then debone the meat, saving the bones, the meat, and the juice in the bottom of the pot.

Return the bones and juice to the pot. Cover and simmer gently for ½ hour. Strain the bones, reserving the stock, and discard the bones. Skim off the excess fat from the strained stock to yield at least ½ cup defatted stock. Make up the difference with Chicken Stock if you do not have enough defatted duck stock. Shred the de-boned duck meat and set aside, covered. Drain the porcini, reserving the liquid. Chop the porcini coarsely.

Heat a large frying pan and add the olive oil, garlic, onion, chopped porcini, and fresh mushrooms. Sauté until the onion is tender. Add the remaining white wine and reserved porcini liquid and simmer, uncovered, for 2 minutes. Add the cream and the ½ cup reserved duck stock. Add the reserved duck meat. Simmer, uncovered, to reduce and thicken slightly, about 5 minutes. Salt and pepper to taste.

Cook the pasta until al dente and drain well. Return the pasta to the kettle and add the duck and porcini sauce. Toss all together and garnish with grated parmesan cheese and chopped parsley.

SPAGHETTINI WITH SAND
(From Saleh al Lago)
SERVES 6 TO 8 AS A PASTA COURSE

The name is fun, but the dish is very good. While I have included this dish for the sake of the very young cooks in the household, I can see them making it for everyone.

This dish is a gift from a Middle Eastern cook who runs an Italian restaurant in Seattle. His name is Saleh, and since his fine institution is by Green Lake, he calls his place Saleh al Lago. I have eaten there many times and I have never been the least bit disappointed.

This dish is not on his regular menu, but he will make it for you if you would be so kind as to ask.

The sand, of course, is the bread crumbs.

1 pound spaghettini
¼ cup olive oil
2 cloves garlic, peeled and crushed
⅛ teaspoon crushed red pepper flakes (or less if you have little ones at the table)

½ cup freshly ground French bread crumbs (not too fine)
Salt to taste

GARNISH
Chopped parsley

Bring a large pot of water with a pinch of salt to a boil. Add the pasta and cook until just tender.

Heat a large frying pan and add the oil, garlic, and red pepper flakes. Sauté a few seconds but don't burn. Drain the pasta and add it, along with the bread crumbs, to the frying pan. Toss together with salt to taste until the pasta is coated with the bread crumbs.

VARIATION: If you wish to add cheese to this dish, go right ahead . . . although Saleh does not.

POTATO GNOCCHI LIDIA
SERVES 6

Lidia Bastianich was raised in Istria, that region between Italy and Yugoslavia. She speaks I do not know how many languages but when she speaks with food, I listen and understand. She was featured on the *Great Chefs of New York* PBS television series and is the author of a fine cookbook entitled *La Cucina di Lidia*. I have been eating in her res-

taurant for years and I am in love with her. That's all right
. . . she knows this!

She came out to Seattle to teach the children on my show
to make a food product that is such fun . . . gnocchi, or
hand-formed potato dumplings. This is the result of our
efforts and you will find this dish absolutely irresistible.

GNOCCHI DOUGH
6 **large russet
   potatoes**
2 **tablespoons plus 1
   teaspoon salt**
2 **eggs**

**Dash of freshly
ground white
pepper**
4 **cups unbleached
all-purpose flour**

Boil the potatoes in their skins, about 40 minutes, until
easily pierced with a skewer. Carefully drain the potatoes
in a colander so that they don't break up. When they are
cool enough to handle, peel and rice the potatoes. Spread
the riced potatoes out on the countertop to cool completely
(a marble work surface is best for this).

Bring 6 quarts of water with 2 tablespoons of salt to a
boil.

Gather the cold riced potatoes into a mound and form a
well in the center. Beat the eggs with the remaining 1 teaspoon of salt and the white pepper. Pour into the well in
the center of the riced potatoes. Work the potatoes and eggs
together with your hands, gradually adding 3 cups of flour.
Knead together until a smooth dough is achieved. Knead
in additional flour as necessary until the dough is no longer
sticky. Keep your hands and the work surface dusted with
flour the whole time. Cut the dough into 6 equal parts.
Continue to dust dough, hands, and work surface as long
as the dough feels sticky. Roll each piece of dough into a
rope ½-inch thick. Cut the ropes of dough into ½-inch
pieces called gnocchi. Indent each gnocchi with the end of
your thumb, or press the gnocchi with the tries of a dinner
fork to produce a ribbed effect. You can also roll the gnocchi between your hand and a box grater to make a pattern
on them.

Drop the gnocchi into boiling water a few at a time until you have the desired number of portions (don't try to cook too many at one time as you will lose the temperature of the boiling water). Stir the gnocchi gently and continuously with a wooden spoon. Cook 2 to 3 minutes or until they rise to the surface. Remove the gnocchi from the water with a slotted spoon or skimmer and transfer to a warm platter. Boil the remaining gnocchi in batches. The gnocchi can be frozen for later use, providing that they are dusted with enough flour so that they won't stick together.

SAGE SAUCE

- 1 cup butter
- 12 fresh sage leaves
- 6 portions cooked gnocchi
- ½ cup grated Parmesan cheese
- Freshly ground black pepper to taste

Cut the butter into pieces to facilitate melting. In a skillet, distribute the butter and sage and stir over low heat until the butter has melted. Add the cooked gnocchi and cook over moderate heat, turning gently with a wooden spoon until the gnocchi are coated with sauce and heated through, about 1 to 2 minutes. Transfer to serving plates, sprinkle with Parmesan cheese and pepper, and serve immediately.

GNOCCHI AND PEPPERS
SERVES 4 TO 6 AS A MAIN COURSE, OR MORE AS A PASTA COURSE

Perhaps I can get you into making gnocchi often if you understand that the potato dumplings can be served just as you would serve any other pasta. Spaghetti sauce is fine, as is pesto sauce, or perhaps simply oil and garlic. This variation relies upon peppers, and it is delicious. It was suggested by a young bachelor friend in Waukegan, Illinois. Stephen, ya done good!

1 recipe Gnocchi
   Dough (page
   223)
2 tablespoons butter
2 tablespoons olive
   oil
2 cloves garlic,
   peeled
1 medium green bell
   pepper, cored,
   seeded, and
   julienned
1 medium red bell
   pepper, cored,
   seeded, and
   julienned

2 tablespoons capers,
   drained
1 egg yolk, beaten
½ cup heavy cream
1 tablespoon grated
   Parmesan cheese
1 tablespoon
   chopped parsley
Salt and freshly
   ground black
   pepper to taste

Prepare the gnocchi and set aside, but don't cook.

Heat a large frying pan and add the butter, oil, and garlic and sauté a few seconds. Add the bell peppers and sauté until tender. Add the capers and cook 2 minutes more. Set aside and keep warm.

Whisk the egg yolk and cream together and set aside.

Boil the gnocchi 2 to 3 minutes until tender. Drain well. Place the drained gnocchi in a large bowl along with the sautéed pepper mixture, the egg yolk and cream, and the remaining ingredients. Carefully fold this together until all is incorporated (a large rubber spatula works well for this). Serve at once!

MARION'S SKOKIE CASSEROLE
SERVES 6 TO 8

Marion is the woman to whom this book is dedicated. She came to me as a volunteer when I first started doing shows in Chicago some nine years ago. Her husband of forty years had just died and so she set about redoing her life-style.

I have learned a lot from Marion.

One of the most beautiful things that she taught me was that when you are lonely you can always cook up a dish for someone who is ill or more lonely than you. Thus Marion's Skokie Casserole. All right, so it is not fancy . . . nor does she have the cash to do fancy cooking for older and single friends. All right, so you recognize the recipe, or something close to it, from your own childhood. The dish is included here because it is frugal and hot and tasty and because you can make it for others when they need some support. There! That's why this dish is here. Besides, your kids can make this and they will think they are geniuses.

½ pound elbow macaroni

3 tablespoons olive oil

1 pound ground beef

2 cloves garlic, peeled and crushed

1 medium yellow onion, peeled and chopped

1 medium green bell pepper, cored, seeded, and chopped

2 14½-ounce cans stewed tomatoes

1 10-ounce box frozen corn kernels, thawed

Salt and freshly ground black pepper to taste

1 cup crushed potato chips

¼ pound Cheddar cheese, grated

GARNISH
Parsley

Cook the macaroni until al dente and drain. Rinse in cold water and drain well.

Heat a large frying pan and add 1 tablespoon of the oil. Brown the ground beef until crumbly. Remove to a colander and drain the fat.

Heat the pan again and add the remaining 2 tablespoons of the oil. Add the garlic, onion, and green bell pepper. Sauté until tender and remove to a large bowl.

Combine the cooked macaroni and browned ground beef

with the sautéed vegetables. Add the stewed tomatoes, thawed corn, and salt and pepper to taste. Mix together until all is incorporated. Place the mixture in a large greased casserole and top with the crushed potato chips and cheddar cheese. Bake in a preheated oven at 350° for 1 hour, or until hot and bubbly. Sprinkle with parsley and serve.

Everyone should get along in the kitchen. No cats and dogs at the same time! (That's Carrots, Jason Smith's cat. What a bore!)

STUFFED SHELLS
SERVES 8

Every time that we have cooked stuffed pasta shells on the air my local Italian markets call and complain that they have run out of jumbo pasta shells within an hour. Once you find a shop that stocks these, buy a bunch because they are easy to cook, fun to stuff, and you will get the kids into the kitchen right away.

If you don't like our stuffing, think up one of your own. Anything goes in this book and in the kitchen of the nineties. Anything!

½ pound jumbo pasta shells
½ pound mild Italian sausage, casings removed
1 pound lean ground beef
3 cloves garlic, peeled and crushed
1 medium yellow onion, peeled and finely chopped
2 tablespoons olive oil
1 pound spinach, washed and chopped

2 tablespoons grated Parmesan cheese
Salt and freshly ground black pepper to taste
3 cups Italian Tomato Sauce (page 216)
1½ cups grated mozzarella cheese
Additional Parmesan cheese for topping
2 eggs, beaten
½ cup bread crumbs

Cook the pasta shells until al dente. Drain and rinse with cold water. Drain well.

Sauté the sausage and ground beef until crumbly. Drain and discard the fat.

In a large frying pan, sauté the garlic and onion in the oil until transparent. Add the spinach and cook until the spinach collapses and the liquid is evaporated.

Combine the sautéed meat and sautéed spinach mixture in a bowl. Add the remaining ingredients except the tomato sauce and mozzarella cheese. Mix together very well, using your hands.

Place 2½ cups of the tomato sauce into two separate 13×9-inch glass baking dishes. Fill the shells with the meat mixture, close them, and place them seam-side down in the sauce. Top the shells with the remaining sauce and cover with mozzarella and additional Parmesan cheese. Cover the baking dishes with foil and bake at 375° for 30 minutes or until hot throughout and bubbly. Uncover the dishes and broil a couple of minutes to brown the cheese slightly. Garnish with chopped parsley.

Vegetables

And the people of Israel said,
"We remember the fish we ate in Egypt for nothing,
the cucumbers, the melons, the leeks,
the onions, and the garlic; but
now our strength is dried up,
and there is nothing but
this manna to look at."

Numbers 11:5–6

In the ancient world vegetables seem to have been more important than they have been during our recent past. We took to canning and freezing virtually everything and our appreciation for fresh foods seemed to wane . . . but we are back, and we are back with a vengeance.

I dislike canned vegetables of any kind, especially those special sins called canned asparagus and canned beans. How could you . . . why would you . . . your mother never liked them either! In our time even frozen are better but the fresh are the best.

When you consider what you get for your money per pound in fresh vegetables, you realize that they are much cheaper than any kind of meat . . . though we should use a little meat for flavoring.

This section offers a few new ideas and some old ideas that will make you recall a time when you felt that you were not so disgustingly busy that you would eat fresh goodies from the garden. Please, in our time the frugal family needs to think about fresh things for the sake of nutrition, value, and finally, the most important thing, flavor.

I think you will enjoy the vegetable dishes in this section since none of them takes much time to prepare and all of them are really quite good. Your kids should never grow up as I did, eating canned asparagus (Oh, Lord, save me

and perish the thought!) and they should learn that fresh
things taste best. Always!

GRILLED TOMATOES

Grilled vegetables are just delicious. Instead of boiling or
microwaving everything, try bringing out your stove-top
grill (page 39) and cooking vegetables with a bit of infused
olive oil.

Remember that a grill is different from a griddle in that
the grill has ridges so that the food does not lie flat on the
cooking surface. A griddle, on the other hand, is simply a
flat cooking surface.

Ripe tomatoes that are still a bit firm work best for this.
Remove the core from a tomato and cut it in half crosswise.
Brush the tomato with either Infused Oil for Grilling Meat
(page 197) or Infused Oil for Grilling Fish (page 152).
Baste the tomato with the oil while grilling. Grill just until
they are hot and tender, but not overly soft.

GRILLED ACORN SQUASH

I love acorn squash, but the only way I had it as a child
was baked. Try grilling this wonderful vegetable. It will
have fewer calories than the version baked with butter,
brown sugar, and bacon that we all remember having when
we were growing up.

Cut an acorn squash into ½-inch-wide rings crosswise.
Remove the seeds from the rings and brush with Infused
Oil for Grilling Meat (page 197) or Infused Oil for Grilling

Fish (page 152). Grill both sides over medium heat until tender. Baste with the oil while grilling. Do not have the heat too high or the outside will color and burn before the middle is tender.

These are just great done on the barbecue grill.

GRILLED EGGPLANT

I really think that eggplant is one of the most delicious vegetables available. Many Americans turn up their noses at this great purple egg-shaped jewel, but I think they would be quickly converted if they would simply learn to cook this vegetable properly. The secret to getting rid of the bitterness is to salt the flesh and allow it to drain for a bit. The salt is then rinsed from the eggplant and you are ready to cook. This works every time.

Try the following dish on your barbecue as well as your kitchen grill (page 39).

Cut an eggplant into ½-inch-wide slices crosswise. Sprinkle both sides of the slices with salt. Place the slices in a colander and allow to drain for 30 minutes. Rinse the slices with cold water and pat dry with paper towels. Brush the slices with either Infused Oil for Grilling Meat (page 197) or Infused Oil for Grilling Fish (page 152). Grill over medium-high heat for a couple minutes on both sides. Baste with the oil while grilling.

TONY'S FRIED ENDIVE

Tony is a great cook and a fine man. His wife of over forty years passed away recently, so he has had to make some major changes in his life. You can understand this. However, he considers food to be very important, so he eats well, as he and his wife always had. He has the grandkids over for dinner often and he does the cooking. After all, he is Italian.

This recipe is a neat trick that he offers those who live

alone. From a head of endive he comes up with two dishes. Pretty clever, Tony.

Head of endive	½ cup water
2 tablespoons olive	Salt and freshly
oil	ground black
2 cloves garlic,	pepper to taste
peeled and	
chopped	

Use the darker green outer leaves of a head of endive for this dish. Save the tender light-colored leaves for Tony's Endive Salad (page 131). Wash the head of endive well and drain. Break off the outer leaves. Heat a small pot and add the oil and garlic. Add the endive and sauté for 3 minutes. Add the water and cover the pot. Reduce the heat and cook until tender, about 15 to 20 minutes. Stir the endive occasionally. Add salt and pepper to taste and serve.

The best rule for safety in the kitchen is to remember that many things are hot and dangerous. I burned my tail once. . . . I can't believe I told you that.

PRIDE OF DEER CAMP
BARBECUED POTATOES
SERVES 4

Everyone loves potatoes, and we always welcome new ways to make them. This one is simple if you have made a batch of wonderful Pride of Deer Camp Barbecue Sauce. You can use it for all sorts of dishes, as these potatoes will show.

2 large baking
    potatoes, washed
½ cup Pride of Deer
    Camp Barbecue
    Sauce (page 186)

¼ cup grated
    Parmesan cheese

Cut the potatoes in half lengthwise. Cut each half into 3 long wedges. Place the potato wedges in a bowl with the sauce. Toss together and allow to marinate for 30 minutes. Toss a couple times while marinating. Place the potatoes skin-side down in a greased 13×9-inch glass baking dish. Bake at 375° for about 40 minutes. Baste the potatoes with the sauce while baking. When the potatoes become barely tender, sprinkle on the grated cheese. Turn the oven to medium broil and brown the tops of the potatoes.

STUFFED POTATOES
SERVES 6

During the frugal nineties I think we are going to come back to an appreciation of the potato. I remember the first time that I tasted a stuffed potato such as you will find in this recipe. It was in a rather mediocre restaurant, but I thought I was in heaven. You know from this story that I was very young at the time, since stuffed potatoes were dumped in the American restaurant business for the sake of a newer, somewhat cutesy vegetable line. Well, I want my stuffed potatoes to come back and thus Craig and I offer this recipe.

If you cook the potatoes the night before they are to be

served, just cook them while you are preparing dinner, then on the night of serving you will be able to mix in the other ingredients and serve them in very little time.

3 large baking potatoes	½ cup butter, melted
2 tablespoons olive oil	½ cup sour cream
Kosher salt to taste	1 teaspoon Worcestershire sauce
¼ pound bacon	Salt and freshly ground black pepper to taste
1 bunch scallions, chopped	Paprika to taste

Wash the potatoes and drain. Place in a bowl and rub with olive oil and kosher salt. Place the potatoes directly on an oven rack in the center of the oven. Bake at 375° for 1 hour. Remove and allow to cool until the potatoes can be handled.

Fry the bacon until crisp. Drain on paper towels. Chop the bacon coarsely and set aside.

Cut the cooked potatoes in half lengthwise and scoop out the insides, leaving about ¼ inch of potato attached to the skins. Set the skins aside. Beat the potato with the bacon, scallions, and half the butter. Add the sour cream, Worcestershire, and salt and pepper.

Refill the skins and place on a baking sheet. Drizzle the tops with the remaining melted butter and sprinkle with paprika. With the oven on broil, bake the potatoes in the center of the oven until nicely browned and hot throughout, about 10 to 15 minutes.

ITALIAN FRIED POTATOES
SERVES 4 TO 6

Now and then a young person sends me a recipe. Some are great! Some are just recipes. However, when Margaret Brown sent me this one I felt I had to share it with you.

Margaret is very young but she loves to spend time in the kitchen. Try this one. It is simple and delicious. The fact that you cook the potatoes twice means that they will be crunchy and delicious.

2 pounds russet potatoes, peeled	**2 cloves garlic, peeled and crushed**
¼ cup olive oil	**Salt to taste**

Slice the potatoes thinly. Heat a large nonstick frying pan and add half the olive oil. Add the garlic and the sliced potatoes. Pan-fry on one side until lightly browned. Turn and brown the other side. Remove from the pan and allow to cool. Heat the pan again with the remaining oil and cook again on both sides until nicely browned and tender. Salt to taste and serve.

SANTA FE SPUDS

In our time there is no such thing as a leftover potato that goes to waste. In the frugal kitchen there is no such thing.

This recipe came about when Jeff Wollam, my chef's brother, went to the refrigerator and found some leftover baked potatoes. With the ingenuity that must mark every bachelor in our time he created this dish. Well, I suppose you must claim that all people who live alone must be this ingenious . . . or starve! In any case, Jeff came up with the dish. You will probably have the stuff sitting in your refrigerator, so there is little pain here. A good dish!

Dice up baked potatoes left over from the day before. Sauté the potatoes in garlic and olive oil until crispy. Season with sweet paprika, Worcestershire sauce, and salt and freshly ground black pepper to taste. Serve garnished with guacamole, sour cream, salsa, and chopped coriander.

PEAS IN ACORN SQUASH
SERVES 6

Sara Little, a dear friend who has taught me more about the implications of eating than perhaps anybody else, suggested this dish. She was anxious to talk to children about eating out of edible containers in our time. Thus this dish. The kids will have fun with it and you can serve it at a dinner party.

SQUASH
- 3 acorn squash
- 4 tablespoons butter, melted
- Salt and freshly ground black pepper to taste

FILLING
- 2 tablespoons olive oil
- 1 medium yellow onion, peeled and chopped
- 2 10-ounce boxes frozen peas, thawed
- Salt and freshly ground black pepper to taste

Cut the squash in half lengthwise and dig out the seeds. Place the halves skin-side down in a baking dish and brush with melted butter. Salt and pepper to taste. Bake at 350° until tender and lightly browned.

When the squash is almost done, heat a large frying pan and add the oil and onion. Sauté until tender and add the thawed peas. Sauté together a few minutes and salt and pepper to taste. Fill the cooked squash halves with the pea mixture and serve.

CRUCIFEROUS VEGETABLES

The name for members of this cabbage, kale, and mustard family comes from the fact that the plants have a flower that is in the shape of a cross. Therefore, they carry a cross, just as does the crucifer in church.

While most kids refer to this family as the "yuck!" vegetables, there is good evidence that they help inhibit certain forms of cancer. So, eat your Brussels sprouts!

CABBAGE SAUTÉED WITH CARAWAY
SERVES 6

This method of cooking cabbage keeps the flavor fresh and bright. Overcooked cabbage is not a joy to any youngster, or to any of us oldsters. The kids will enjoy this healthy, easy-to-do dish.

3 tablespoons olive oil	1½ teaspoons caraway seeds
3 cloves garlic, peeled and crushed	**DRESSING**
1 medium yellow onion, peeled and sliced	½ cup olive oil Juice of ½ lemon Salt and freshly ground black pepper to taste
2½ pounds green cabbage, cored and sliced ⅛-inch thick	

Heat a large frying pan and add the oil, garlic, and onion. Sauté over medium-low heat for 5 minutes, until the onion becomes tender. Do not brown. Add the cabbage and caraway seeds and sauté 3 to 4 minutes until the cabbage just becomes tender but still a bit crisp. Pour onto a sheet pan and spread out to cool completely.

Combine the ingredients for the dressing in a mixing bowl and add the cooled cabbage mixture. Toss well, chill, and serve.

BREADED BRUSSELS SPROUTS
SERVES 6 TO 8

When I was very young my mother insisted that I eat Brussels sprouts . . . and she always cooked them too long. Mushy little green cabbages. This method of cooking the little rascals will keep them firm and flavorful.

If using fresh sprouts, simply blanch them a bit until they are tender but still firm.

2 10-ounce boxes frozen whole Brussels sprouts, thawed
2 cups all-purpose flour
Salt and freshly ground black pepper to taste
4 eggs

3 cups bread crumbs
¼ cup olive oil
4 cloves garlic, peeled and crushed

GARNISHES
Salt to taste
Juice of ½ lemon

Cut the Brussels sprouts in half lengthwise and place in a bowl with the flour and salt and pepper to taste. Toss about so that they are evenly coated with flour. In another large bowl, beat the eggs. Sift the floured Brussels sprouts through your hands and add to the bowl of eggs. Toss to coat evenly. Place the bread crumbs in another large bowl and add the egg-coated Brussels sprouts. Toss to coat evenly with the bread crumbs.

Heat a large frying pan and add the oil. Sift the Brussels sprouts through your hands and add to the pan. Fry over medium heat, turning the Brussels sprouts to cook evenly. Stir in the garlic and continue pan-frying until golden brown, about 4 minutes. Be careful not to burn the garlic! Remove the mixture from the pan and drain on paper towels. Serve on a platter and garnish with salt and lemon juice.

BAKED CAULIFLOWER
SERVES 6

Patty and I fell in love with baked cauliflower when I was in graduate school in theology. A local greengrocer of Italian descent was concerned that we did not purchase his beautiful heads of cauliflower. I explained that I disliked cauliflower . . . and he inquired as to how I had had it cooked. "Boiled to death," I replied. He took after me and I have been enjoying baked cauliflower ever since.

Even the kids will enjoy this one.

1 1¾-pound head cauliflower
2 eggs, beaten
1 tablespoon chopped fresh tarragon

½ cup bread crumbs
¼ cup grated Parmesan cheese
Salt and freshly ground black pepper to taste

Preheat the oven to 375°.

Trim off any leaves on the cauliflower. Trim the base of the core so that the head will stand upright. Set up the remaining ingredients so they are ready to use. Bring a large pot of water with a pinch of salt to a boil. Blanch the head of cauliflower in the boiling water for about 5 minutes. Remove and drain. Place the cauliflower in a deep casserole and top with the remaining ingredients. Cover and bake for 15 minutes.

CAULIFLOWER WITH CHEESE
AND SOUR CREAM
SERVES 6

The sesame seeds add a wonderful flavor to this dish,
though I will admit that the vegetable is a tad rich when
served in this manner. My theory is simple. Either get the
kids to eat their cauliflower with a little cheese and butterfat
or they will not eat the white blossom at all. Try this. It is
great!

1 2½-pound head cauliflower	1 cup sour cream
1 teaspoon salt	½ pound sharp
2 teaspoons sesame seeds	Cheddar cheese, grated
Salt and freshly ground black pepper to taste	

Remove the outer leaves and core of the cauliflower. Break
the head apart into 1-inch florets. Heat a large pot of water
and add the salt and the cauliflower. Blanch until just
tender, about 5 minutes. Drain and rinse with cold water to
stop the cooking. Drain well.

Toast the sesame seeds in a small frying pan until lightly
browned. Do this over medium heat while shaking the pan.
Set aside.

Place half the cauliflower in a 13×9-inch baking dish
and even it out. Salt and pepper to taste. Spread half the
sour cream over the top. Add half the cheese and sprinkle
with half the sesame seeds. Repeat with another layer and
bake at 350° for 30 minutes, or until bubbly and melted.

CAULIFLOWER SALAD, RUSSIAN STYLE
SERVES 8

This is not at all complex and it points to the fact that in Eastern Europe people eat many more cruciferous vegetables than do we. The same is true of China. Why? Because these vegetables keep well during the winter. Further, if you don't overcook them they are delicious.

I think that you will find this one to be a family favorite. Craig and I developed it after meeting with and reading about our friends in Russia.

1 2- to 2½-pound head cauliflower
2 cups thinly sliced radishes
1 bunch scallions, chopped
¾ cup sour cream
¾ cup mayonnaise

Salt and freshly ground black pepper to taste

GARNISH
2 hard-boiled eggs, peeled and grated

Cut out the core of the cauliflower with a paring knife. Break the cauliflower into small florets. Bring a large pot of water to boil. Add a pinch of salt and the florets. Blanch for about 4 minutes until just tender. Drain and rinse with cold water. Drain very well and place in a large bowl. Add the radishes and scallions.

In a separate bowl, mix together the sour cream, mayonnaise, and salt and pepper to taste. Mix until smooth and add to the bowl of cauliflower. Toss together and chill. Garnish with grated hard-boiled eggs and serve.

MUSHROOMS

Give me mushrooms in a thousand variations . . . and strangely enough the Creator has done just that. Nothing so convinces me of the wisdom of the King of the Universe as when I march through a field covered with horse dung and there I see them! Upright and lovely, white and inviting, these fungi call to me to pluck them up. And here is the theological truth of the mushroom. Out of that which we call ruin and waste the Holy One can call forth one of the most blessed foods that I know.

MARINATED BUTTON MUSHROOMS
SERVES 6 TO 8 AS AN APPETIZER

Yes, we are getting back to basics in this book. But remember that we are encouraging every member of the family to help in the cooking event, and thus this dish.

I still love these things and you will like them much better than those that you find premarinated and soaked in too much vinegar . . . those little rascals found in a bottle at the supermarket.

1 pound large button
   mushrooms
½ cup olive oil
2 tablespoons lemon
   juice
2 tablespoons white
   wine vinegar
3 cloves garlic,
   peeled and
   crushed

2 tablespoons
   chopped parsley
1 teaspoon dried
   oregano, whole
Salt and freshly
   ground black
   pepper to taste

Trim the stems off the mushrooms and save for another use. Bring a large pot of water to a boil and blanch the mushrooms for 2 minutes. Remove and drain very well.

Mix the remaining ingredients together in a medium-sized bowl and add the drained mushrooms while they're still hot. Toss together and allow to marinate in the refrigerator for 4 hours. Toss the mushrooms a couple times while marinating. Serve as an hors d'oeuvre with toothpicks.

MUSHROOMS AND RICE
SERVES 8 AS A SIDE DISH

This is so rich that you will wonder about my own health. To me, mushrooms cry for cream, but if you wish to substitute half-and-half or milk, go right ahead. It will still be an easy and tasty dish.

3 tablespoons olive oil

3 cloves garlic, peeled and crushed

1 medium yellow onion, peeled and chopped

¾ pound mushrooms, sliced

4 cups Chicken Stock (page 109) or use canned

2 cups Uncle Ben's Converted Rice

1 cup heavy cream, half-and-half, or milk

1 egg, beaten

2 tablespoons chopped chives

3 tablespoons freshly grated Parmesan cheese

Salt and freshly ground black pepper to taste

Heat a large frying pan and add the oil, garlic, and onion. Sauté a few minutes and add the mushrooms. Sauté until just tender. In a 4-quart pot, bring the Chicken Stock to a boil and add the mushroom mixture and the rice. Return to a boil and reduce to a simmer. Cover and cook for 20 minutes. Stir in the remaining ingredients off the burner. Serve immediately.

STUFFED MUSHROOMS
MAKES ABOUT 24 JUMBO STUFFED MUSHROOMS

This is Craig's recipe. We have all had stuffed mushrooms but Craig uses really large mushroom caps and mixes pesto sauce with Italian sausage. If you use these as an appetizer for the evening meal, I promise no one will make it to the dinner table!

24 jumbo mushrooms (nice, very large caps are best)

2 cloves garlic, peeled and chopped

2 tablespoons olive oil

1½ pounds mild Italian sausage (if the sausage is in casings, squeeze the sausage out)

1 cup peeled and chopped yellow onion

2 tablespoons Pesto Sauce (page 266)

2 eggs, beaten

¼ cup grated Parmesan cheese

4 scallions, finely chopped

Salt and freshly ground black pepper to taste (easy on the salt)

GARNISH
Additional grated Parmesan cheese

Remove the stems from the mushroom caps and chop; set aside. Heat a large frying pan and sauté the mushroom caps and garlic in olive oil for a few minutes until slightly browned. Remove the mushrooms to cool. Heat the pan again and add the sausage and onion. Brown the sausage until very crumbly. Add the chopped mushroom stems and cook a few minutes more. Drain off the excess fat. Remove the mixture to a bowl and allow to cool a bit. Mix in the remaining ingredients until all is incorporated. Pat the filling mixture into the sautéed mushroom caps so that they are full and slightly mounded.

Lightly oil a shallow baking dish and arrange the mushrooms in it. Top with additional grated cheese. Bake at 400° for 20 to 25 minutes, or until the center of the mushroom cap is tender when pierced with a knife. Turn the oven to high broil and toast the tops until nicely browned and bubbly. (Do not leave these unattended when broiling as they can burn quickly!)

MUSHROOM CAVIAR
MAKES 2 TO 3 CUPS

This is not anywhere near caviar in terms of flavor, or in color or texture. It is just a name for a very delicious spread that mushroom lovers really appreciate. If you have some of this in the refrigerator, you are set . . . at least for a couple of days. It will be eaten in less time than that!

4 anchovy fillets
¼ cup milk
1 tablespoon olive oil
2 cloves garlic, peeled and crushed
2 pounds white button mushrooms, finely chopped
¼ pound dried Italian olives, pitted and chopped
2 tablespoons chopped parsley
Freshly ground black pepper to taste

Soak the anchovies in the milk for 20 minutes. Drain and rinse with cold water. Heat a large frying pan and add the oil and garlic. Add the mushrooms and sauté over high heat about 5 minutes. Cook until tender and the excess liquid has evaporated. Remove to a bowl. Mince the drained anchovies and add to the mushrooms, along with the olives, parsley, and pepper to taste. Mix all together and refrigerate for 2 hours. Stir once while chilling. Serve for hors d'oeuvres with toast rounds or crackers.

CREAM OF MUSHROOM SOUP

I love this soup and I therefore have placed it in both the soup and the mushroom sections so that you will not miss it. The use of dried mushrooms along with fresh make this dish rich with the earthy flavor that I appreciate so much.

No, Jason will still not eat mushrooms!

The recipe is on page 102.

MUSHROOMS ON TOAST
SERVES 2

During the Second World War my father introduced me to gravy on toast. No meat . . . just gravy on toast. He practically lived on the stuff when he was a child. The family numbered eight and my beloved grandma Nettie Smith kept them alive on cornmeal mush and gravy on toast. Dad still enjoyed eating such things even when he did not have to. This souped-up version still needs no meat and it makes a fine dinner when served on toasted English muffins. Really!

2 tablespoons olive
   oil
2 cloves garlic,
   peeled and
   crushed
½ pound mushrooms,
   sliced
¼ cup dry white wine
2 tablespoons
   chopped parsley

1 cup heavy cream or
   half-and-half
Salt and freshly
   ground black
   pepper to taste
4 English muffins,
   split and toasted

Heat a large frying pan and add the oil, garlic, and mushrooms. Sauté over high heat for 5 minutes until tender. Add
the wine and parsley and simmer for 1 minute. Add the
cream and simmer for 7 to 10 minutes to reduce and thicken
slightly. Salt and pepper to taste. Serve over the toasted
English muffins.

Grains and Legumes

Man can live without spices,
but not without wheat.

Jewish proverb

In our time there is a new emphasis on eating grains. It has something to do with a new interest in healthy eating, less animal fat, and all of that. But, the truth is that grains are delicious. It may take your family a short time to change from potatoes to pasta, rice, barley, bulgur wheat, lentils, and the like, but the group will be happy that they did.

No, I am not claiming that you should give up potatoes. I would never do such a thing since potatoes are healthy and versatile as well as being delicious. However, there are so many other wonderful food products, such as grains, that will put starch and substance into our lives.

255

PEAS AND LENTILS
SERVES 8 TO 10 AS A SIDE DISH

This is a great dish that resembles something from the Middle East. If you were to add a bit of curry powder to this dish you would have something from India. As it is, this recipe is fine for everyone in the modern family and it points to the fact that we should blend grains and vegetables together. This is a practice that goes clear back to Ancient Rome.

3 tablespoons olive oil
3 cloves garlic, peeled and crushed
1 medium yellow onion, peeled and sliced
4 cups Chicken Stock (page 109) or use canned
1½ cups lentils
Salt and freshly ground black pepper to taste
1 16-ounce bag frozen green peas, defrosted

Heat a frying pan and add the oil, garlic, and onion. Sauté until just tender. Place the Chicken Stock and lentils in a 4-quart pot and bring to a boil. Cover and simmer for 15 minutes. Add the sautéed onion to the pot of cooking lentils and simmer 10 minutes more or until the liquid is absorbed. Salt and pepper to taste. Stir in the peas and cover. Turn off the heat and allow to stand for 5 minutes.

RICE TIMBALES
MAKES 12 TO 16, DEPENDING ON THE SIZE
OF THE MOLDS

Rice is great for dinner and easy to prepare. It is so easy that I simply cannot understand why people buy instant rice. The flavor is closer to that of a cardboard box than to rice. You can mix rice with vegetables, serve it with gravy or spaghetti sauce, pan-fry it with chopped meats, or just serve it with a little melted butter and grated Parmesan or Romano cheese.

To cook rice, simply put 2 cups of the grain in a medium saucepan. The pan should have a tight-fitting lid. Add 4 cups of water, a pinch of salt, and bring to a boil with the lid off. When it boils, cover with the lid and turn the heat to very low. Cook for 15 minutes and then, without removing the lid, turn off the heat and let the pan sit on the burner for another 10 minutes. That is it! While the rice is cooking, go ahead with the rest of the dinner preparations. The rice will be perfect, so don't worry about it. By the way, rice doubles in volume when cooked.

2 tablespoons olive oil

2 cloves garlic, peeled and crushed

1 cup peeled and coarsely chopped medium yellow onion

1 stalk celery, coarsely chopped

½ cup peeled and coarsely chopped carrots

½ cup cored, seeded, and coarsely chopped red bell pepper

½ cup coarsely chopped mushrooms

½ cup heavy cream

2 eggs, beaten

1 cup grated Monterey Jack cheese

2 tablespoons Parmesan cheese

1½ cups long-grain rice (cook this; you will have 3 cups cooked rice)	Salt and freshly ground pepper to taste Peanut oil for greasing the molds

Heat a frying pan and add the oil, garlic, and onion. Sauté a few minutes and add the remaining vegetables. Sauté until all are tender. Remove to a mixing bowl and allow to cool. Fold in the remaining ingredients.

Lightly grease the timbale molds with the peanut oil and fill with the rice mixture. Each mold should hold about ½ cup. Level off the molds but don't pack them too tightly. Place the timbales in a baking pan and fill the pan with enough hot water so that it comes halfway up the sides of the molds. Cover the pan first with parchment or waxed paper and then with aluminum foil. Bake at 350° for 25 to 30 minutes.

Allow the timbales to cool enough so that you can handle them. Remove them from the water and run the back edge of a table knife around the inside edge of the molds. Invert onto plates and serve.

FLANK STEAK AND LENTIL SALAD

This is another one of those dishes that is hard to place in terms of our normal food categories. Is it to be under meats or under grains and legumes? I think this salad has to be under both camps.

I am mentioning this recipe twice in order to point to the fact that lentils will stretch out a meat dish: more grains and legumes and less animal fat. That is the current rule for the whole family kitchen. Don't get me wrong, though, as I love meat and we must all learn to use it along with grains and beans and pasta . . . instead of eating meat all by itself.

Craig developed this recipe after I described such a thing

to him. Took him no time at all, and the results are impressive. I would serve this at a formal dinner party as a first course or as a main course at home in the summer.

You will find the recipe on page 119.

BARLEY WITH CHICKEN AND ONIONS
SERVES 4 TO 5

Barley is a most interesting and frugal grain. The flavor is delicious and you can put it in soups, stews, casseroles, even salads. I have used it in every cookbook that I have done and I want you to think about using it more in your whole family cooking. Rice swells and doubles when it cooks, but barley grows to three to four times its original size. Good stuff, that barley!

3 tablespoons olive oil
2 cloves garlic, peeled and chopped
2 medium yellow onions, peeled and sliced
8 chicken thighs
Salt and freshly ground black pepper to taste

1 cup barley, rinsed and drained
6 cups Chicken Stock (page 109) or use canned
2 tablespoons chopped parsley

Heat a large frying pan and add 2 tablespoons of the oil. Add the garlic and onion and sauté until tender. Remove

from the pan and set aside. Season the chicken with salt
and pepper to taste. Heat the frying pan again and add the
remaining tablespoon of oil. Brown the chicken on both
sides and set aside.

Place the rinsed barley and 3 cups of the Chicken Stock
in a 6- to 8-quart pot. Bring to a boil, cover, and simmer
30 minutes, or until the liquid is absorbed. Add the remaining 3 cups of Chicken Stock, the browned chicken,
onion, and parsley. Bring to a simmer and cook, covered,
over low heat until the liquid is absorbed and the chicken
is tender. Salt and pepper to taste.

BULGUR WHEAT
WITH ANYTHING!

Bulgur wheat is a fine food product that we need to use
more often. It is also a very old type of processed grain
that goes back to the Ancient Middle East. The wheat is
steamed and dried, then milled, so that it cooks very
quickly, just like rice.

You can find it in any Middle Eastern or Greek grocery.
Many health food stores carry it as well. Buy it in bulk—
it is quite cheap. You will find it in three different grind
sizes: fine, for baking or thickening soups; medium, for
stews and salads; and coarse, for eating as a starch such as
rice.

You can eat it raw in salads if you just soak medium-
grind in warm water for a few minutes and then drain the
water. Add it to any salad you like.

Stir it into soups and allow it to cook, stirring often, for
about 30 minutes. The soup will have a wonderful nutty
flavor and will be quite rich.

Cook it as you would rice and then serve it on the side
as a starch course. With gravy it is great. Mix the cooked
grain with cooked meats and gravies or with cooked vegetables such as peas or beans, or cook it along with rice for

a very tasty side dish. Add herbs or spices, cook it with a chicken or beef stock just as you would a pilaf, and you are on your way to converting your whole family crowd to very healthy and creative eating.

Try using bulgur along with mushrooms for a side dish with just about any kind of meat that you might offer.

Herbs

And thou beholdest the earth blackened;
then, when We send down water upon it, it quivers,
and swells, and puts forth herbs
of every joyous kind.

The Koran

When I was a child we used few herbs in our cooking. Norwegians don't do much with herbs. As my mother continued to grow in her own cooking abilities I began to understand how important herbs are in the kitchen. Now I believe they are the most important tool you have when it comes to healthy and creative eating in our time. After all, you can cut down on salt and fat and sugar, etc., but if the food does not have good flavor no one is going to care about the evening meal. All will take to snacking on the things we call "American junk food," not because they are hungry for fillers in the stomach but because they are hungry for flavor.

Herbs will provide the flavor in your cooking if you begin to cut down on salt and fat.

Some herbs you can grow in your kitchen window, if you are into that sort of thing. Otherwise, find fresh herbs at a good supermarket. Basil, thyme, oregano, mint, parsley, dill, cilantro, rosemary, and tarragon should all be available year-round these days. Otherwise, use dried, but buy them in a spice shop where they are stored in bulk, thus retaining their flavor.

Soups, meat stews, salads, grain dishes, omelets, meat roasts, infused oils, vinegars, fish dishes, vegetable dishes . . . in other words, just about any dish you are preparing will be improved with good herbs. Experiment and you will come up with some good ideas.

PESTO SAUCE
MAKES ABOUT 2 CUPS

This lovely green sauce comes from Genoa, in northern Italy. I can no longer think of running my kitchen without this condiment. If you have some in your refrigerator, you will begin to use it to bolster good vegetable soups, to flavor garlic toast, to add depth to salad dressings, and of course, to add to pasta.

I grow my own basil during the summer and then prepare a beginning sauce and freeze it. This recipe is for fresh sauce, but if you wish to freeze basil for the wintertime, simply chop the leaves in a food blender with enough peanut oil (not olive oil) just to make a paste. Freeze in heavy plastic bags or cartons and then use that paste to prepare this recipe during the winter. You will not have to add quite as much olive oil due to the peanut oil that you used to preserve the basil.

4 cups tightly packed fresh basil, leaves only
½ cup olive oil
2 cloves garlic, peeled and crushed
6 sprigs parsley leaves

Salt and freshly ground black pepper to taste
¼ cup pine nuts, walnuts, or almonds
½ cup freshly grated Parmesan or Romano cheese

Place the basil in a food blender (don't bother trying this with dried basil; it won't work). Add the oil, garlic, parsley, and salt and pepper. Blend until all are chopped very fine.

Add the nuts and chop a bit more. Remove from the blender and stir in the grated cheese.

PESTO TOMATO SAUCE
MAKES ABOUT 2 CUPS

For a quick pasta sauce, heat a frying pan and add 2 tablespoons olive oil, 2 chopped cloves garlic, and ½ cup peeled and chopped yellow onion. Sauté until the onion is clear. Add 2 tablespoons Pesto Sauce (opposite) and one 14½-ounce can crushed tomatoes. Bring the sauce to a simmer and salt and pepper to taste. Serve with your favorite pasta.

MINTED PEAS AND ONIONS
SERVES 6 TO 8

This is a simple and flavorful way of dressing up your kids' favorite vegetable. The youngsters can easily cook this dish and they will be quite proud of themselves.

- 3 tablespoons olive oil
- 2 medium yellow onions, peeled and sliced
- 2 10-ounce boxes frozen peas, thawed
- 2 tablespoons chopped fresh mint
- Salt and freshly ground black pepper to taste

Heat a large frying pan and add the oil and sliced onion. Sauté until transparent. Add the thawed peas and cook over medium heat until the peas are hot. Add the mint and salt and pepper to taste. Toss together and serve.

BASIL, TOMATO, AND
ONION SALAD WITH CHEESE
SERVES 6

Tomatoes and fresh basil simply belong together. What a marriage! This is one of my favorite summer salads, especially if you can bring the tomatoes in from your garden while they are still warm from the summer sun.

3 ripe medium tomatoes	½ cup olive oil
2 medium white onions	2 tablespoons lemon juice
1 large bunch of fresh basil, leaves only	1 tablespoon fresh oregano
1 cup grated mozzarella cheese	Salt and freshly ground black pepper to taste
	1 tablespoon grated Parmesan cheese

Core and slice the tomatoes about ⅛-inch thick. Peel the onions whole and cut into same-size slices. Shingle the tomato and onion slices with basil leaves on a platter. Place the grated mozzarella in the center of the platter. Mix the oil, lemon juice, oregano, and salt and pepper to taste. Pour over everything and sprinkle with grated Parmesan cheese.

GARLIC HERB SOUP
SERVES 10

I received a letter the other day from an elderly woman who must be a beauty. What a sense of humor. She simply wrote to congratulate me on the fact that I had done a recipe on television that did not contain garlic!

I cannot help it. I love garlic beyond all sense or reason. This soup will prove my point.

2½ quarts Chicken Stock (page 109) or use canned

2 tablespoons fresh rosemary

1 tablespoon fresh oregano

1 cup chopped parsley

2 teaspoons fresh thyme

2 large heads (yes, whole heads) garlic, cloves peeled

½ cup dry white wine

6 tablespoons butter

½ cup all-purpose flour

½ cup heavy cream or half-and-half

2 tablespoons chopped fresh chives

Salt and freshly ground black pepper to taste

GARNISHES
Garlic croutons (see Note)
Grated Parmesan cheese

Place the Chicken Stock, rosemary, oregano, parsley, and thyme in a 4-quart pot. Bring to a boil, cover, and simmer for 1 hour. Strain, reserving the stock. Discard the cooked herbs and return the stock to the pot.

In a small saucepan, place all but 2 of the peeled garlic cloves (they will be used later). Add just enough water to cover the garlic and simmer, covered, for 15 minutes.

Puree the cooked garlic and liquid until smooth. Add to the pot of stock along with the wine and bring to a simmer.

Melt the butter in a small frying pan and stir in the flour. Cook together to form a *roux*. Do not brown.

Whisk the *roux* into the hot stock until smooth and thickened. Crush the 2 reserved garlic cloves into the pot. Simmer for 5 minutes. Add the cream, chives, and salt and pepper to taste. Serve garnished with garlic croutons and grated Parmesan cheese.

NOTE: It's easy to make your own garlic croutons simply by toasting small French bread cubes with a bit of olive oil in a frying pan. Toss them about until golden brown and crunchy. Add some crushed garlic toward the end and toast them a bit longer. Don't burn the garlic.

ROASTED GARLIC BUTTER

Don't back away from me on this recipe! It is not at all as strong as it sounds. The roasting of the garlic mellows out the sharpness of the bulb and gives the butter a soft but bright garlic flavor.

2 whole heads (not
   cloves) garlic (the
   whole head
   unpeeled)

2 sticks butter, at
   room
   temperature

Place the heads of garlic in a small baking dish and bake at 375° for 35 minutes. Allow to cool, then squeeze the cloves out of their skins into a small bowl. Mash the garlic up with a fork and add the softened butter. Mix together until smooth. Spread on bread or crackers.

You can also enjoy this on all kinds of meat and fish.

HERBED ONION RELISH
MAKES ABOUT 3 CUPS

This simple condiment is to be served on the side of the
plate as a relish for just about anything. I developed this
one night because my herb garden was in full bloom and I
thought the dinner plates needed some extra flavors. This
is my solution. You can even eat this on sandwiches.

3 tablespoons olive
oil

2 cloves garlic,
peeled and
crushed

3 medium yellow
onions, peeled
and thinly sliced

1 teaspoon chopped
fresh sage

1 teaspoon chopped
fresh basil

1 teaspoon chopped
fresh rosemary

1 teaspoon chopped
fresh thyme

2 teaspoons chopped
parsley

¾ cup dry white wine

1 teaspoon
Worcestershire
sauce

Salt and freshly
ground black
pepper to taste
(easy on the
pepper)

Heat a large frying pan and add the oil, garlic, onion, and
herbs. Turn the heat to low and cover the pan. Cook for 15
minutes, stirring frequently. Add the wine and Worcestershire sauce. Cover and simmer gently for 10 minutes more,
or until most of the liquid is gone and the onion is tender.
Salt and pepper to taste. Serve as a condiment with roasted
or grilled meats. Can also be served with fish.

HERBED ZUCCHINI QUICHE
SERVES 6

I love quiche and it is really very useful to the contemporary household cook. You can use this dish for entertaining or for a quick meal for your family.

1 recipe Basic Easy Crust (page 318)
2 tablespoons olive oil
2 cloves garlic, peeled and crushed
1 medium yellow onion, peeled and diced
1 tablespoon chopped fresh basil
1 tablespoon chopped parsley
2 teaspoons chopped fresh rosemary
6 eggs
¼ cup sour cream
⅓ cup heavy cream
Salt and freshly ground black pepper to taste
3 medium green zucchini, thinly sliced

Prepare the Basic Easy Crust. Roll out three quarters of the dough to ⅛-inch thickness, then wrap the remaining quarter of the dough and refrigerate for another use. Place the dough in a deep 9-inch pie dish and trim it so that there is ½ inch of excess around the edge. Poke the bottom of the dough all over with a fork. Form an attractive edge around the dish by pinching the overhanging dough between your fingers. Bake in a preheated 375° oven for 10 minutes. Remove and allow to cool.

Heat a large frying pan and add the oil, garlic, and onion.

Sauté until the onion is clear. Add the herbs and cook a couple of minutes more. Allow to cool. Beat the eggs in a mixing bowl. Beat in the sour cream, heavy cream, and salt and pepper to taste.

Place some of the egg mixture in the bottom of the pre-baked pie shell. Add a layer of the onion mixture and a layer of sliced zucchini. Continue layering, finishing with the egg mixture. Bake at 400° for 30 minutes, then reduce the heat to 350° for 15 to 20 minutes until the quiche is set. Remove and allow to cool a bit before cutting.

HERB BREAD

The simple addition of herbs to a basic bread dough produces something that can be used as the central point of an entire meal. Serve it with wine and a fresh salad and you are set.

Prepare a batch of Basic Bread Dough (page 291). Follow the recipe up to the ''batter'' stage, the point before the remaining flour is added. Add ½ cup chopped sautéed onion. Add to taste fresh chopped herbs such as sage, rosemary, parsley, or basil. Whatever you like. Add freshly ground black pepper to taste. Add the remaining flour as called for, plus an additional ½ cup flour so the dough won't be sticky. Form into loaves and bake as instructed.

HERBED OILS

Herbed oils, or ''infused'' oils, are very popular at the moment. They can be used in all kinds of grilling and pan-frying, as well as a dip for your French or Italian bread. Many restaurants are now serving these oils at the table in place of butter. I like the practice.

Further, these oils help make a quick but rich salad dressing. Try these oils on toast at lunch or at the evening meal.

I have offered two examples of infused, or herbed, oils. The Infused Oil for Grilling Meat is on page 197 and the Infused Oil for Grilling Fish is on page 152. Do not be limited to meat and fish since oils will work well in all of the ways I have suggested.

GARLIC TOAST WITH GORGONZOLA SAUCE
MAKES ABOUT 1¾ CUPS

This is not a toasted cheese sandwich! Gorgonzola is so rich that this is a full meal. My garlic meets Gorgonzola! This is almost too much. . . .

2 tablespoons butter
4 tablespoons all-
  purpose flour
½ cup milk
½ pound Gorgonzola,
  crumbled
⅓ cup olive oil

3 cloves garlic,
  peeled and
  crushed
Sourdough bread
  slices or cocktail
  rounds

Heat the butter in a 2-quart saucepan. Add the flour and cook together to form a *roux*. Do not brown! Add the milk and whisk together until smooth. Bring to a simmer, stirring regularly until thickened. Add the Gorgonzola and stir until all is incorporated but still a bit lumpy. Allow to cool. Combine the oil and garlic. Toast the bread under the broiler until crisp on one side. Brush the untoasted side with the garlic oil. Toast under the broiler again until crisp on both sides. Spread the cheese mixture on the garlic toast and broil until bubbly and lightly browned.

Fruits

All millionaires love a baked apple.

Ronald Firbank

I t seems to me that it is a very good thing that we are placing a new emphasis on fresh fruit in today's diet. And please understand that I am not just talking about health. I am talking about wonderful flavors.

When I was a child the variety of fruits that were available to us was very limited. My mother and I would go pick strawberries and wild blackberries and she would can peaches and pears. These were all great, but aside from an apple or orange that was about it. You walk into a fruit market in our time and you are totally confused by the wonderful and vast selection of fresh fruits from all over the world. What a good time can be had in the fruit section of the market.

When my boys were growing up, Patty refused to feed them snacks of cookies and sweets after school. Instead, fruit was always available and offered after a day of hard work with the books and the playground. This is still the way that they snack. A good habit for all of us!

FRIED FRUIT SALAD
SERVES 8

I thought this kind of thing would work well. I love fruit fried in a little butter, and so I described this dish to Craig, my assistant. He marched into the kitchen and took my original thinking several steps closer to glory when he added the orange liqueur and then topped the whole thing off with blueberries. The blueberries sort of bleed a wonderful color and flavor all over this dish.

This is fine for parties and great for a summer evening meal. On the other hand, all of these fruits are available in the dead of winter, so this dish really knows no season.

3 Red Delicious apples
1 medium-sized pineapple
4 bananas
3 tablespoons butter
¼ cup Grand Marnier (orange-flavored liqueur)
1½ tablespoons fresh lime juice
2 cups fresh blueberries
⅓ cup fresh mint leaves

Peel, core, and cut the apples into wedges. (If you are not going to prepare this dish right away, hold the apple wedges in cold water with a little lemon juice. This will help prevent them from turning brown. Drain well before using.)

Cut off the top and bottom of the pineapple. Trim off

the outside skin and cut the pineapple in half lengthwise and then into quarters. Trim out the tough core. Cut the pineapple into 1-inch pieces.

Peel the bananas and slice them into ¾-inch pieces.

Heat a large frying pan and add the butter and apple wedges. Sauté over high heat for about 3 minutes and add the pineapple. Sauté about 2 minutes and add the bananas. Sauté all over high heat and add the Grand Marnier. Continue cooking and tossing the fruit to burn off the alcohol. Add the remaining ingredients and toss together over the heat for about 1 minute until the blueberries begin to color the dish. Serve immediately.

BAKED APPLES
SERVES 4

This is a very good version of an American classic. Mark Hogan, one of our assistants on the *Whole Family Kitchen* series, loves to cook for his children. This is so simple that your kids can make their own. If you behave yourself, they might make one for you!

4 Red Delicious apples	¼ cup sugar
6 tablespoons butter, melted	2 teaspoons cinnamon
¾ cup chopped walnuts	

Core the apples, leaving them whole. Place them upright in a small baking dish and drizzle with the butter. Combine the chopped walnuts with the sugar and cinnamon. Sprinkle the mixture into the centers and over the tops of the apples. Bake at 375 for 1 hour.

FRUIT COBBLER
SERVES 6

This recipe can be used with almost any of your favorite fresh fruits. This is an easy way to prepare a great fruit dessert and you can use just about any fruit that you wish.
Peel, core, and pit the fruit before using if necessary.

4 cups fresh fruit (whole blueberries, blackberries, sliced peaches, pitted plums, whatever you like)	**¼ cup sugar**
	6 tablespoons cold butter, cut up
	¾ cup apple juice
	2 tablespoons cornstarch
⅓ cup all-purpose flour	**1 tablespoon cold water**

Place the fruit in an 8×8-inch glass baking dish. Combine the flour, sugar, and butter in a small bowl. Using a fork or a pastry blender (page 46), cut the butter into the flour and sugar until crumbly. Bring the apple juice to a simmer in a small saucepan. Place the cornstarch in a small glass and stir together with the cold water until smooth. Whisk the cornstarch and water into the hot apple juice until smooth. Simmer a couple of minutes until clear and thickened. Pour over the fruit in the baking dish. Sprinkle the crumbled flour mixture over the top. Bake in a preheated oven at 350° for 45 minutes or until bubbly and golden brown.

PEAR TART
SERVES 6 TO 8

A tart, I used to tell my sons, is a very fancy big cookie
with class. That was enough for them. If you will bother
to take a minute to arrange the fruit in an attractive manner
on the top of this very rich dough, you will impress everyone in the neighborhood.

DOUGH	FILLING
¾ cup butter, at room temperature	4 ripe pears
3 tablespoons confectioner's sugar	2 tablespoons granulated sugar
1½ cups all-purpose flour	⅓ cup apple jelly

Cream the butter and confectioner's sugar together for the
dough. Add the flour and cut together with a pastry blender
(page 46) until coarse and grainy. Place in a plastic bag
and refrigerate for 30 minutes. Press the dough into the
bottom and sides of a 10-inch tart pan. Place on a sheet
pan and bake in a preheated oven at 425° oven for 10
minutes. Remove and cool.

Peel and core the pears. Slice the pears into thin wedges
and shingle them on the bottom of the cooled tart shell.
Sprinkle with the sugar and bake at 350 degrees for 50
minutes.

Melt the jelly in a small saucepan. Brush the top of the
cooked tart with the jelly. Allow to cool and serve.

PEACH TART
SERVES 6 TO 8

Prepare the dough and tart shell as for the Pear Tart (page 283). Fill the cooled tart shell with peeled and sliced peaches (about 4 to 5 peaches will do). Sprinkle with 2 tablespoons sugar and bake as instructed for the Pear Tart. Glaze with melted apple jelly and allow to cool.

JAM TART
SERVES 6 TO 8

Prepare the dough and tart shell as for the Pear Tart (page 283). Fill the cooled tart shell with about 1 cup or so of your favorite jam and bake at 350° for about 35 minutes, or until the crust is lightly brown and the jam is bubbly. No additional sugar or apple jelly is needed.

BROILED GRAPEFRUIT
SERVES 4

Why am I putting things in this cookbook that you ate as a child? I am doing it because your mother probably had time to cook for you . . . and I am hoping that you will take time to cook with your family. This dish is so simple that anyone in the family can do it. And I will bet that you still remember how delicious and special this dish was when you were a kid.

2 ripe grapefruit   **GARNISH**
4 tablespoons dark   **Fresh mint sprigs**
    brown sugar

Cut the grapefruits in half crosswise and place on a sheet
pan. Using a paring knife, trim around the outside of each
individual grapefruit section so that it is loosened but still
intact. Sprinkle the sections of the grapefruit halves with
the brown sugar. Place under a broiler on high and cook
until bubbly and caramelized. Remove and allow to cool to
room temperature. Garnish the center of each with a fresh
mint sprig.

When someone is carrying a
pot filled with hot stuff, tell
them to warn everyone. If
they don't, you just go sit on
the porch and eat a bone.

STRAWBERRIES WITH
BALSAMIC VINEGAR
SERVES 4

Sometimes the description of a dish leaves you in anticipation of a flavor in total confusion. This is such a description. Vinegar on strawberries? We are using that very old
and mild and deep and rich vinegar from Modena, Italy,
the balsamic vinegar that is aged for twenty years. What it
does for a ripe strawberry can only be tasted, not described.
I dare you to try this one on your household. Just great.

1 pint ripe
    strawberries
	2 tablespoons
	    balsamic vinegar

1 tablespoon sugar (or more to taste)	

Hull the strawberries and cut them in half lengthwise. Place
in a bowl and carefully toss with the sugar and vinegar.
Toss just before serving and offer them in fancy glasses.

Breads

Give us this day our daily bread . . .

The Lord's Prayer

I n Biblical times bread was not served as an addition to the meal as we do in our time. In those days bread *was* the meal! Everything else to eat centered around the bread—three meals a day. So bread in the Bible does not refer so much to food as it does to total and complete daily sustenance.

I know of few cultures that do not make a bread of some sort. In most ancient cultures a grain of some sort was ground up and mixed with water. Sometimes a leavening was used and sometimes it was simply allowed to ferment. Then it was baked in loaves or patted into pancake shapes and fried on the tops of hot stones. In all cases the invention of bread meant salvation for the tribe. That is what the Bible is talking about when it talks about bread. Bread is a gift from God and without it we will most likely perish. Whether it be a raised loaf, a corn pancake, or a steamed roll, it is the staff of life.

I see nothing but glory and awe in the baking of bread.

Families and living groups that buy all of their bread at the supermarket miss out on the wonderful experience of tasting . . . no, first smelling the rising yeast and then tasting bread in your own kitchen.

Bread baking is easy, I swear. Patty, my wife, has never gotten into it because she claims that she "never cooks with anything that is alive!" True, yeast is alive, but you can have great fun cooking bread together.

Some basic rules for good bread baking:

• Use a thermometer for the water in which you place the yeast. It should be about 110°, no hotter.

- Use unbleached white flour for better flavor in your bread.

- Always beat the batter for a good 10 minutes. Use your electric mixer. Mixing the batter this long assures you of the development of the gluten that is so necessary to a good crust.

- Use a rapid or quick-rising dry yeast. It cuts the process down in terms of time.

- Use a very large stainless-steel bowl as a cover for the dough, which can then be left on a plastic counter, covered, to rise.

- To get a fine crunchy crust, spray the loaves with water in the oven a couple of times during the baking process. Use a plastic plant sprayer or clothes sprayer. Avoid hitting the elements of an electric stove with water.

- Quick yeast or not, be patient. Allow the dough to rise beautifully and fully each time.

BASIC BREAD DOUGH
(From The Frugal Gourmet*)*
MAKES 3 OR 4 LOAVES

This makes wonderful French bread. The secret is the use of a scale and your spraying the loaves with a mist of water during the baking. See the preceding basic rules for good bread baking and then go at it.

2 envelopes quick-
    rising dry yeast
2½ cups tepid water
    (110°)
2 pounds 3 ounces
    hard wheat
    flour, mixed
    with
    unbleached
    white flour
    (mix them half
    and half), or
    just unbleached
    white flour

1 teaspoon salt
    dissolved in 1
    teaspoon water
Cornmeal for
    baking (optional)

Dissolve the yeast in the water. (Tepid: not hot, not cool, but barely warm.) Let stand for 5 minutes. Stir to dissolve.

Using a small paper bag on your scale, weigh out a total of 2 pounds 3 ounces flour. (If you can't get hard wheat flour, use a good unbleached flour.)

Make a batter of the water and yeast, together with 4 cups of the weighed-out flour. Beat for 10 minutes with an electric mixer. The batter will pull away from the sides of the mixing bowl.

Add the salted water. Add the remaining flour and knead for 5 minutes in a good mixer (I use my KitchenAid), or 15 minutes by hand.

Place on a Formica counter, or on a piece of plastic wrap, and cover with a large metal bowl. Let rise until double in bulk, 1 to 1½ hours. Punch down, and let rise for another 1½ hours.

Punch down again, and mold into 3 or 4 loaves. Let the loaves rise. I use an extra oven with a pan of hot water in the bottom. This allows for steam heat, perfect for raising dough. Place the loaves on a greased baking sheet before letting them rise; you may wish to sprinkle cornmeal on the greased baking sheet.

Preheat the oven to 450°. When the loaves have risen to double their original bulk, place them in the upper one third of the oven. *Important:* Place a pan of hot water on the bottom shelf. This will assure you of a great crust.

Bake for about 25 minutes, or until the bread is nicely browned and the loaves sound hollow when you thump their bottoms with your finger.

If you wish your bread to have an Old World look, simply dust the loaves with flour before the final rising. You can use an egg and water glaze, but I am convinced that you will get a much better crust if you simply use flour.

This bread is so rich that you need not put butter on it. The French rarely eat butter on bread. And if you wish to reduce or eliminate salt in the bread, simply cut down on the amount of salt in the recipe. It is tasty without.

SALAMI, OLIVE, AND
CHEESE BREAD
MAKES 2 LOAVES

Now you can begin to have real fun with your kitchen helpers. You can fold all kinds of delicious things into Basic Bread Dough and come up with wonderful flavors. This is one of my favorites.

1 recipe Basic Bread Dough (page 291)	1 cup coarsly grated provolone or mozzarella cheese
½ cup chopped salami	¼ cup grated Parmesan cheese
¾ cup pimiento-stuffed olives, drained on paper towels	Cornmeal for baking

Follow the recipe for the Basic Bread Dough up to the point where you achieve the initial batter. Add the above ingredients to the batter except the cornmeal, and blend until smooth. Knead in the remaining flour. After the dough has risen twice, punch down the dough again and form into 2 loaves. Sprinkle a little cornmeal on a sheet pan and place the loaves on it. Allow the dough to rise again. Dust the loaves with a bit of flour and bake at 450 degrees for 30 minutes. Remove the loaves from the pan and allow them to cool on a rack.

MINCEMEAT BREAD
MAKES 2 LOAVES

I did this on a lark one day, and my mother declared it to be just great. You see, she loves toast. This will make some of the best breakfasts you have ever eaten.

> 1 recipe Basic
>   Bread Dough
>   (page 291)
>
> 1¼ cups mincemeat

Follow the recipe for the Basic Bread Dough, but add the mincemeat after the initial batter has formed. Blend until smooth. Then add the remaining flour as instructed. If the dough seems a little too sticky when finished, knead in a little additional flour by hand. To bake, grease and flour two 9×5-inch loaf pans. Tap out the excess flour. Divide the dough into 2 equal loaves. Place the dough in the pans and allow to rise again. Bake in a preheated 425° oven for 40 minutes, or until nice and brown. Remove the loaves from the pans and allow them to cool on a rack. You may return the loaves to the pans once they are cooled to prevent them from drying out.

CARAWAY RYE BREAD

I thought there was some deep secret to making a good rye, but as you see from this recipe, there is no secret at all. I love this with a slice of Bermuda onion, salt and pepper, and a touch of mayonnaise. Yes, I am a goy!

Follow the recipe for Basic Bread Dough (page 291), but first measure out 2 cups rye flour. Then make up the balance of the flour for the recipe with regular wheat flour. The total weight of both flours together should be 2 pounds 3 ounces.

Once you have achieved the batter as instructed in the recipe, blend in 1½ tablespoons caraway seeds. Proceed with the recipe as usual.

Do not bake in bread pans. Just form a couple of round loaves and let them rise. Bake as for the Basic Bread Dough. Be sure to mist the loaves with water while baking.

PRIVATE LOAF PANS

Miniature bread-loaf pans can be purchased in a good cookware shop. Kids love them because they are just the right size. Just make a batch of Basic Bread Dough (page 291) and place enough of the dough to come halfway up the sides of a mini-pan. Allow the dough to rise to the top of the pan. Bake in a preheated 450° oven until nicely browned on top, about 20 to 25 minutes. Remove the loaves from their pans and cool on a rack.

It is fun for the kids to each have their own loaf of bread!

BREAD IN FUN SHAPES

I will never forget my first alligator. My father was busy losing his shirt in the bakery business in Canby, Oregon. I was about six or seven years old and worked in the bakery peeling apples for two bits an hour. No, I didn't do it often. In any case, Dad hired a new baker and in order to get on the good side of the boss's kid, the new fellow baked me a French loaf in the shape of an alligator. I still remember the open mouth and the green icing inside. He was wonderful. I made friends with a loaf of bread!

Bread in fun shapes is great for the whole family. These three that follow are Craig's treasures and I cannot take any credit for them. The Turtle Bread (page 298) is a stroke of genius, I swear!

BEAR PAWS
WITH SAUTÉED ONIONS
MAKES 6 BIG BEAR PAWS, REALLY BIG

If you use sweet onions, this bread tastes just as good to a
child as does candy.

3 tablespoons olive oil
1 large yellow onion,
    peeled and thinly
    sliced
Salt and freshly
    ground black
    pepper to taste
1 egg

2 tablespoons water
1 recipe Basic Bread
    Dough (page 291)
Cornmeal for
    baking
2 tablespoons dark
    soy sauce (page
    58)

Heat a large frying pan and add the oil. Sauté the onion
until transparent. Add the salt and pepper to taste and allow
to cool. Beat the egg and water together and set aside.

Prepare the Basic Bread Dough. Punch down the dough
after it has risen twice and cut it into 6 pieces. Cut each
sixth in half and form into rounded triangles about 6 inches
long and ½ inch thick (see illustration). Place a little bit of
the sautéed onion on a piece of the formed dough, leaving
a ½-inch border around the outside. Brush the border with
the egg wash and place another matching piece of dough
on top. Press the edges together to seal. Continue with the
remaining dough. Sprinkle a sheet pan with a little cornmeal and place the formed dough on it.

Make 4 cuts about 1 inch long into the large end of the
formed dough (see illustration). This will form the claws.

Allow the bear paws to rise again. Brush with dark soy sauce and bake in a preheated 450° oven for 25 minutes until nice and brown.

SNAKE BREAD
MAKES 2 SNAKES

Given the popularity of gruesome things among the young, this should be a great hit. Be sure to let the little ones in on the shaping of the snake.

1 recipe Basic Bread Dough (page 291) Cornmeal for baking	1 egg, beaten with 2 tablespoons water

Prepare the Basic Bread Dough. After the dough has risen twice, punch it down again. Cut the dough into 2 pieces. Roll 1 of the pieces into a 24-inch rope with one larger end about 2 inches wide for the snake's head and the other end tapering off to become the tail. Sprinkle a sheet pan with cornmeal. Place the roll of dough on a sheet pan. Form the dough into an **S** shape to resemble a snake (see illustration above). Make a horizontal slit with a knife or scissors in the large end of the snake to form a mouth. Make 2 slits in the snake's head to form eyes. You may want to cut off a tiny bit of dough from the tail to make a forked tongue and press it into the snake's mouth. Re-form the tail and make another snake with the remaining dough. Allow the snake bread to rise again. Score the top of the snakes with a paring knife to form a pattern on top. Brush with egg wash. Bake in a preheated 450° oven for 25 minutes, or until golden brown. Remove to a cooling rack.

TURTLE BREAD
MAKES 1 TURTLE

I must warn you: Craig's Turtle Bread is so much fun to make that the kids may decide that they will never eat the thing. So much for a good bread-baking class!

1 recipe Basic Bread Dough (page 291)	1 egg
Cornmeal for baking	2 tablespoons water
	½ cup Pesto Sauce (page 266)

Prepare the Basic Bread Dough. After the dough has risen twice, punch down the dough and divide it into thirds. Dust the counter with flour and press out one of the pieces into a 10-inch round, leaving it slightly mounded in the center. Sprinkle a sheet pan with a little cornmeal and place the round dough on it. Cut another third of the dough into 5 pieces, with 1 of the 5 pieces much larger than the others (see illustration). The larger piece will form the turtle's head. The remaining smaller pieces will become the 4 legs. Cut off another small piece of dough to form the tail. Beat the egg and water together and set aside. Shape the pieces of dough to resemble a head, legs, and tail. Attach the pieces of dough to the round piece on the pan. Do this by brushing the dough with the egg wash in the appropriate areas and pressing the head, legs, and tail into place. Brush the body, head, legs, and tail with half the Pesto Sauce. Press out the remaining dough into a round large enough to cover the turtle's body. This piece becomes the turtle's shell. Pinch the shell and body together in several places and brush all with the remaining Pesto Sauce. Using scis-

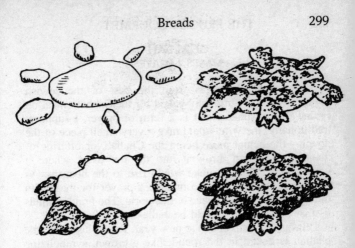

sors, make vertical cuts in the legs to represent claws (see illustration). Make a horizontal cut in the turtle's head to form a mouth, and make 2 slits in the head for eyes. Use your paring knife to make a crisscross pattern on the top of the shell.

Allow the Turtle Bread to rise again. Bake in a preheated 425° oven for 30 minutes. Carefully remove to a cooling rack.

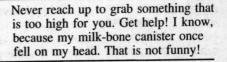

Never reach up to grab something that is too high for you. Get help! I know, because my milk-bone canister once fell on my head. That is not funny!

CHALLAH
MAKES 2 LOAVES

This wonderful bread is from the best of the Jewish traditions. It is traditionally baked for the Sabbath meal on Friday before sundown. It is a form of prayer, I suppose; traditionally, the wife would take a very small piece of the dough—the actual piece being the Challah, or offering of thanksgiving—and throw it into the hot oven, where it would burn and the smoke would rise to the heavens. As this is occurring, she is to breathe a prayer for the health of her family and for peace in the world. The braid reminds us that Sabbath joy should be endless.

During the festival of the new year, Rosh Hashanah, the challah is baked in the round, like a crown, symbolizing the kingship of God. The loaf again is endless, and it is eaten with sweet things such as honey and apples in anticipation of a new year filled with endless sweet events and caring.

You do not have to be Jewish to fall in love with this bread or with the traditions behind it.

DOUGH
2½ cups tepid water
   (about 110°)
3 teaspoons salt
3 tablespoons sugar
3 envelopes quick-
   rising dry yeast
3 eggs, at room
   temperature,
   beaten
½ cup vegetable oil

3 pounds unbleached
   white flour
   Cornmeal for
   baking

EGG WASH
2 egg yolks
1 tablespoon water

GARNISH
1 tablespoon sesame
   seeds

Place the water, salt, and sugar in the bowl of a heavy-duty electric mixer (KitchenAid K5A2 model works best). Stir to dissolve the sugar. Add the yeast and stir to dissolve. Stir in the beaten eggs and the oil. Beat in 5 cups of the

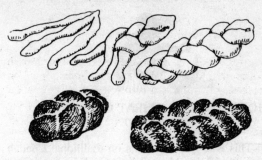

weighed-out flour to make a batter. Beat for 5 minutes or until the batter begins to pull away from the sides of the bowl. Knead in the remaining flour by machine until smooth. Place the dough on a clean countertop and cover it with a large metal bowl. Allow the dough to rise until double in bulk. Punch the dough down and allow it to rise again. Punch the dough down again and divide it in half. Cut each half into thirds. Roll 3 of the pieces into ropes about 16 inches long with your hands. Join 1 end of each rope and press together with the heel of your hand (see illustration). Alternately, braid the 3 ropes together and press the other 3 ends together with the heel of your hand.

Sprinkle a large sheet pan with a little of the cornmeal. Place the braided dough on the sheet pan and allow it to double in bulk again. Repeat the process with the remaining dough. Allow the dough to rise until double in bulk.

Beat the 2 egg yolks and 1 tablespoon of water together for the egg wash. Lightly brush both risen braided doughs. Sprinkle with sesame seeds. Bake in a preheated 350° oven for 50 to 55 minutes, until the loaves are deep golden brown and sound hollow when tapped on the bottoms with your finger. Remove to a cooling rack.

HONEY WHOLE-WHEAT CHALLAH
MAKES 2 LOAVES

Get ready! This is a great variation on traditional Challah and it is the gift of Rabbi Marc Gellman of New York City. This charming man claims the original recipe came to him through his dear friends Levi and Naami Kelman.

We have made a few small changes in the recipe so that it can be more easily understood. You must try this—it is delicious.

2 cups tepid water
  (about 110°)
4 envelopes quick-
  rising dry yeast
2 teaspoons kosher
  salt
2 tablespoons light
  brown sugar
3 large eggs plus 1
  egg yolk, at
  room
  temperature
⅓ cup peanut oil
½ cup honey
3 cups unbleached
  white flour

3 cups whole-wheat
  flour
Cornmeal for
  baking

EGG WASH
1 egg
1 tablespoon honey
1 tablespoon water

GARNISH
1 tablespoon sesame
  seeds

Place the water in the bowl of an electric mixer (I use my KitchenAid). Add the yeast, kosher salt, brown sugar, and stir to dissolve. Beat the eggs and egg yolk together and add to the mixing bowl, along with the oil and honey. Stir together until smooth. Add 2 cups each unbleached flour and whole-wheat flour. Beat together for 10 minutes to form a batter. Replace the beater with a dough hook and knead in the remaining 1 cup of each kind of flour.

Knead for 10 minutes until a smooth dough is formed. Knead in additional unbleached flour a bit at a time if the dough sticks to your hands. Place the dough on the countertop in a warm place and cover with a large bowl. Allow the dough to rise until double in bulk. Punch the dough down and allow to rise again. Punch the dough down again and divide in half. Divide each half into thirds. Roll each third into a rope about 16 inches long. Press the ends of 3 ropes together, using the heel of your hand, and braid the ropes together as in the preceding recipe. Repeat the process with the remaining dough. Sprinkle a little cornmeal on 2 sheet pans and place a loaf on each. Allow to rise until doubled in bulk.

In a small glass, beat together the egg, honey, and water for the egg wash. Brush the risen loaves with the egg wash and sprinkle with sesame seeds. Bake in a preheated 350° oven for 1 hour, or until the loaves are deep golden brown and sound hollow when the bottoms are tapped. Carefully remove to a cooling rack.

DEEP-DISH PIZZA DOUGH
(From The Frugal Gourmet Cooks American)

This is straight from Chicago. That is to say, this is my variation on that wonderful crust from the Windy City. The secret is in the oil that is added to the dough. It is so rich and short that you need not roll it. As a matter of fact, you cannot roll it. You must push it out with your fingers. A clue to success—keep your fingers oiled a bit with olive oil as you spread and stretch the dough in the oiled pan. It will work—I promise.

2 envelopes quick- rising dry yeast	4 tablespoons olive oil
2 cups tepid water (about 110°)	½ cup cornmeal
½ cup salad oil	5½ cups all-purpose flour

In the bowl of your electric mixer (KitchenAid is perfect for this), dissolve the yeast in the water. Add the oils, cornmeal, and 3 cups of the flour. Beat for 10 minutes with the mixer. Change the batter attachment to a dough hook and mix in the remaining 2½ cups flour. Knead for several minutes with the machine. It is hard to do this by hand since the dough is very rich and moist.

Pour out the dough onto a plastic countertop and cover with a very large metal bowl. Allow to rise until double in bulk. Punch down and allow to rise again. Punch down a second time and you are ready to make pizza!

Push some of the dough into an oiled round cake pan. With oiled fingers, poke the dough about until it covers the bottom of the pan. The dough should be about ⅛ inch thick. Add your favorite toppings and bake in a preheated 475° oven until golden brown, about 35 to 40 minutes.

PIZZETTA WITH
HERBS AND ONIONS

This is a simple little pizza, or Pizzetta, that enjoys the flavor of onions and herbs. It is simple to prepare and will remind your kids that pizza does not have to have tomato on it to be delicious.

If you want to buy small pizza pans, I suggest a restaurant supply house in any large city.

1 recipe Deep-Dish Pizza Dough (page 303) Olive oil for pizza pans	1 recipe Herbed Onion Relish (page 271) Grated Parmesan cheese for topping

Prepare the dough as instructed. Lightly oil several small pizza pans or sheet pans. Push some of the dough into each of the pans and spread it out using your fingers. Top with some of the Herbed Onion Relish and a sprinkle of Parmesan cheese. Bake in a preheated 475° oven until nicely browned on top. The cooking time will depend on the size and thickness of the pizzas.

FOCACCIA
(From The Frugal Gourmet Cooks Three Ancient Cuisines)
MAKES 2 SHEET PANS, ENOUGH FOR 10 TO 12 PEOPLE

This wonderful pan-baked bread is a cross between a pizza and a flatbread. It is the ancestor of what we now call pizza, and it has been baked in this fashion in Rome for hundreds of years. Prepare it according to the full recipe and enjoy, but if you are going to use this dough for the Rolled Pizza recipe (page 307), omit the topping.

DOUGH
2 envelopes quick-
   rising dry yeast
2 cups tepid water
   (about 110°)
1 tablespoon sugar
4 tablespoons olive
   oil
½ cup vegetable or
   salad oil
1 teaspoon salt
5½ cups unbleached
   white flour

TOPPING
3 cloves garlic,
   peeled and
   crushed
¼ cup olive oil
1 tablespoon dried
   rosemary, whole
1 tablespoon kosher
   salt

Dissolve the yeast in tepid water. Add the sugar, olive oil, salad oil, and salt. Mix in 3 cups of the flour and whip until the dough begins to leave the sides of the mixing bowl, about 10 minutes. (I use my KitchenAid for this whole process.)

Mix in the remaining flour by hand or with a dough hook and knead the dough until it is smooth. Allow the dough to rise twice, right in the bowl, and punch down after each rising.

Oil 2 baking sheets, each 18 by 13 inches, and divide the dough between the 2 pans. Using your fingers, press the dough out to the edges of each pan. Allow to rise for about 30 minutes and brush with the crushed garlic mixed with the oil for topping. Sprinkle the rosemary and kosher salt on top. Bake in a preheated 375° oven for about 20 minutes.

VARIATION: Top with green onions instead of rosemary.

ONION CUSTARD BREAD
MAKES 2 SHEET PANS, ENOUGH FOR 10 TO 12 PEOPLE

This is good, really good! The sour cream and egg form a kind of custard on the top. While this is not a normal pizza topping, you will enjoy the flavors.

This does not keep well for the second day.

1 recipe Deep-Dish Pizza Dough (page 303)	2 teaspoons chopped fresh rosemary
TOPPING	Salt and freshly ground black pepper to taste
4 tablespoons butter	2 eggs, beaten
6 cups peeled and thinly sliced onion	1½ cups sour cream

Prepare the dough as instructed. After the dough has risen twice, punch it down and divide it in half. Press the dough out into two 18×13-inch lightly oiled sheet pans.

Heat a large frying pan with the butter, and sauté the onion with the rosemary until tender. Add salt and pepper to taste. Allow to cool. Spread half of the cooled onion on each sheet pan of dough. Beat the eggs and sour cream together until smooth. Pour over the onion on both sheet pans and spread out evenly. Bake in a preheated 375° oven for 35 to 40 minutes, until lightly browned on top. Remove to a cooling rack.

ROLLED PIZZA
MAKES 2 LONG PIES

This is a wonderful variation on normal pizza that I think you will want to try the minute you read this recipe. It is quite simple to prepare and the presentation is nothing short of spectacular. This is our variation on an idea sent us by a fan—a very creative fan! Remember to prepare the vegetables and herbs and have everything ready to go for the filling.

DOUGH

1 recipe Focaccia
  dough (page
  305) (omit the
  topping)

FILLING

4 tablespoons olive
  oil
6 cloves garlic,
  peeled and
  crushed
4 medium yellow
  onions, peeled
  and sliced
8 medium red bell
  peppers, cored,
  seeded, and
  sliced

½ cup chopped
  parsley
2 teaspoons dried
  oregano, whole
¼ teaspoon crushed
  red pepper
  flakes or to taste
Salt to taste
1 cup Parmesan
  cheese
1 28-ounce can
  whole tomatoes,
  crushed, with
  their juice

Prepare the dough as instructed and press the dough out onto two 18×13-inch lightly oiled sheet pans. Omit the topping in the recipe.

Heat 2 large frying pans and divide the oil, garlic, onions, and peppers between the 2 pans. Sauté a few minutes, cover, and reduce the heat to low. Cook the pepper mixture over low heat for 20 minutes, stirring occasionally. Add the remaining ingredients for the filling and simmer gently, uncovered, for 20 minutes, until the excess liquid evaporates. The peppers should be very tender and the mixture not watery. Allow the pepper mixture to cool completely.

Spread one quarter of the pepper mixture lengthwise down the center of a pan of pressed-out dough. Fold one layer of dough over the pepper mixture. Spread another quarter of the pepper mixture on top of the fold. Fold the remaining layer of dough over the top. Repeat with the remaining pepper mixture and the other sheet pan of dough.

Bake both in a preheated 375° oven for 45 minutes. Allow to cool and slice.

The pies can be refrigerated overnight and warmed up or sliced and eaten cold.

Desserts

> *An I had but one penny in the world,*
> *thou shouldst have it to buy gingerbread.*

Shakespeare, *Love's Labours Lost*

I refuse cheesecake unless it has been made by my wife. She, being a New Yorker, knows what cheesecake is. I refuse burnt cream unless it has been made from one of my favorite recipes. For the most part I think we are dependent on sugar at the end of the meal out of sheer habit.

I receive letters every now and then asking me why I do not do more with heavy desserts. I suppose it is because I do not particularly care for sugar, nor does my family. There is one place in my beloved Seattle in which I will often order the most flamboyant dessert I know . . . and that is at Kaspar's on First Avenue. He does something he calls a signature plate and he actually signs the plate in chocolate! This is too much, and I often give in.

The dessert dishes that you will find in this section are not difficult to prepare and most stem from old favorites.

No, Patty's cheesecake is not in this book. It is in our very first book, simply called *The Frugal Gourmet*.

STRAWBERRIES AND
BALSAMIC VINEGAR

I have placed this recipe under both the fruit and the dessert
categories. The youngsters will think this is odd when they
help you prepare it, but I promise you that they will love
the dish. The recipe is found on page 286.

FRUIT COBBLERS

Don't forget fresh fruit cobblers. They are simple for anyone in the family to prepare and one of those dishes that
carry a lot of memories of our own youth. See page 282.

FRUIT TARTS

The dough that we use for these tarts is close to a butter
cookie dough, so these fruit tarts are certainly to be included in the desserts section. See pages 283 and 284.

MARION'S SUGAR COOKIES
MAKES ABOUT 6 DOZEN COOKIES

Marion, the woman to whom this book is dedicated, symbolizes for me several of the camps to which we are trying to address this book. She is a widow, she lives alone most of the time, she has what she considers to be the greatest grandchildren ever produced, she worries about her sick friends and neighbors and cooks for them, she is up to her neck in her church, and so on. Further, she has become our set mother, and whenever we are taping shows Marion is there to keep everyone calm.

This cookie recipe is one of her gimmicks for keeping the crew in line. On the first day of studio taping she shows up with a big box of these treats and passes them around the studio. Marion is then in charge. We love her.

She is also very opinionated about brands and products when it comes to baking. I listen to her because she really is a fine baker. She will be tickled to know that your kids get into preparing these cookies.

1 cup granulated sugar	4½ cups all-purpose flour
1 cup confectioner's sugar	1 teaspoon baking soda
1 cup margarine (Marion prefers Imperial brand)	1 teaspoon cream of tartar
1 cup Wesson oil	1 teaspoon vanilla extract
2 eggs	Additional sugar for baking

Cream both sugars together with the margarine and oil. Add the eggs and beat until smooth. Add the flour, baking soda, cream of tartar, and vanilla. Beat together until a smooth dough is achieved. Refrigerate for 2 hours. Roll the dough into walnut-sized balls and place on a cookie sheet. (Marion prefers Wilton Even-Bake pans.) To flatten the cookies, use a water glass with a textured bottom or the rough side of a meat pounder. Dampen the bottom of the glass or pounder with water and dip it in additional sugar. Press the sugar into the ball of cookie dough and flatten. Bake in a pre-heated 375° oven for 10 to 12 minutes. Allow to cool on a rack.

FROZEN CHOCOLATE BANANAS
MAKES 4

I receive recipes from young people regularly and some of them are a kick. This one is from 10-year-old Jennifer Reiffer, who lives in New York State. It is a clever bit and I placed it in the dessert section rather than in the kids' section because of the great chocolate craze in our time. Adults will enjoy these as well as the youngsters.

8 ounces Baker's semisweet chocolate	4 Popsicle sticks
2 bananas	1 cup sweetened shredded coconut

Melt the chocolate in a small pan. Cut the bananas in half crosswise. Peel the bananas and insert a Popsicle stick lengthwise in each. Roll the bananas one at a time in the melted chocolate. Remove from the chocolate and roll in the shredded coconut. Place on waxed paper. Freeze for 2 hours. Save any leftover chocolate for another batch.

BURNT CREAM FROM BLOOMINGDALE'S
(From Le Train Bleu)
MAKE 12 SERVINGS

Bloomingdale's, in New York City, remains one of the great department stores in the nation. I always stop in whenever I am in the city and I always enjoy myself.

During a recent book signing at Bloomies, I was invited to have lunch at their restaurant on the sixth floor. It is called Le Train Bleu. It is a great train dining car built high in the sky and it is very much like eating on the *Orient Express.* You will be tickled with the service and the surroundings, but the food is outstanding. This Burnt Cream was so fine that I marched out to the kitchens and pleaded for the recipe. It was most graciously offered.

Yes, the recipe is rich. But it is very simple to make and it does serve 12 people. Further, you are not going to make this that often anyhow. Try it soon, however.

11 egg yolks	1 quart heavy cream
6 ounces sugar	Additional sugar
1 teaspoon vanilla	for caramelizing
extract	

Beat the egg yolks, sugar, and vanilla together in a mixing bowl. In a saucepan over low heat, bring the cream to a gentle simmer (be careful not to let the cream boil over). Using a wire whisk, slowly whisk 1 cup of the hot cream into the egg yolk mixture. Whisk in the remaining hot cream, stirring constantly.

Ladle into twelve 5-ounce ramekins. Set the ramekins in a roasting pan and fill the pan with enough hot water to come halfway up the sides of the ramekins. Bake in a preheated 300° oven for 60 minutes until firm. Remove the custards from the pan and allow to cool.

Well before serving, sprinkle additional sugar on top of the custards and caramelize by placing them under a broiler on high heat. The sugar will melt and should form a brown glaze. You may also brown these with a small propane blowtorch. Cool to room temperature and serve.

BASIC EASY CRUST
MAKES ENOUGH DOUGH FOR ONE 9-INCH PIE WITH TWO CRUSTS, TOP AND BOTTOM

I am proud of the youngsters who write and tell me that they can do a good pie crust. It is really no big deal, but you must remember that the shortenings used in the recipe should be fairly cool when you are working the crust. And learn to use a pastry blender (page 46).

This is a very easy pie crust, though you might wonder about my use of margarine and Crisco when I told you in the healthy eating section that I do not use hydrogenated oils in cooking. I do not—at least not for pan-frying or sautéing. In baking, however, I am not quite so concerned, since the temperatures in preparation are so much lower than in stove-top cooking.

This will make a very good pie crust.

3 cups all-purpose flour	1 egg
1 teaspoon salt	1 tablespoon white vinegar
½ cup margarine	3 to 4 tablespoons ice water
½ cup Crisco	

In a medium-sized bowl, stir the flour and salt together. Cut in the shortenings using a pastry blender (page 46). Keep working the flour and shortenings until the mixture is rather grainy, like coarse cornmeal. In a small bowl mix the egg and vinegar together and, using a wooden fork, stir the mixture into the flour. Add enough ice water so that the dough barely holds together. Place on a marble pastry board or a plastic countertop and knead for just a few turns, enough so that the dough holds together and becomes roll-able. I roll my dough out on waxed paper. It is easy to handle that way. If you have a marble rolling pin, this will be easy. If you use a wooden one, be sure to dust a teaspoon of flour on it a couple of times when you are rolling the dough.

NOTE: If you wish to use this recipe for a sweet pie, simply stir in 1 tablespoon sugar along with the flour and salt.

COOKING WITH KIDS

Each child brings his own blessing into the world.

—Jewish proverb

I cannot remember when I first began playing in the kitchen. I can remember cooking with my mother when I was a very small boy, but that was certainly not the first time I was in the kitchen. I can also remember my mother's earliest instructions concerning cooking. She would yell from the front room, "Jeffey, don't forget to clean up after yourself!" A good first rule for all children.

When we did a special show with Elmo, the little red monster from *Sesame Street*, he cracked up the staff by running around behind the counter with a small stainless-steel bowl on his head and yelling, "Where did everybody go?" I told Patty, my wife, about how funny this was and she reminded me that Channing and Jason, our two neat sons, used to sit on the floor in the kitchen while Patty and I were cooking. They would each put a bowl on their head, a bowl that would come down over their eyes, and then act as if we could not see them. "They seemed always to be sitting there with a bowl on their heads,'' recalled Patty. A good way to get your kids to be comfortable in the kitchen.

I have no pat rules about teaching children to cook. Well, maybe a few. Safety is important, so please go through the rules for kitchen safety (pages 27 to 31) with your children from the very beginning. And do it often as they grow. Add your own safety tips to the list—and you might even send them to me.

I also think it is important to give the kids jobs that are not too complex so that they can complete them. This whole section has very simple recipes, though some need an adult's guidance.

Don't let your kids use powerful electric appliances, such as a fine KitchenAid mixer, without your being present and in charge. They could hurt their little hands.

Find fun stuff for them to prepare. Craig's Bread in Fun Shapes will make a baker out of your little genius. Gus's favorite dog cookies will also prove to be a hit.

Finally, organize your kitchen so that there is a place for the child, perhaps a special spot where he or she can store a small cutting board and a bowl or two, along with an apron. Please, please, do not put a woman's apron on a small boy. You need to help him understand that cooking is a nonsexist activity. Find him a chef's apron . . . that is the only way he is going to feel comfortable growing up knowing that someday he will be cooking for himself or the person he loves.

GUS'S FAVORITE MILK BONES

By this time I hope you know who Gus is. This odd dog, of questionable parentage (Are not all favorite dogs of questionable parentage?), considers himself an authority on most subjects, certainly safety in the kitchen and how to con your master. This recipe is for him. He prefers to eat these cookies while sipping a light Burgundy and listening to Bach.

Your kids will have a great time cooking these for the household dog. It isn't that the dog is going to notice a lot of difference in the flavor of such foods, since dogs eat so fast that they seem to taste nothing. However, the youngsters will take great delight in preparing something very creative for that furry creature that offers them so much special affection.

These are healthy for the pup. The recipe is a variation on one from a book by Frances Sheridan Goulart called *Bone Appétit*, published by Pacific Search Press in 1976.

1½ cups barley flour
   (find in health
   food stores)
2 tablespoons
   bonemeal
   powder (find in
   health food
   stores)
½ teaspoon salt
2 teaspoons baking
   soda
1½ tablespoons
   vegetable oil
1 egg yolk
½ cup milk
2 tablespoons honey

Cream the dry ingredients together with the oil. In a separate bowl, beat together the egg yolk, milk, and honey.

Gradually mix into the dry ingredients. Knead into a dough. Roll the dough out on a lightly floured surface to about ½ inch thick. Cut into any shape you like. (You may also find bone-shaped cutters at a good gourmet shop.) Prick the bones with a fork and place on a greased cookie sheet. Bake in a preheated 375° oven for about 20 minutes. Turn once to brown evenly.

SPAGHETTI SAUCE BREAD DIP

I hope you will help your kids understand that snacks after school are necessary, but they should be healthy. Fruit is great and leftovers are generally just fine. Here is one that was a favorite of my wife when she was a child growing up in Brooklyn.

Oftentimes you'll have leftover spaghetti sauce in your refrigerator. This makes a great after-school snack for your kids instead of junk food. Just dip bread into the cold sauce right out of the refrigerator. If you have time to heat up the sauce, it will be even better.

TORTILLA ROLLS

These are great fun to make and are just different enough from a normal sandwich that the kids will think themselves clever.

Follow the recipe for Lettuce Rolls (opposite) and simply start with a wheat tortilla and then begin layering with lettuce.

There are no laws against what can be placed in one of these tube sandwiches. Leave the youngsters to their own imaginations and you may see some strange concoctions.

LETTUCE ROLLS

This is a quick way for a young person to entertain friends after school with something that is just a bit different. Wash the leaves ahead of time and store them in the refrigerator in a sealed plastic bag. Keep a paper towel in the bottom. The leaves will keep a good 2 days this way.

Mayonnaise to taste
Butter lettuce leaves,
   washed and patted
   dry
Thinly sliced mortadella,
   salami, or any other
   cold cut

Dijon mustard to taste
Thinly sliced tomato
Freshly ground black
   pepper to taste
Toothpicks for securing

Spread a thin layer of mayonnaise on the inside of a lettuce leaf. Add a couple of slices of mortadella or salami. Spread a small amount of mustard on top of the meat. Top with tomato and freshly ground black pepper to taste. Roll up like a burrito and secure with a toothpick.

VARIATIONS: Substitute leftover meat loaf cut into sticks instead of cold cuts, or substitute scrambled eggs instead of meat as the filling. The possibilities are endless.

LITTLE SANDWICHES

I can just hear you. "Smith is telling me to teach my child to make tea sandwiches!" Why not? They will learn a good deal about the proper use of a knife and they can create interesting shapes and flavors. This sort of stuff is great if your little one wishes to entertain some friends.

Trim the crust off square white bread slices and cut into fancy shapes. You can cut the crustless bread slices into 4 squares or cut diagonally to form 4 triangles, cut into 3 rectangular strips, or you can punch out little round circles with a cookie cutter. Serve with assorted toppings as below.

CUCUMBER WITH MAYONNAISE AND DILL

Spread a bit of mayonnaise on a little round circle of bread. Add a slice of cucumber. Top with a dollop of mayonnaise and a tiny sprig of fresh dill.

PEANUT BUTTER WITH POTATO CHIPS

I had never heard of this one, but Craig claims he ate them often as a child. I tell you this is delicious!

Spread peanut butter on whatever shaped bread you like. Top with crushed potato chips.

OLIVE RELISH ON TOAST
MAKES ABOUT 2½ CUPS

Now this is a little more sophisticated, but you can always let the kids make this for you if they do not care for it. My bet is that they will like it if they make it. That is true for most dishes that young people prepare.

Don't worry about a strong anchovy flavor as the soaking in milk will take away the sharpness, I promise.

4 anchovy fillets
¼ cup milk
1½ cups drained, pitted black olives
¼ cup peeled, finely chopped onion
¼ cup finely chopped parsley

3 tablespoons olive oil
2 hard-boiled eggs, grated
Salt to taste (not much if any— taste first)
Freshly ground black pepper to taste

Soak the anchovies in the milk for 20 minutes. Drain and pat dry with paper towels. Place in a food processor and chop fine. Add the drained olives and chop them fine, but do not puree. Do this by pulsing the machine on and off and scraping down the sides several times. Remove to a mixing bowl, and add the onion, parsley, oil, and grated eggs. Fold together and add salt and pepper to taste. Toast the fancy bread shapes listed opposite. (Do this under a broiler on both sides.) Spread a layer of the olive mixture on top and serve.

NEW YORK ONION SAUCE
FOR HOT DOGS
MAKES ABOUT 4 CUPS

I have got it, and this is legit! Even my wife from Brooklyn claims that this is the real stuff.

There are three kinds of hot dogs in this country: Chicago hot dogs with vegetables and peppers on them, New York hot dogs with this sauce, along with sauerkraut and mustard, and everything else everywhere else in the country. That's it!

Help your children prepare this sauce for a hot dog that they will not forget. Use good-quality franks, preferably kosher, as they contain much less fat and no fillers.

3 tablespoons olive
  oil
3 cloves garlic,
  peeled and
  crushed
3 medium yellow
  onions, peeled
  and sliced
½ cup commercial
  bottled
  marinara sauce

Pinch of crushed
  red pepper
  flakes (careful
  with this if it is
  for the kids)
1½ tablespoons
  paprika
Salt to taste

Heat a large frying pan and add the oil, garlic, and onion. Sauté until the onion is very tender. Add the marinara sauce, red pepper flakes, and paprika. Simmer for 15 minutes. Add salt to taste. Serve over hot dogs in steamed buns.

In New York City, street hot-dog vendors also offer sauerkraut and mustard along with the sauce. With all three, it is New York heaven!

TUNA SALAD SANDWICH
MAKES ABOUT 3 CUPS

I thought that everyone was raised on tuna salad sandwiches. I know I was. But I often meet kids who don't know what I am talking about. They live on stuff from the deli case at the supermarket or on frozen foods prepared in the microwave. I include this sandwich so that young people can have their own recipe and prepare something that I just love.

1 6½-ounce can tuna fish, packed in water, drained
¼ cup mayonnaise or more to taste
3 scallions, chopped
¼ cup chopped celery
Salt and freshly ground black pepper to taste

Mix everything together using plenty of mayonnaise so the salad isn't dry. Serve on your favorite bread.

VARIATIONS: You might try adding a bit of sweet pickle relish. Or a pinch of curry powder is good in this sandwich. If you have fresh chives about, replace the scallions with the chives. That's delicious!

PITA BREAD PIZZAS

This is much more creative than the melting of a frozen pizza. You kids think up your own toppings and go to it!

Spread some tomato or marinara sauce on a round of pita bread. Add your favorite toppings plus cheese. Broil until bubbly and nicely browned.

Use leftover lunch meats, chopped meat loaf, sausage, and anything left in the refrigerator.

FIRST-CLASS TOASTED CHEESE

I love toasted cheese sandwiches, but not the grilled kind. I think this is much easier to make and much more delicious.

Toast a thick slice of caraway rye bread on both sides. Spread one side with plenty of mayonnaise and a little Dijon mustard. Top with grated white Cheddar or Monterey Jack cheese. Broil until the cheese is melted and lightly browned.

TOASTED CHEESE SANDWICH

This is a bit from my childhood, and I am sure from yours. I have included this recipe so that the young cook can prepare his/her own toasted cheese classic from the days of the soda fountain lunch counters.

Spread one side of two pieces of bread with butter. Place the buttered side of one slice in a medium-hot frying pan.

Add a couple of slices of Cheddar cheese. Spread one side of the other piece of bread with butter. Place it, buttered-side up, on top of the cheese. Toast the sandwich on both sides until golden brown.

If you add a bit of Dijon mustard to this sandwich just before toasting, it might be a welcome improvement.

FRUITED FRENCH TOAST

This is a simple trick that will help your children do something a bit different with good old French toast.

Stir some raspberry jam or other favorite into French toast egg batter. Dip a piece of bread in the fruited batter and fry in butter or oil. Don't let the heat get too high as it can burn the jam.

JAM IN YOUR PANCAKES

Another quickie that will help the kids understand that you don't have to have it the same old way every time.

Stir some of your favorite jam into pancake batter. Cook as usual, being careful not to let the heat get too high. It can burn the jam.

DATE-NUT BREAD WITH
CREAM CHEESE AND WALNUTS

This is very New York. There was a chain of quick eating houses in Manhattan called Chock full o' Nuts and years ago this used to be one of their specialties.

It is totally simple. Cream cheese is mixed with chopped

walnuts and spread upon slices of date-nut bread. This is very rich and delicious, and actually quite good for you.

If you do not know what date-nut bread is, or if you cannot find it in your local supermarket, the following recipe is terrific. It is from a television cooking person who I used to watch as a boy. I watched Bea Donovan on KING NBC Seattle even before I watched Julia Child.

Help the kids with the recipe. This stuff keeps well when wrapped in plastic wrap and stored in the refrigerator.

1½ cups chopped, pitted dates
1 cup boiling water
½ cup dark brown sugar
1 egg, beaten
3 tablespoons melted shortening
1 teaspoon vanilla extract

2 cups sifted all-purpose flour
1 teaspoon salt
½ teaspoon baking soda
1½ teaspoons baking powder
½ cup coarsely chopped walnuts

Place the dates in a mixing bowl and add boiling water. Let stand until fairly cool. Then add the brown sugar, egg, shortening, and vanilla. Stir the flour, salt, baking soda, and baking powder into the mixture. Add nuts. Stir until well mixed. Bake in a greased and floured loaf pan in a preheated 350° oven for 1 hour. Remove to a cooling rack.

PORCUPINE BALLS
SERVES 4 TO 6

These are a part of my childhood, though this recipe is much better then the one I remember as a kid. Don't think that this dish is a child of the American Depression of the 1930s as the Greeks have been eating a similar dish for many generations.

The kids can have fun molding these and watching them cook up into prickly little creatures.

3 tablespoons olive oil
2 cloves garlic, peeled and crushed
1 medium yellow onion, peeled and chopped fine
¾ cup long-grain rice
½ cup water
2 teaspoons dried sage, whole
2 tablespoons chopped fresh parsley
¼ cup bread crumbs
2 eggs, beaten

1 pound lean ground beef
½ pound lean ground pork
Salt and freshly ground black pepper to taste
1½ cups Chicken Stock (page 109) or use canned
½ cup heavy cream, half-and-half, or milk
2 tablespoons chopped fresh dill
Salt and freshly ground black pepper to taste

Heat a large frying pan and add the oil, garlic, and onion. Sauté until the onion is transparent. Remove the sautéed onion to a mixing bowl and allow to cool. In a small saucepan, place ¼ cup rice and the water. (The remaining ½ cup raw rice will be used later.) Bring the rice to a simmer, cover, and cook for 15 minutes. Allow to cool and add the cooked rice to the bowl of onion. Add the rest of the ingredients, except the remaining raw rice, the Chicken Stock, cream, and dill. Mix very well with your hands.

Form into 1¼-inch balls and roll in the raw rice. Pack the balls with your hands so the rice will stick. Return the frying pan to the burner and add the Chicken Stock, cream, and dill. Bring to a simmer and add salt and pepper to taste. Add the rice-coated meatballs and simmer very gently, covered, for 30 to 35 minutes. Carefully turn the meatballs so they cook evenly. Remove the meatballs with a slotted spoon to a warm plate. Cook to reduce the sauce until thickened slightly. Pour over the meatballs.

ANIMALS BURIED IN DIRT

Does this sound a bit strange to you? One of the wonderful things about cooking with children is that they will come up with names for dishes that just crack you up!

This one is from Christopher Thompson. Chris was five-and-a-half years old when he sent me this recipe. He lives in Illinois where he runs his family.

This is as close as I can come to a translation of the recipe that he and his friends enjoyed at their school.

Break up 2 graham crackers and place them in a single serving bowl. Add a few miniature marshmallows. Pour some chocolate pudding over this. Then stick some animal crackers into the pudding. Be sure to leave their heads sticking out of the pudding so that you have "Animals in Dirt."

Thanks, Chris.

CRAIG'S JAM-STUFFED
CORNBREAD
MAKES 9 PIECES

People are always asking Craig, my chef, and I how we got into the kitchen. We both agree that it was our mothers who brought about this event. I rarely met a chef who claims he was brought to the kitchen by his father. It is always Mama. So this is a salute to mamas—all of them.

Now, the interesting part. When Craig was very young his mother realized that he was innately capable in the kitchen so she let him go at it. One night his parents went off to a meeting and Craig announced that he would cook dinner for his two brothers. Well, he forgot until the last minute, but he did find two packages of Jiffy Corn Muffin Mix in the pantry. Innate indeed! This is what he did. It is delicious, and there is nothing wrong with your kids using a mix if it is the quality of products like Jiffy.

2 8½-ounce boxes Jiffy Corn Muffin Mix	1 8-ounce jar raspberry jam

Blend the two packages of mix together as instructed for corn muffins on the box. Grease an 8×8-inch glass baking dish and place half of the batter in the bottom of the dish. Spread the jam evenly over the batter. Top with the remaining batter. Take a chopstick and make a swirl in the batter here and there, perhaps four or five times total for the dish of batter and jam. Bake in a preheated 350° oven for 35 minutes. Cool and cut into squares.

P.S. His brothers, who are well beyond the early twenties' camp, still enjoy this dish when Craig prepares it.

Cook fresh food for your baby. Then, grind it up in a food blender and freeze it in ice-cube trays. The cubes are stored in a plastic bag in the freezer and you can put together a wholesome meal for the baby in nothing flat. Anchor Hocking has a little tray with four containers in it (I think they want you to use it for muffins), and it is perfect for microwaving food for that little one who always seems to get in my way. Besides, if you serve the little squealer fresh food from these containers, he is not as likely to pour that stuff from those little bottles upon my head.

I have had enough of that!

ADDITIONAL RECIPES FOR KIDS

You might also look at the following recipes; they are suitable for young people in the kitchen.

Fish Paste with Cookie Cutters (page 143)
Egg Salad Sandwiches, Old-fashioned Style (page 205)
Chicken Drumettes for Kids (page 176)
Chicken Cacciatore (page 172)
Private Loaf Pans (page 295)
Frozen Chocolate Bananas (page 316)
Bread in Fun Shapes (page 295)
Spaghettini with Sand (page 221)
Spaghetti with Peanut Butter Sauce
   (page 217)
Corn Salad (page 132)
Potato Peel Soup (page 106)

LETTERS FROM
CHILDREN

We get sacks of mail at our office each week. Most letters are kind and affectionate . . . now and then a letter complaining about my pronunciation of a foreign term or something about the fact that I have never cooked Czechoslovakian food. But the fun letters come from the kids. Little comment is needed for the following epistles from the little crowd. Incidentally, we have the largest children's audience of any television cooking show, ever. I am very proud of that fact.

If you are a younger person and have written to me, I hope that I received the letter and have already sent you an answer. Just because your letter does not appear in this article certainly does not mean that I didn't appreciate your letter. We can write again to each other, I am sure.

Dear Jeff Smith,
My name is Kate. I am 5 years old. I saw your show where you were cooking a duck and I am very upset. Ducks are nice and friendly and you can throw food at them. I don't want you to do any more duck shows. Just food.

Kate

I offered the following reply:

Dear Kate,
I thank you very much for your letter of July 22nd. I especially liked your drawing of the "Space Monster"!

I read carefully your remark about your being upset over the fact that I was cooking a duck. I agree with you that some ducks are nice and friendly and that you can throw food at them. I have done that too. I have also fed chickens, cows, rabbits, lambs, and turkeys. Kate, I think it is important for us to always remember that every time we eat we are eating off of the kind creation of God. Even when we eat vegetables we are eating from God's creation and we must always give thanks. I always thank the duck and I always give thanks to the cow when I have a hamburger. These things are all food and I am sorry that you are fond of this particular creature. I think I know how you feel.

You were kind to be concerned and in my upcoming children's series that we will do next year I promise that I will not cook any ducks or rabbits. But would it be all right for me to cook chickens and turkeys and beef? Do you like those foods?

I wish you well and I certainly hope that you will continue to watch the shows.

Your friend,
Jeff Smith

THE FRUGAL GOURMET

Dear Jeff Smith,
I really like your show. I'm eight years old. I help my mom make breakfast, lunch and dinner.

I make my own snack. It's Ants on a Log. It's made with celery, peanut butter, and raisins. You put the peanut butter in the celery, than put some raisins on it.

Your friend,
Hannah

Dear Mr. Smith,
My name is Chelsea and I am seven years old. My mom
is writing this for me. I love your show on Channel 11.

I thought you would like to know that because of you I
am $25 richer. I won the money at a Halloween costume
contest for the most original costume. My mother made the
hair and beard; my dad carved the carp out of soap, and I
helped sew the apron. I hope you will get a kick out of the
pictures enclosed. Everyone thought I looked like you. I'm
glad the judges thought so, too. I used the money to buy
Christmas presents for everyone in my family.

Say hello to Channing and Jason for me.

Your Friend,
Chelsea

Dear Mr. Smith,
I had a tragety in my life my brother was mowing our yard
and mowed my garlic plants down by accident. I was
shocked but I forgave him. My family doesn't like garlic
that much. Not like you or I.

Thank you for answering my last letter. When I get in a
bad mood I read your letter and it puts me in a good mood.

I wish you well and until I hear from you again . . .
I bid you peace
(Sorry I stole your line—Ha, Ha.)

Singed
Ron

Dear Froogy,
I like your show

Becky
Age 6

Dear Jeff Smith,
Thank you for the wonderful food. I watch your new show brefist lunch and diner it is great.
 I like your peanut butter waffles my mom makes them.

Love,
Sarah

Dear Frugal Gourmet,
I watch your show every saturday at 6:00 p.m.
 My mother forgets to get a piece of paper and a pencle. I love your show!

Sensearle,
Joy

Dear Jeff Smith,
I am 5 years old. And I love to watch your show. And would love to cook with you I love garlic. And everything you cook.

Jacob

Dear Jeff Smith,
I watch your show a lot. My mom and I wonder what "MSG" is. We got your book at the library. After that we watched your show and read along with you. Mom might cook some of your recipes. I learned a lot of history from your show. I liked the show when you told us a bout the red dried eggs, the animal egg, and the Buffalo. I like the show a lot. Keep up the good work.

Jennifer
Age 7

P.S. My Dad likes your pizza.

Dear Mr. Smith, I am Carrie. I am 8 years old. I like watching your shows. The one I liked the best was the cranberry. It made me jealous when you tasted the ice cream. do you try everything first? I like watching your shows becuse you are funny. What was your favorite show? The stuf you don't finish do you finish? Pleases write back.

Well bye.

Carrie

Finally, a letter from one of the oldest children I know. Dr. Simon Klein is a retired dentist and we have become great friends through the years. Most of the relationship has been conducted through the mail. He is charming and funny and this note is typical of his mindset.

What goes through the mind of a six-year-old child while sitting in the dental chair, having a tooth filled? It must be a combination of fear and anxiety, but also a deep trust. If this confidence is not betrayed, we shall have a grateful and cooperative patient.

Cindy was a lovely, intelligent child, who was having a sensitive baby tooth prepared for filling. An encounter like this is always challenging for patient and dentist alike.

"Let me know if you want me to stop. Just lift your hand as a signal."

Up went her hand. "It hurts," she exclaimed.

At this point I told her the story of a six-year-old Chinese boy who accepted treatment without blinking an eye. He explained that he "thought away" the pain.

"Do you think you could do this, Cindy?" I asked. "We could still use the hand signal."

"Think very hard about something nice," I repeated, as I raised the drill, and began to complete the preparation. In a few moments it was all done . . . with no interruption.

"Did it bother you?" I queried.

"Nope . . . not at all," said Cindy.

"And . . . what did you think of?"

"Pizza," was the prompt reply.

"What did you put on it?"

"Pepperoni," she murmured.

Such is the kingdom of childhood. What a shame that we should ever lose it.

THE MICROWAVE

Yes, I do have a microwave. As a matter of fact, I own four of them. Two are in my test kitchens, one is in the studio, and one is at home. No, I do not use mine much more than the average microwave owner. I defrost, melt, and heat in mine most of the time.

The story of the invention of this machine carries a funny bit. Percy Le Baron Spencer, a researcher working for the Raytheon Company, was exploring the emission of short-wave electromagnetic energy when he noticed that microwaves had melted a piece of candy in his pocket. Wow! How did the candy melt in his pocket without the microwaves severely burning him? It must have been some pocket!

When this oven was invented in 1946 the Raytheon Company rightly predicted that it would change the cooking habits of the nation. However, almost fifty years later Americans are still a bit reluctant to cook full meals in these metal boxes due to a simple lack of flavor. This is understandable as flavors take time to develop. Meat that is not properly browned has very little flavor, and the same problem occurs when a casserole is not colored on the top. Bread turns to goo. Still this machine can be a blessing in our time if we use it on the dishes that it does well. That is what this section is about. Don't expect your microwave to take the place of a good oven. These two appliances have very different jobs in the kitchen.

A microwave will do a good job on some vegetables, and it is fine for cooking certain egg dishes. Fish can be poached in nothing flat. I am quite sure that Barbara Kafka, a serious authority on the use of the microwave, is amused that I am finally catching up. It is predicted that by the end of the century there will be microwave ovens in the bedroom and in each of the kid's rooms. I had best catch up, indeed!

If you are not using your microwave, I suggest you look at one of two books, perhaps both. *Betty Crocker's Microwave Cookbook* is helpful, though the author implies that everything is going to taste great. It will not. The book does give helpful insight into the use of the machine, as does *Let's Cook Microwave* by Barbara Harris. I think Harris is a tad more realistic. In addition, Barbara Kafka has a couple of fine books out on this subject.

I have learned the following helpful rules:

- Cut food into equal-size pieces. They will cook more uniformly.

- Reduce the quantity of liquid called for in the recipe since the liquid is not going to cook long enough to evaporate.

- Use a lower power setting for delicate foods such as fish.

- You can cut down on oils and butter since you are not browning and nothing is going to stick.

- Volume is important. If you double the volume on a recipe, you are going to have to double the time. You might want to cook the dish in a conventional manner.

- If the food is cold from the refrigerator, it is going to take longer to cook in a microwave than had the food been at room temperature ... just like your regular oven.

- Better to undercook a dish rather than overcook it,

since it will continue to cook a bit after you take it from the microwave.

- Arrange the food in a circular pattern when possible, as the food near the outside of a rounded dish is going to cook more quickly than the mass in the center.

- Stir foods that are liquid, or close to liquid, once or twice during the cooking. This will help even out the temperature of the dish.

- Cover the food with plastic wrap to keep moisture in. Remember that a microwave primarily steams your food. Poke a small hole in the plastic to allow some of the steam to escape.

- Plastic cooking bags are great, but remember to leave a corner of the top open a bit for a steam vent.

- You have to think time, not temperature, when using the microwave. It is just like steaming in some senses. Time is the issue, not the temperature of the oven.

- Utensils for the microwave are very creative in our time. I just saw a line of plastic cooking containers with lids that go from the refrigerator into your microwave or oven. Perfect for those who live alone! Anchor Hocking makes them.

- Precook meats, such as spareribs, before grilling. Remember that it is just like steaming them a bit first, a common practice in much of the South.

- Children should not be taught to use a microwave until they are capable of using normal ovens and stove tops in your kitchen. They must learn kitchen safety first, as the rules for the microwave are a bit different. While the container may not be hot, the contents are very hot. Children need to respect the dangers of microwave cooking because it is somewhat confusing to a young person.

CRUSTLESS QUICHE
SERVES 4 TO 6

This is very simple and quite delicious. You can vary the vegetables, of course, but when using frozen vegetables be sure that they are melted before use.

½ pound Monterey
Jack cheese,
coarsely grated
5 eggs
½ pound cottage
cheese
¼ cup all-purpose
flour

⅛ teaspoon salt
½ teaspoon baking
powder
¼ cup butter, melted
½ 10-ounce package
frozen peas and
carrots
3 scallions, chopped

Grate the cheese and whip the eggs in a mixing bowl until fluffy. Stir in the cottage cheese and half the Monterey Jack cheese. Mix the flour, salt, and baking powder together and stir into the egg and cheese mixture. Stir in the melted butter. Add the vegetables and top with the remaining Monterey Jack cheese and scallions. Place in a greased deep-dish pie plate and microwave at 9 for 15 minutes, turn one-quarter turn, and then cook at 5 for 5 minutes.

Be sure to cover the quiche with a sheet of waxed paper so that the dish will not spatter. Allow to cool a bit before serving.

POACHED TROUT IN A BAG

This will work with any small fresh fish. Since you are not using a great deal of oil for frying, this is a very healthy dish. Further, since you are using white wine and lemon juice you can eliminate salt altogether; this dish will not need it.

1 tablespoon olive oil
1 fresh trout (about 6 to 8 ounces)
1 tablespoon chopped parsley
½ teaspoon dried dillweed, whole
2 tablespoons dry white wine
2 teaspoons freshly squeezed lemon juice
Freshly ground black pepper to taste

Brush a bit of olive oil on the trout. Sprinkle the remaining ingredients on the trout and place in a plastic cooking bag. Be sure and poke a hole in the bag. Cook at 5 for 8 to 10 minutes, turning once during the cooking. Let stand for a few minutes before removing from bag.

SOLE AS A PIE
SERVES 4 AS A FISH COURSE

This dish has a bright Italian flavor. The fish is not over-cooked due to the fact that we prepare it so quickly in the microwave. Remember, do not overcook when using a microwave. Turn off the machine and let the food just sit in there until you are ready.

½ cup bread crumbs
1 teaspoon chopped fresh oregano
1 tablespoon chopped parsley
Salt and freshly ground black pepper to taste

1 pound fresh sole fillets
½ cup canned tomatoes
2 tablespoons olive oil
Fresh lemon juice to taste

Mix the crumbs, oregano, parsley, and salt and pepper together. Dredge the fish in this mixture and place in an oiled glass pie plate. Top with the remaining crumb mixture. Squish up the tomatoes with your hand and pour over the fish. Top with the olive oil.

Cover with plastic wrap and poke a hole in the wrap. Microwave at 9 for 5 to 7 minutes. Top with a bit of fresh lemon juice before serving.

CHINESE MEATBALLS
SERVES 4

I like this dish very much, though I usually steam it. The microwave works great because this is precisely what it does . . . it steams this dish. You can do this with all kinds of meatball recipes.

1 pound lean	1 teaspoon grated
hamburger meat	fresh ginger
1 tablespoon dry	½ teaspoon sugar
cocktail sherry	1 egg white
1 tablespoon light	Mustard greens or
soy sauce (page	fresh spinach
58)	

Mix all the ingredients together with the exception of the greens. Mold into 8 meatballs and place on a bed of fresh mustard greens or fresh spinach leaves in a glass pie plate. Cover with plastic wrap. Be sure and poke a small hole in the wrap.

Microwave at 10 for 9 minutes, turning once. Allow to sit for 2 minutes before serving.

GREEN PEAS ITALIAN
SERVES 2 TO 3

I offer this simply because I want you to know that a microwave does a great job on frozen vegetables. I have planned this cooking time so that the vegetable is still frozen when you put it into the casserole.

1 10-ounce package	½ teaspoon dried
frozen peas	oregano, whole
2 tablespoons	¼ teaspoon dried
chopped parsley	basil, whole
½ tablespoon olive oil	2 tablespoons water
1 clove garlic, peeled	
and crushed	

Mix all the above ingredients in a 1-quart casserole. Microwave, covered, at 9 for 5 to 7 minutes, stirring once and turning one-quarter turn during the cooking. Let sit a moment before serving.

VARIATION: Try this with green beans or corn kernels.

I never chase the cat in the kitchen. The kitchen is a place for serious business and it can be dangerous. . . . I'll get the cat later.

LOW-SALT/LOW-FAT
CHICKEN ITALIAN
SERVES 3 TO 4

I know that the words "low-salt/low-fat" usually scare us to death because we feel that the dish will be low in flavor, not just salt and fat. Not to worry! This amounts to a poached chicken with lots of herbs and flavor. And since you have removed the skin, which contains most of the fat of the chicken, the dish is low in everything but flavor.

1 whole 3-pound chicken, skin removed	½ teaspoon dried oregano, whole
1 tablespoon olive oil	½ teaspoon dried basil, whole
2 cloves fresh garlic, peeled and crushed	Paprika to taste
Freshly ground black pepper to taste	2 tablespoons freshly grated Parmesan cheese

Cut the chicken through the breastbone completely, so that the bird can be opened and spread out flat on the counter. Remove the wings. Pull off the entire skin beginning at the neck and pulling clear to the ends of the legs.

Lay the chicken in a baking dish. Brush with the olive oil and garlic. Sprinkle with the remaining ingredients.

Cover the end of each leg with a 2-inch square of aluminum foil to prevent overcooking of the smallest part of the leg. Cook at 9 for 25 minutes, turning once. Allow to sit several minutes before serving.

SHIRRED EGGS
SERVES 4

Normally, I do not like microwaved eggs as they are usually overcooked. However, if you use this recipe and do not overcook the eggs you will have a treasure. I like to use plain white Chinese teacups for this dish. They work great in a microwave. Just be sure and watch them and turn them around.

4 **Chinese teacups
without metal
design (without
gold-painted
trim, etc.)**
1 **tablespoon butter**
4 **eggs**
1 **teaspoon dry sherry
for each egg (not
cooking sherry,
just decent dry
sherry)**

**Freshly ground
black pepper and
salt to taste
Sprinkle of grated
Parmesan cheese**

Melt the butter quickly in one of the teacups in your microwave. Distribute butter evenly among the 4 cups and brush each cup with the butter. Break 1 fresh egg into each cup and top with the sherry, a bit of salt and pepper, and a sprinkle of cheese. Cover each cup with a little plastic wrap and then carefully poke one small hole in the center of the wrap, using a toothpick. Poke the toothpick clear down into the yoke. The yolk must have this tiny hole in the membrane in order to cook properly.

Microwave 2 minutes on 9, changing the positions of the cups in the oven after the first minute. Check to see if the eggs are done to your liking. If not, cook a moment longer.

Please remember that these eggs should be underdone when you turn off the oven. Since the cups are hot, the eggs are still cooking. Serve immediately.

THE AMERICAN
SODA FOUNTAIN

*Jerk a bridge through Georgia,
shake it to the right, and pull a
long one, hold the hail.*

Soda jerk, 1950

It is ours. Soda pop and the soda fountain are American inventions, and the old soda fountain played a major role in the social life of this country. Since the turn of the century people have been meeting around the soda fountain, but in the 1950s we began to close them all down. I consider this to be a great American tragedy.

When I was a kid, during the early 1950s, the guys who were active with me in Boy Scouts would always gang up at our local soda fountain. It was in a drugstore, of course. Soda fountains were always in drugstores since the original inventor of soda water first claimed that it was medicinal . . . and he sold it in his drugstore. I knew the story of the soda fountain even as a small child when I would save my allowance and walk across the street to Keener's Drug Store on upper Fremont Avenue. Mr. Keener, the pharmacist and owner, would come out from behind his drug cabinets and wander up to the soda fountain to serve me and the neighborhood kids. To this day I believe that he always gave me an extra squirt of syrup in my root beer float. Lord, I miss those times!

The history of the soda fountain has something to do with the invention of ice cream, since that is what the soda

THE DRINKJOY.   THE NIAGARA

fountain finally did with the soda. It was mixed with ice cream!

We know that Nero Claudius Caesar (A.D. 54–68) had runners bring in snow from the mountains. It was then flavored with honey and fruit juices and pulps for the Caesar, who sat back on his couch and enjoyed what must have been one of the first forms of fruit ices.

During the 1200s Marco Polo returned from the Far East with a recipe for something like sherbet. Sherbet is different from a fruit ice in that it contains milk.

During the 1700s the American colonists celebrated ice cream, an invention that they apparently got from the British and French. It was Thomas Jefferson who first began serving his ice-cream creations at formal dinner parties while he was President.

So we had ice cream.

Now to the soda.

In 1767 Joseph Priestley, an Englishman who is credited with the discovery of oxygen, also succeeded in making carbonated water from the gases that came off the brewery

Ornate nineteenth-century soda fountains like these reflected the incredible popularity of the soda jerks' concoctions.
SMITHSONIAN INSTITUTION

THE MONITOR

vats in Leeds. Nothing more occurred with this "soda water" until 1825, when Elias Magliore Durand, a pharmacist in Napoleon's army, opened the "first modern drugstore" in America. He sold soda water for medicinal purposes. And in 1838 a French perfumer named Eugené Roussel began adding flavors to his soda. Soon many persons were flavoring the bubbling water, but catch these flavors! They flavored the water with birch beer, pepsin, ginger, lemon, kola, cherry, sarsaparilla, champagne, and claret. Some selection!

The first widely used soda fountain was put together by the English immigrant Joseph Matthews. He opened it in New York in 1832 and used scrap marble from New York's Saint Patrick's Cathedral for carbonating the water. In those days simple acid was put upon limestone rocks, such as marble, and the gas produced was used to make the soda water. Matthews got enough scrap marble from the cathedral to carbonate 25 million gallons of water. The soda water business was off and running, literally!

Blakely's Blizzard Soda: All-male soda hangouts were not uncommon toward the end of the nineteenth century, as this 1890 advertisement indicates.

THE NEW-YORK HISTORICAL SOCIETY

Soda fountain at the Studio Inn at Universal Studio
CULVER PICTURES, INC.

Philadelphia was to see the first formal freestanding ornate and marble-studded soda fountain. It was in 1903. It was not like its predecessors as it did not stand against the wall but was actually a counter with a vast array of draft arms, syrup pumps, and deep ice-packed wells for ice cream. Within a few years every major city in America had one of these beautiful fountains designed by Gustavus Dows. They were like beautiful freestanding altars!

The City of Brotherly Love also has another soda fountain discovery that must be properly credited. In 1874 Robert Green, a pharmacist there, invented the ice-cream soda. He simply placed a scoop of ice cream in the fruit-flavored soda. It was not long before people were filling his establishment and enjoying the new soda and ice-cream drink, even on Sundays! The local clergy were horrified and spoke

A drugstore in Staten Island at Wall Street and Stuyvesant
Place, 1928
CULVER PICTURES, INC.

out against the "foul sin of sucking soda on Sunday"!
It took only a few years to deal with this gross charge
of immorality. In 1890 some pharmacists in Evanston,
Illinois, and in Two Rivers, Wisconsin, decided that they
would get around the rule that "outlawed the Sunday
Soda Menace." They simply removed the soda from the
concoction and served ice cream with syrup on top.
Thus the Sundae.

The St. Louis Exposition of 1904 was to see the invention of the ice-cream cone. Mr. Hamwi, who had come
from Syria in 1903, had a stand next door to an ice-cream
peddler. The ice-cream man ran out of glass dishes, and
Mr. Hamwi, who was selling salabias, cooked like a thin
waffle, offered his product, rolled up like a cone, to his
neighbor. Instant hit!

The Home Soda Fountain

Since it does not seem possible for you young people to go to a soda fountain, I should like you to make one of your own at home. Oh, I know that you buy milk shakes made in a big machine at the local drive-in . . . or drive-through. A real milk shake, as I knew it, is not served from a wax-covered paper cup. It is served from an old-fashioned milk shake glass, with the can from the mixer sitting alongside. I cannot tell you how many of your ancestors proposed to one another over this very drink.

If you wish to know the flavors from those times, then you must know the recipes and the language.

Step 1: Simple Syrup

Make some simple syrup. Stir 2 cups sugar into 1 cup of water and just heat until all dissolves and is clear. This sweet syrup is added to concentrates to make your own soda syrups or it is added to jams or jellies to make your own sundae toppings.

Example: Root beer soda syrup is made by adding 1 tablespoon of root beer extract to the above syrup recipe. You can find Hires Root Beer Extract in many fancy groceries or in shops that sell supplies for home beer and wine making. Soda water is added when you are ready for the drink and you are in business.

Step 2

Check out the selection of ready-made syrups that are available at good Italian markets or delicatessens. Two brands that I trust are Toranni from San Francisco and Ferrara's from New York City.

You will find all kinds of syrups including: cherry, strawberry, cola, lemon-lime, vanilla, raspberry, blackberry.

Root beer syrup, as made above, is to be added to the list, along with chocolate syrup, which you can buy in a plastic squirter dispenser from Hershey's.

If you mix an ounce or two of every syrup you have in

the place, you wind up with a favorite from my childhood.
It is called a Zombie or sometimes a Graveyard.

Step 3: The Soda

Now we are ready. Two ounces of flavored syrup are placed
in a 12-ounce soda glass. Add a little ice and soda to fill:
8 ounces of soda to 2 ounces of syrup. Stir only once so
that you don't work out the carbonation.

Soda can be purchased in quart bottles or you can buy a
seltzer bottle and use household water and CO_2 cartridges.

Step 4: The Ice-Cream Soda

Half a scoop of vanilla ice cream is placed in a soda glass.
The syrup is added and then you stir the syrup into the ice
cream. Soda is then added and a scoop of ice cream tops
it off.

Step 5: The Milk Shake

In Boston a milk shake is simply milk with flavored syrup
in it. It is whipped on a milk-shake machine. (You can still
buy this machine from Hamilton-Beach, though an old-
fashioned one works a bit better than the new lighter
models.)

A Brown Cow milk shake is made by "shaking" together 2 ounces of evaporated milk along with 2 ounces of chocolate syrup. Mix this with a bit of ice and drain into the soda glass. Fill with root beer and top with chocolate shot. This is a Boston classic!

From Chicago on out West, a milk shake is made by placing 2 scoops of vanilla ice cream in the milk shake canister. Add 2 ounces of flavored syrup and just enough milk to cover. Mix until thick and frothy. Serve in a soda glass. In Boston this is called a frappe, pronounced frap.

An Awful Awful is made by adding more ice cream to the milk shake. It is called this because it is "awful rich and awful good"!

Step 6: The Malted Milk

A malted milk is made by adding a teaspoon or two of malted milk powder to your milk shake. My favorite was always a root beer malted milk shake. Use root beer syrup and malted milk and go to it. Gad, I am beginning to feel like a teenager!

Step 7: The Sundae

A scoop or two of vanilla ice cream is placed in a tulip sundae dish and a thick syrup is added for a topping. A dollop of whipped cream used to be added and then a maraschino cherry for a topping. If you wanted chopped nuts you had to pay 10 or 15 cents extra!

Common flavor toppings for sundaes were chocolate, strawberry (made from regular strawberry jam thinned a bit with your simple syrup), marshmallow (buy in the supermarket), along with butterscotch (supermarket as well) and pineapple (jam thinned with your simple syrup).

Great combinations were created by the soda fountain artists.

A black and white was a sundae of chocolate ice cream topped with marshmallow syrup.

A Purple Cow was a sundae of wild blackberry ice cream topped with chocolate syrup.

A Dusty Miller was a vanilla ice-cream sundae topped with both chocolate and marshmallow syrup, along with a dusting of malted milk powder. Wow!

Step 8: Graduation Time for the Jerk

The young fellow who popped the soda spigot back and forth, or who jerked it about, was called a soda jerk. If he really knew his stuff and was respected by the rest of the crew they called him Jerk. If he did not know his stuff, the staff referred to him as Pop Boy. But after a few years of dealing with the soda fountain and at least a hundred recipes, one might attain the respectable title of Professor. He was then responsible for thinking up new ice-cream and soda creations, thus the name.

Jeff Wollam, one of Craig's brothers, submitted this one. I vote for professorship for him for this one.

Black Top Sundae

Coffee ice cream is allowed to melt just long enough so that you can stir in some coarse but freshly ground espresso coffee. Yes, stir it into the ice cream and refreeze. When ready to serve, the scoops of ice cream are topped with chocolate syrup, along with a garnish of ground coffee. Thank you, Professor Jeffrey!

Banana Splits

A banana split was made properly in the fifties. One scoop of vanilla ice cream, along with a scoop of chocolate and strawberry, was placed in a glass banana split dish. Marshmallow syrup was placed on the chocolate ice cream, pineapple on the strawberry, and chocolate on the vanilla. A banana was split and placed on the sides of the dish. This was all topped with whipped cream, chopped nuts, and a cherry. I think I am going to cry!

Phosphates

A phosphate was a soda to which the Jerk added a few drops of citric acid so that the soda had a tart and fresh taste. You can make phosphate liquid by dissolving 2 tablespoons of sour salt (find in any good spice shop) in 1 cup water. All you will need is a few drops in a soda.

Floats

Floats were made by floating a scoop of ice cream on the top of the soda. No ice cream was mixed into the soda syrup as in an ice-cream soda. The ice cream was just floated on the top. My favorite always has been a root beer float.

Step 9: The Egg Cream

Extra-credit examination by Patty, my wife, who was raised in Brooklyn, New York: "Make an egg cream!"

I'll help here. You do not need an egg nor do you need cream.

A regular chocolate soda is prepared with a bit of milk

Joe E. Brown plays a soda jerk in the 1938 movie
Wide Open Faces.
CULVER PICTURES, INC.

in it. That's it. Egg cream? Well, the best explanation I
have ever heard is that this drink from the Lower East Side
of New York City, the home of Orthodox Jews, is that it
is so called because the term for pure, as in pure cream or
pure milk, is *ekht* in Yiddish. So a soda with pure cream
or milk in it became known as an ekht cream or an egg
cream. Everyone agrees that there was never an egg in an
egg cream.

All of this can be done in your home without much
preparation. Buy good-quality ice cream. The glasses for
the old-fashioned soda fountain are still being made by
Anchor Hocking, just as they have done for years. You
can find them at any restaurant supply house and you will
have your own old-fashioned soda fountain counter in
nothing flat.

Soda Jerk: This unidentified young man, caught in the act in Corpus Christi, Texas, in 1939, was probably drafted into World War II, along with the manufacturers of soda fountain equipment, who were making airplane parts, rafts, gasoline tanks, etc.
LIBRARY OF CONGRESS

The Soda Fountain Luncheonette

One of the most interesting things to come from this whole soda fountain movement was the luncheonette. I read the paper this morning and learned that Kress's Dime Store is closing one of their last ones.

What was this institution? Well, it was hardly based on what we call a full restaurant menu, but it was the beginning of the fast-food lunch in this country. It was a soda fountain with a long counter, and in addition to the fountain drinks they offered a limited breakfast menu and a lunch menu filled with sandwiches. You could grab a quick soda and a sandwich and be on your way in nothing flat.

The sandwiches? They served egg salad, tuna salad, toasted cheese, date-nut bread with cream cheese and walnuts, and of course, the old ham on white bread sandwich. All of the above sandwiches are included in this recipe book with the exception of the ham on white. Nope!

One of the most wonderful things about such places was the language that the counter gals used when placing an order with the sandwich or grill person. It became an art form and was really very amusing to the ear and to the heart. As for the food, well, nostalgia is usually most happy when not totally investigated.

Great names for common foods. Here are some favorite cries that you might have heard in a soda fountain luncheonette during the forties and fifties, with translations.

Everyone that worked in the place had to know these terms, from the Professor down to the Pop Boy. You would hear the waitress yell for one or several of the following.

You will not really appreciate these ingenious titles unless you yell them out loud when you read them. I don't care if your wife or husband is asleep. Yell 'em out or we can't hear the order!

ADAM'S ALE!	Water
BABY!	Glass of milk
BELCH WATER!	Glass of seltzer
BLACK STICK!	Chocolate ice-cream cone
BREAK IT AND SHAKE IT!	Put an egg into a drink
CITY JUICE!	Glass of water
CLEAN UP THE KITCHEN!	Hash
CONEY ISLAND CHICKEN!	Hot dog
FLY CAKE!	Raisin cake
GENTLEMAN WILL TAKE A CHANCE!	Hash
GO FOR A WALK!	Take-out order
GRAVEYARD STEW!	Milk toast
HOLD THE HAIL!	No ice
HOUSEBOAT!	Banana split
LOOSENERS!	Dish of prunes

LUMBER!	Toothpick
MUD!	Chocolate ice cream
NERVOUS PUDDING!	Jell-O
ONE ON THE CITY!	Glass of water
ONE ON THE COUNTRY!	Buttermilk
ON WHEELS!	To go
PAIR OF DRAWERS!	Two coffees
PATCH!	Strawberry ice-cream cone
PEST!	Assistant manager
PIG BETWEEN TWO BLANKETS!	Ham sandwich on white bread
PINK STICK!	Strawberry ice-cream cone
SAND!	Sugar
SINKERS AND SUDS!	Coffee and donuts
SQUEEZE ONE!	Orange juice
THIRTEEN!	One of the big bosses is around
WHITE COW!	Vanilla milk shake

This is the sort of thing you would hear in a fountain/luncheonette some thirty years ago. I have a favorite story of a very famous Boston clergyman who used to frequent one of these counters regularly. He often ordered two eggs on toast. The girl would yell, "Adam and Eve on a raft!" One morning after she called in his order, he said, in a mischievous manner, "Oh, I would like them scrambled, please." Without a moment of hesitation, she yelled, "On that Adam and Eve on a raft—wreck 'em!"

Those were fun times.

You can do all this in your own kitchen. The kids and all will love it and perhaps they will think up food names that are more zany than the ones I have offered you. For more help in this area I refer you to the experts. Please see the Bibliography.

Food and Color

Look at that antipasto buffet.
Just the colors alone convince you that
you are starved!

Craig Wollam
Frugal Gourmet's chef

What place does color have in terms of food and the table?

Years ago I read about a dinner party at which the host served food that was blue. I mean everything was blue. Blue is a terrible color for food as it just does not seem natural. What food is blue? No one at the party ate a thing.

I was so taken by the story, I think it was Alfred Hitchcock who threw the party, that I had to try the same silly stunt. I had my chance on live television in Seattle a few years ago. I made a whole buffet of fine-tasting food. . . . but everything was dyed blue. One member of the audience was blindfolded while things were put in place. He tasted several dishes and pronounced them delicious. When I took off the blindfold and he saw the color of the food, he began to cough and burp. He was horrified.

My Norwegian ancestors go for white food on white plates covered with white cream sauce. If you add parsley for color, they know you are an outsider!

381

I began thinking about how children react to the color of certain foods. If the color is bizarre enough they laugh. If it is a normal food product with an unappetizing color they reject the food. White fish is a good example. Pea soup seems to be another color that shuts them off. So, I decided to do a show on food and color.

Color is terribly important when it comes to appetite. The plate must offer three kinds of enticement before it can really be called successful. The food must smell good, it must be attractively arranged, and, most important, it must look good in terms of color. We all know this is true.

Consider the wonders that an artist does with color. When I first saw a Monet painting of a lake I was amused with the fact that he thought the water on the lake offered many colors . . . purple, pink, orange. Everybody knows that water is blue. Always. No, after you see a Monet you begin to look again and realize that the artist is right. An artist can actually change your perception of reality and thus reality itself by offering you a new insight into color. My favorite lake, Green Lake, in Seattle, is not green at all. I now see that it is purple, pink, orange . . . well, it has happened to you as well, I am sure.

In preparation for the show on children and how they react to food and color, we decided to discuss the issue with one of the finest artists I know. Dale Chihuly, a world-famous artistic glassblower, has been a friend for years. His studio is a furnace of colors and shapes and artistic frenzy, all of which come together in the most beautiful forms of glass that I have ever seen. Craig and I discussed the food and color issue with Dale and he immediately offered an invitation to come to his glassblowing school, where a glass plate would be produced . . . a glass plate that would serve as an example of attractive food presentation.

We took a bunch of kids up to the Pilchuck Glass School and watched the production of the platter. I hope you saw the show or will see it soon. What an experience! Leno Tagliapietra, one of the world's truly great glassblowers from Venice, Italy, was in residence at the school, and between Leno and Dale the young people witnessed the production of a plate that is so beautiful you hesitate to place food upon it. We were urged to use it and we offered the kids a lesson on food and color. Craig thought the plate looked like coral from the sea, and he claimed he could see the waves in the glass. He then wisely prepared a Seafood Salad (page 153) that looked like the plate had been made for the dish. It had!

While the kids loved the Seafood Salad, we realized that another thing had happened in this process. None of these kids had ever seen a serious or world-famous artist at work. That is tragic. The Pilchuck School was founded by Mr. Chihuly in 1971 and it now boasts some of the most famous glassblowers in the world among its alumni. Since it is nonprofit—we are talking art—it needs the support of the general public if it is to survive. (Get ready for the touch!) If you were taken by what you saw on the show on food and color, and if you want to become a supporter of the ancient art of glassblowing, then contact this world-famous school. The address is below. Finally, you can visit this incredible place during one of the yearly open houses and tours. My tour changed my life . . . just as Monet changed Green Lake.

> The Pilchuck Glass School
> 107 South Main, #324
> Seattle, Washington 98104
> 206–621–8422

This has become one of my favorite projects. Jump in and join us.

Now, you might try a fun menu on your kids, or they might like to try such a buffet on their friends. It is really quite simple. Go to a restaurant supply house and order a bottle of blue food coloring. The little bottle you get in the supermarket will not be enough. So you don't want to do a blue buffet? Try green, yellow, or brown. The sameness of color will have the same effect.

Add a bit of the coloring to each of the following dishes.

All will appear just ghastly but will taste fine. This could be real fun for a family get-together, especially if you invite relatives whom you really do not care for.

All of the following can be served "blue" . . . or some other color.

Milk

Wine

Mashed potatoes

Cream gravy (white cream sauce with grated cheese)

Blue mayonnaise on boiled egg halves (disgusting looking but delicious!)

Pasta and sauce (make your own pasta and use the cream gravy above)

Bread

Blue-cheese spread

Blue Jell-O with blue whipped cream

Blue ice cream

The whole point of such a strange party centers around the need to educate children and make them more sensitive to their surroundings. Educating the palate is certainly connected to educating the eye, though that might sound strange to some. In the end we wish to create meals that lead to increased sensitivity to flavors and colors and . . . well, the world. That is the point when it comes to cooking with your whole family.

Epilogue

What is the function of the table?

In the long run we have to admit that the table must offer something more than just food. Gathering for the process of eating also involves nuturing and communication, as well as sustenance. Therefore I am convinced that "being at table" means that you are most often with and concerned about someone else.

When I was a college chaplain years ago I worked with students who were so hungry to come to table that they did so even when little food was offered. Companionship and insight were often the meal. That is serious feasting!

This book is certainly less complicated than anything else we have done, and it is somewhat more basic because I want everyone to feel both comfort and comfortable in the kitchen and thus at table. Children should certainly be taught to cook so that they do not grow up having to depend upon someone else for their food. The ability to cook also gives one a sense of self-confidence and independence, two gifts that can be returned to friends and family when they gather for a feast.

I have nothing against prepared foods or fast foods, except that they are often boring. Cook fresh foods several times a week, even if you live by yourself. You will feel better in terms of your health and the friends with whom you share your food will continue to feed your friendship.

Thanks again to everyone who helped with this book and with the television shows. I know of no table that is large enough to hold all of us, but the book has been a feast in itself.

Bibliography

American Demographics. March 1991, pp. 44–46; September 1990, p. 2; January 1991, p. 10.

Bastianich, Lidia, and Jay Jacobs. *La Cucina di Lidia.* New York: Doubleday, 1990.

Betty Crocker's Microwave Cookbook. New York: Prentice-Hall, 1981.

Bland, Jeffrey. *Your Health Under Siege: Using Nutrition to Fight Back.* Brattleboro, Vt.: Stephen Greene Press, 1981.

DeGouy, Louis P. *Soda Fountain and Luncheonette Drinks and Recipes.* New York: Dover, 1940.

Dickson, Paul. *The Great American Ice Cream Book.* New York: Atheneum Press, 1972.

Donovan, Bea. *Bea Donovan's Favorites.* Seattle: Bea Donovan and M. B. Sawyer, 1962.

The Futurist. September–October 1990, pp. 53–54.

Gellman, Marc. *Does God Have a Big Toe?* New York: Harper & Row, 1989.

Goulart, Frances Sheridan. *Bone Appétit*. Seattle: Pacific Search Press, 1976.

Harris, Barbara. *Let's Cook Microwave*. Portland, Ore.: Barbara Harris, Inc., 1974.

Kafka, Barbara. *Microwave Gourmet*. New York: William Morrow and Company, 1987.

Monthly Labor Review. March 1990, pp. 4–12.

Robbins, Maria Polushkin (ed.). *The Cook's Quotation Book*. Wainscott, N.Y.: Pushcart Press, 1983.

Rosten, Leo. *Leo's Rosten's Treasury of Jewish Quotations*. New York: McGraw-Hill, 1972.

Taylor, Jennifer (ed.). *The Gourmet Quotation Book*. London: Robert Hale, 1990.

Index